For A Woman's Love

Which would be worse?
To live as a monster or
To die as a good man?

Danyl A. Doyle and Ron Kop

Not just another Vietnam War story, "For A Woman's Love" redefines what courage and honor mean. Imagine Rowdy's heart-wrenching decision to desert, not out of cowardice, but for a woman's love when he asks, "Which is worse: To live as a monster or to die as a good man?" Rowdy's girlfriend, Dove, demanded that he join the Army to kill Vietnamese communists in return for her love, and to the delight of Rowdy – her virginity.

Foreword

I want the horror of the Vietnam War to be so deeply impressed on the mind of the reader that they will never allow the U.S. to do again what they did to the Vietnamese people. Had I known, I would never have enlisted for any reason and especially for the love of a woman.
Ron Kop 1970

In April 2014, Ron was in a nursing home dying of cancer caused by Agent Orange from when he was in Vietnam. For years he tried to write this story but couldn't because it was too emotionally tough.

Ron looked up at me. "You have to write it. You're the only one who can. You have to promise me that you'll put it together and finish it."

He offered his hand and we shook.

I have reconstructed his story from audio tapes that I recorded during several red wine evenings, his many emails and letters to me, and the chapters he had roughed-out while attempting to write this story about a young idealist man in love with a young woman who talked him into joining the Army to "Kill Communists for God."

All the character's names have been changed to protect those who don't want their name in print.
Danyl A. Doyle 2025

1. Jump Rowdy, Jump

I shut the tractor down for a break from picking up boxes of sour cherries. The newscaster's voice was tight with stress, "It has just been learned that Robert Kennedy, who was shot late last night by Sirhan Sirhan, has died."

Devyn said, "Kennedy should have been our next president; he promised to end our involvement in the Vietnam War."

"Yeah, I'm with you," I said. "The good men in politics are being killed in America – just last month some idiot assassinated Martin Luther King Junior."

"I know. All we're going to have left are men without a vision." Devyn went on, "My dad is mister hardcore Marine and he thinks we ought to take territory in North Vietnam. He says the strategy of trying to win by getting body counts will never work. We're winning battles but losing the war."

I nodded in agreement. "My dad was in the Dutch resistance during World War Two. He says the North Vietnamese are like the Nazi Germans when they over-ran Holland. He thinks we have to take the battle to North Vietnam."

Big Owl leaned against the rear tractor tire. "My brother was in the Army just like my dad and grandpa during the world wars. He spent a year in 'Nam."

Devyn asked, "Where is he now?"

"He's in San Jose." Owl slapped his leg. "Hey, that's what we oughta do. Get out of Cedaredge and go see him!"

"Yeah, California dreaming. My older brother is in the Army at the Presidio in San Francisco," I said. "There's no point in me going back to high school. I flunked the second semester this year, and the counselor said I can't graduate with my class." I frowned. "I'll be two years behind. I got held back in first grade when we came from Holland because I didn't know English. They stuck me in with my younger sister who started first grade in the US."

Big Owl said, "Me too. I flunked third grade and now I flunked eleventh grade. I ain't going back for more donkey poop."

"Well," Devyn said, "I'm glad you guys were held back because otherwise, you'd a pounded on me like the other upperclassmen."

"Hey, made you tough didn't it?" Big Owl shoved him.

He fell backward and plopped on his butt. His face turned bright red and his eyes narrowed. He attacked Owl with everything he had, his fists flying.

With one hand, Big Owl picked him up by the shirt neck and held him straight out from his chest.

Dev failed in the wind.

I said, "Dev, calm down, take a breath, easy now. Owl's not your dad; your dad isn't here." Devan's arms slowed. "That's right, relax. Owl won't hurt you." I told Big Owl, "Sit him on the ground slow and gentle; his dad knocks him around. The old marine taught him to fight at the drop of a hat. Tell him you won't hurt him."

Big Owl grinned like a coyote as he sat Devyn on his feet. "I thought you was getting better about blowing up."

He panted. "I'm sorry man. I get these flashes of my old man pounding me. I didn't mean to go after you."

Big Owl smiled great big and patted him on the back. "We're buds for life." He laughed. "But you better be careful 'cause someday, somebody gonna make you eat his shorts!"

It was a hot, dry June day in western Colorado near a wide spot in the road called Eckert. I jammed the transmission into gear of the Ford 9N since it was challenging to engage. The tractor lurched forward, belching smoke. I pointed. "Hey Dev, there are six lugs in the tall grass."

Big Owl and Devyn fetched and stacked sour cherry boxes, gathering them from tree rows where three-legged ladders stood underneath freshly stripped limbs.

Devyn didn't hear me over the noisy tractor so I got off and picked up the cherry lugs. I stacked them near the front of the load. The wagon was already loaded four high. I started a fifth tier. We usually stopped at three levels and hauled them to the semi-truck to unload. However, this was cleanup time and the upper orchard was picked. Not much was left but for scattered lugs of cherries, ladders, and forgotten picking buckets so we stacked the boxes of cherries higher and higher.

I rolled the smoke-belching tractor up to the end of the row and stopped for Big Owl to set boxes on the wagon. His real name is Alvin or Al for short. He was six feet six inches tall and nobody messed with his two hundred-seventy-pounds of solid muscle. He sported curly red hair, freckles, and baby white skin except for a pink blush from the sun. His arms were as thick as my legs. He reeked from a beer and grain alcohol hangover. His T-shirt said, "Coors Breakfast of Champions." Everyone called him Big Owl because in junior high he had shot a great-horned owl and kept the talons for a key chain. It was a pun since he was anything but wise.

He waited with three cherry lugs weighing thirty pounds each under each arm like a stack of books. At school, girls had fun hanging off his huge arms, sometimes two or three at a time. He laughed and laughed, loving the feeling. It sounded like "Yuck, yuck." Piling the boxes on top of the wagon in a single lift, he moved two lugs around to even the load.

"Dev's got four boxes," I said to Big Owl. "And there's a stack of a dozen there," I pointed.

He took a breath and grinned. "Hey you skinny prick, how about bumming me a smoke?" His vocabulary development stopped the day he learned to cuss back in first grade. Swearing made him feel a touch smarter than he was.

"Sure." I pulled a pack of Camel filters from my shirt pocket. I had black Beatle-length hair, fair skin, and brown eyes. Like Mom, I didn't have a mean bone in my body. I hated my angry, bragging father who hit us eight kids. I often stepped in to take whippings from Dad to protect the younger ones. I shut off the tractor and flicked on Devyn's transistor radio. "California Dreaming on such a winter's day."

"What orchard we going to next Monday?" Big Owl asked.

"Not sure, but we're done with this one. Here comes Dev, let's ask him."

Although two years younger, Devyn was the leader since he was smart. He exclaimed, "Like I figured, you guys are jacking off." He rounded the back of the wagon. He wasn't as big as me. He stood five feet, ten inches tall, and was maybe 140 pounds. He had blue eyes, a tense skinny body, and Beatle-length blonde hair. "Look at you two – a couple of slackers sitting in the shade telling lies."

Big Owl said, "Eat my shorts!" He laughed like he just told a great joke.

"Ya got another smoke, Rowdy?"

In 1968, everybody smoked: dentists, teachers, and doctors. Most teens followed suit. Thick grey smoke boiled out of the Cedaredge High teacher's lounge. There wasn't anything like having a teacher lean over your shoulder with foul ciggie breath. Nothing. 'Come up to the fresh taste of Salem' the ad said as a beautiful couple near a waterfall smoked and then kissed.

Devyn said as he lit up, "Look, we're about finished. Once we get unloaded, we can call it a day. Skyland Foods won't pay overtime, so why bust our butts?"

We nodded in agreement.

I started the tractor and drove two rows over to pick up the last boxes. The trailer was six levels high; double the number we were supposed to put on it.

"Let's get the heck outta here," Owl shouted.

I reminded my friends, "Yeah, we got a triple date this evening. Remember, I have you two set up with Dove's sisters. We'll meet them at the Dairy King in Delta at seven."

Owl rubbed his crotch. "Me get pussy."

I shook my head. "Don't go there, Alvin. This is the first time you're meeting them and they're church girls. You gotta be cool. I like Dove and I want to impress her."

Dev and Owl stood with their toes on the back of the wagon, holding onto cherry lugs to keep them from sliding off. The tractor groaned as it pulled over the banks of a dry irrigation ditch. I eased the heavily overloaded trailer out of the orchard and onto the graveled road. As the little Ford wound up to a whining pitch, I shifted into third, then fourth gear and headed for the yard down the hill.

Lush green orchards sat several hundred feet below where another wagon crew crept between the rows of fruit trees picking up cherry-filled boxes. A semi-trailer sat with open water tanks waiting for the day's harvest. We would toss the cherries one box at a time into the tanks. One threw while the other caught the lug and dumped it as the third one rested.

I approached the crest of the hill, stepped on the clutch, and ground the transmission as I shifted lower into second. I let up on the clutch hoping to keep us creeping along for a half mile. The rolling descent caused the braking engine to whine louder and louder until it screamed. I thought about the sharp right turn at the foot of the hill and the open machinery shed. I sure didn't want to end up there.

Suddenly, the transmission snapped out of gear. I pumped the clutch as I tried to force it back into gear. We rolled faster and faster. I kept grinding away. I stood up on the smoking brakes. The overloaded wagon had too much weight and momentum.

Devyn saw what was happening and yelled, "Jump man… It's out of control. We're gonna crash!" He hopped off and Owl followed suit.

Running behind the wagon, they yelled, "Jump Rowdy, Jump! Let it go. Get off! It's gonna kill you."

I ground on the transmission trying to force it into gear. The brakes stank of burning pads and did little to slow the heavy rig.

To my buddies, me, the tractor, and the overloaded cherry wagon disappeared past a hump as they ran after me, yelling, "Jump Rowdy, get off!"

Minutes passed as the tractor spun ever faster down the hill. I saw the machinery shed and turned the front wheels which slid on the gravel. A sickening crash with the sound of splintering wood and I flew off the tractor seat. Things went dark.

Devyn and Owl loped down the road. Dreading the sight, they rounded the corner. The tractor sat upright. It was still attached to the tipped-over wagon with its left corner dug into the gravel. Dust rose in the air. A mass of cherries and boxes were scattered everywhere inside the open equipment shed. I was on my stomach, lying in shock, buried under cherry boxes seeing only red mushy things. The wagon's left front edge had dug a trench twelve feet long through the graveled road and brought the tractor to a sudden halt, tossing me off.

Racing around the tractor, Devyn saw me pushing up from being buried among the splattered and scattered cherry lugs. "Are you okay?" He yelled. Big Owl was close behind him.

"I think so." I stood. My head, face, arms, and chest were blood red. Dizzy, I brushed smashed cherries off my blue jeans and shirt. Feeling through my hair, I found a cherry stuck behind one of my oversized ears.

"Man, you're bleeding!" His face twisted with concern, Devyn stormed over with his arms out.

"I don't know." My eyes were wide with shock. Cherry juice plastered my face, hair, shirt, and pants. I touched my chest, legs, and arms. "Nothing seems broken. This is cherry juice." As I looked around, my face blanched cold. "Oh, man…I'm in trouble."

The boss had lost his lower right leg from shell fragments during the Korean War. Jan came out from the office rapidly swinging his phony leg. He yelled, "What the hell are you guys doing to my equipment?" At six-foot-four inches and two-hundred-forty pounds, he was a force to be reckoned with. Despite his prosthesis, he covered a remarkable amount of ground and was in my face. "Jesus! How am I supposed to explain this to corporate?"

Devyn stepped between us and stared up at Jan. "It's you and Skyland Food's fault. We've been telling you this Ford's transmission pops out of gear when we're going downhill. We also told you it has no brakes." Dev faced off with Jan, his face purple with anger. "You don't even care about Rowdy; look at him – he's bleeding!"

Jan's tone changed. "You hurt Rowdy?" He rubbed the sweat from his short-cropped black hair.

I brushed more smashed cherries from my face, neck, and shirt collar. "I'm all right – its cherry juice." I picked a way through the massive pile of spilled and squashed cherries to the gravel driveway.

Jan said, "Well, check yourself, guy. I don't want a workman's comp claim. They'll fire my ass for sure if I didn't take care of you."

I felt my legs, arms, and shoulders and stretched my back again. "I'm not hurt too bad, just shaken up." I touched my ribs. "A box got me in the side."

They walked around the tractor where Big Owl stood staring at the mess. "Boy, you done 'er up good, Rowdy. There ain't a cherry box left on the wagon!" He laughed loudly.

Jan moaned. "Damn! They'll be all over me for this wreck. Why were you coming off the hill so damn fast?"

"He told you," Dev's voice was frustrated, "It popped out of gear halfway down and without brakes, he couldn't get it back into gear. It just took off."

I added, "I almost made the turn but the wagon tipped and caught the front edge. The tractor went up on two wheels and threw me off and I blacked out for a few." I looked around. "I barely missed that wood post and plow." I pointed.

Dev said forcefully, "You're lucky it didn't take off his head! We hopped off and yelled at him to jump. Rowdy could have been killed but he rode it out. He'll be bruised but he's alive. He's too damned brave for his own good."

Silently, everyone surveyed the damage.

Big Owl said, "Hell, let's tip the wagon back up." He grabbed the upper corner and pulled down with all his weight. The trailer rocked but didn't settle back into place. "Well, eat my shorts!" He laughed and shook his big freckled head.

Jan, me, and Devyn joined to rock the trailer upright without luck.

Devyn said, "I'll start the tractor and see if I can back it from the trench while you guys pull down on it."

It worked and the wagon settled down as if it was never on its side.

Jan paced and then looked at me. "I have to fire you."

Devyn jumped into Jan's face again. "What?" Yelling, "It's the company's fault, it's a defective tractor without brakes!" He ran to pick up an empty cherry lug and pushed cherries into it with his hands. "We can pick these up and put them in the semi-trailer and no one will know the difference."

Big Owl joined him and they filled and stacked boxes on the metal trailer.

"I still gotta write it up," Jan said. "If they find out and I didn't report, I'd be gone."

"So report it but nobody has to get fired." Devyn frantically shoved cherries into boxes.

I walked around in a daze, wondering how I had survived because I didn't remember anything after the front wheels started skidding on the gravel.

"I don't wanna but I gotta fire you, Rowdy. That's policy. If you wreck any equipment, you have to be fired. They'd fire me if I wrecked a tractor or tore up any equipment. You go, or I go, and I got a wife and kid to feed." He slowly turned to me. "Okay, so you're fired. You can pick up your check on Friday."

Devyn flung a box of cherries across the mound of cherries. It bounced off a wood post and ricocheted back at the tractor. "Bullshit! That's not fair. He didn't wreck anything but a few of these old cherry boxes. You fire him, and I quit. We all quit, right Owl?"

Big Owl shrugged his shoulders. "Yeah, I fogging quit."

We stomped off toward our cars, leaving Jan staring at the huge mound of cherries splattered throughout his equipment shed. Had he cooperated, Skyland may have lost only ten boxes not over a hundred.

I stopped at the cherry dump station near the tanker truck to wash with a garden hose. "This sucks," I said, "This is the only job around Cedaredge." Solemnly, I washed cherry juice from my clothes and body. I looked up with a smile. "Hey, remember, we're supposed to meet Dove and her sisters this evening."

In the back of my mind, I'd do anything for the love of that woman. She was living perfection in every way.

2. Dairy King Girls

Several weeks back, me and Devyn were at the Dairy King drive-in diner in Delta. We gawked at the blonde waitress who sashayed out. Blasting from the Dairy King's speakers was, "I'm pickin' up good vibrations. She's giving me excitations,"

Devyn said, "That order pad could ruin a guy's life. Bet every guy in town is chasing her."

Approaching my side, she flipped her long blonde hair and asked sweetly, "May I take your order?"

Looking into her blue eyes, I almost said, *I'll have you.* I wanted to kiss her face all over. Probably most guys were scared of her because she was *too* beautiful and totally sexy. "Hi, my name's Rowdy, what's yours?" I pushed my long black hair from my eyes and looked directly into hers.

"Dove." She flipped her hair again and her eyes sparkled with something. She was going to Western State in Gunnison for nursing. She was nineteen and a former Delta High School cheerleader.

Dove said, "You look like a young David Janssen with thick black hair, fair skin, and broad shoulders." Apparently, my deep brown eyes, square chin, and trustworthy manner had caught her attention. She liked Janssen in "The Fugitive" the TV series and had fallen in love with him in his new movie. "You should see The Green Berets with me – it's really good."

Her beauty took away all reason. "You look like Grace Kelly in *Dial M for Murder*."

Dove's little sister also worked at the Dairy King. Stormy skipped to the passenger side of the faded red Cadillac. "May I take your order?" She smiled as she pushed up her dorky black-framed glasses.

Devyn smiled. "I haven't seen you here before. What's your name?"

She couldn't keep from bouncing. "Stormy. What's yours?"

"Devyn."

"Doesn't that mean bard?" Her eyebrows crinkled above her cute nose. Twisting her legs together, she did a little spin and smiled as she came around.

He grinned. "I'd be your bard. You can be the storm that brings nourishment to my garden."

"You *are* a bard, aren't you?" She shivered. Trying to stand still, she took a breath, "Where are you from?"

He motioned toward the Grand Mesa. "I go to Cedaredge High School. We have an apple farm just north of Eckert." His face was sunburned with freckles. Dev had a chronically sarcastic twist on his upper lip like James Dean. "Are you from Delta?"

She hung on the car mirror, dipping and twisting with energy, "Yes, we don't live far from here."

"How old are you?"

She knelt to his level. "Fourteen this month. How about you?"

"Sixteen."

She asked, "Can we be friends? I can't stand the boys here. They are so mean. They are always teasing me about my thick black eyebrows and these ugly glasses.

"Ah, oh, ah, sure. I don't have a girlfriend." His face turned red. He never had a girlfriend other than liking my sister, Hetty, when we were in seventh grade.

Dove glared across the roof of the car.

Stormy snapped to attention. "May I take your order?"

Bobbie Gentry's song played on the sound system. "Today Billie Joe MacAllister jumped off the Tallahatchie Bridge."

We thought we had died and gone to heaven since no girls in Cedaredge were this nice and pretty. Dove readily gave me her phone number.

The sound system played, "There's a crazy little shack beyond the tracks and everybody calls it the sugar shack." Free love, drugs, and Rock-N-Roll permeated the airwaves in 1968 – a year after the Summer of Love. Everyone wanted to be cool. "I'm in with the in-crowd. I go where the in crowd goes."

I called Dove every other day, then a couple of weeks later, I asked her out. She was hesitant, knowing that most young men only wanted one thing. "Okay, but you'll need to take my two sisters along."

3. A Sliver of a Moon

Naturally, Stormy would be with Devyn. The girls had an older sister, Alayna, who filled in occasionally at the drive-in. She was a tall, husky, blue-eyed redhead who had recently graduated from college with a teaching degree. We set Big Al up with Alayna after deciding their age difference wasn't as important as size.

As we walked the girls out to my old Cadillac, Devyn pointed at the moon. "Hey, check that out." A golden moon sliver rose on the horizon, romantically on its back.

Using a teacher-like voice, Stormy said, "That is a waxing crescent. It is the moon's first step toward fullness. A new moon is invisible until a tiny sliver is illuminated. In folklore, it signifies an opportunity for change and is a call to action."

Devyn's eyes opened like he was impressed.

Stormy wanted to sit next to Devyn and Owl wanted to sit with Alayna. There was no doubt Dove would be next to me. It turned into a Chinese fire drill because Big Owl and Alayna were more than huge. First, it was guys in front and girls in the back, but Big Owl took up half the front seat and Devyn suffocated under my and Owl's arms. Worse, I couldn't turn the steering wheel. Owl and Alayna tried sitting together in the back but that meant the other four of us were squished together in the front. Again, I couldn't steer. Big Owl ended up in the front passenger seat with Dove in the middle. She didn't mind sitting tight to me. Stormy was happy to squeeze against Devyn because Alayna took half the back seat. The Cadillac shocks sagged on the passenger side as if it was an old boat on a lake.

Delta was named for the Gunnison and Uncompahgre Rivers coming together. It was a swampy run-down farm town with two frantically smoking sawmill stacks and a sugar beet factory that reeked to high heaven when the beet harvest was on.

No one knew what to talk about so I cranked on the radio and song lyrics covered the lack of conversation. KOMA from Oklahoma was the best AM station we received – no FM in Delta County. An anti-war song came from the speakers, "War makes us act with cruelty. No mercy, killing with brutality. But we will not give up. Never no, never no - we will not give up."

Devyn sang along in an Irish tenor and moments later, Big Owl added his deep bass. "There's great profits to be made. Handing the rich the spoils of a soldier's pay. But we will not give up. Never no never no we will not give up."

Dove's eyes flashed. "That song makes me so mad. It's anti-American."

We cruised down Delta's main street, joining other teens from Cedaredge, Delta, Hotchkiss, and Paonia. I held back my baritone as the song continued.

Devyn asked Dove, "Why?"

She didn't respond.

I asked, "Seriously, why? Our band plays this song – it has a three-part harmony."

Her eyes hardened. "The Vietnam War is the final fight against Communism – it's our last chance to stop the onslaught. They're killers, atheists, and they are anti-Christian. The communists have burned nearly all churches in Vietnam and we need to defend the Christians. This is a war for political and religious freedom! We must help the Vietnamese or the devil worshippers will take over the world. Do you want Communist Russia and China to rule us? It all depends on who wins the Vietnamese War."

Her intensity surprised me.

I looked in the mirror.

Stormy rolled her eyes. She'd heard it before.

Devyn got a wry smile and tapped a rebellious foot to the tune. His old man, Mr. Marine, also hated the song, and any little way to defy him made him feel a little more in control. He sang along softly, "They'll see how wrong, killing for peace can never be logical. All belong – it's not that radical."

Stormy realized he was poking fun at Dove. Tension was in her voice as she jerked away. "Our brother is in Vietnam."

Devyn said, "Sorry, we're in a band called The Persimmon Tree. I play the guitar, Rowdy plays the harmonica and Big Owl is our drummer." He said, "Hey, I'm not against the Vietnam War – sometimes you have to take out dictators like Hitler."

Dove said with a firm tone, "We have to stop the communists in Southeast Asia. The Viet Cong are brutal. For example when a fifteen-year-old girl gave U.S. Marines information on VC activities, she was beheaded. As a warning to other villagers, they put her head on a pole in front of her home. Her murderers were her brother and two of his Viet Cong comrades." Dove took a breath. "It is up to us to stop those barbarians."

Devyn said, "You're talking about *Just War Theory*. It says war is terrible, but it may not be the worst option. War is justified to prevent atrocities. My dad said that during the Tet Offensive this last January, the commies broke all rules of international warfare." His contribution went over like a lead balloon. Given Delta County's anti-intellectualism, he doubted anyone besides me understood.

Straightening her back, the car rocked as Alayna leaned toward the front seat. "Dove is right, this is good versus evil. It's God versus Satan." She inhaled through her nose, then said very seriously, "U.S. servicemen are warriors for God."

Big Owl perked up and shifted his massive left arm onto the seat, letting it accidently touch Alayna's chest. She didn't jump back. The car wobbled a little.

She said, "It's our patriotic duty to fight for the Vietnamese people's freedom of religion."

I commented, "Sounds like the Nazis herding people into concentration camps." I switched radio channels.

Another anti-war song came through the Cadillac's stereo speakers. "And it's one, two, three, what are we fighting for? Don't ask me, I don't give a damn, the next stop is Vietnam."

Dove's cheeks flushed as she stared at me. "This is God's cause to stop Satan in his tracks. I would never marry a man who was afraid to fight for Jesus!"

Hell, I damned near ran off the highway because her big sparkling blue eyes caught mine. Instead, I hit the radio search button and kept the Caddie on the road.

To the disappointment of Big Owl, Alayna settled back into her seat with a satisfied sigh. The car springs creaked.

The radio played, "Fighting soldiers from the sky. Fearless men who jump and die."

Dove said, "That's more like it!"

My manhood was excitingly saluting her. "My brother is in the Army based in San Francisco," I said, "He's a driver for a General. I'm thinking about dropping out of high school to fight in Vietnam." I wanted this lovely blonde to fall in love with me no matter the cost.

Dove slipped her left hand onto the inside of my right leg. "You can get your G.E.D. in the Army. I'd write you every day. I want to marry a military man who fights for God." She squeezed her bottom closer and pressed her breast into my side. "You could be my *own* war hero," she said.

I damned near rear-ended this farm pickup on Main Street but weaved into the other land.

Dove's voice was sultry, "We should go see the Green Berets movie with John Wayne and David Janssen. I've seen it once but I'd like to see it again."

"Sure." My manhood saluted her so quickly, it hurt. *Wow, if I take her to the drive-in, we will…*

Big Owl glanced back at Alayna. "My brother did a tour in Vietnam as a trucker. I might join up too." His big teeth were like a squirrel biting an acorn.

Alayna leaned forward, again resting her boobs on the seat, hypnotizing him. "Al, I would write you. You can be my personal warrior for God. We girls admire a man who will do anything for the love of his woman."

He said, "That'd be great!"

Devyn said, "My dad was a Marine. He fought in World War Two and again in Korea."

Stormy subtly shifted back to him. "Are you going to join?"

"I'm sixteen. My mom says I should go to college first." Devyn said whatever he thought. "After what combat did to my dad, she doesn't want me to end up like him. He's got a temper you wouldn't believe." Devyn opened his palm to Stormy. She touched her lips with two fingers as if dismayed.

Dove pushed a Pointer Sister into my right tricep. "So when are you signing up, soldier?"

I had to concentrate to keep my eyes on the road. A car full of teens passed and flipped us off. One kid put his bare ass in the rear window. I said, "Maybe soon. I'm sick of the immature punks in this town."

Dove sighed deeply. "I'm proud to date you. When you enlist, I'll tell everyone we're going steady and you're fighting the communists in Vietnam for me."

It felt like we were already engaged. Fine with me! I pulled into the grocery store parking lot. "Anyone want a drink or a snack?"

As we walked around the inside store, Alayna asked about our religious upbringing.

Big Owl said with a laugh, "Well, one time I went to the Assembly of God Church in Cedaredge but my parents ain't too religious."

Stormy asked Devyn, "And you?"

"Guess I'm a Christian. My old man claims he's one but he doesn't act like it. My mom and grandmother go to the Eckert Presbyterian Church." He glanced at me. "Sometimes I go with them. I love my grandma and mom."

Approaching the cash register, Dove looked expectantly at me.

"I'm Presbyterian." Although it had been years, I said, "We go to church in Cedaredge." I put the sodas onto the conveyor belt, eyeing Dove's rosy complexion. "But I'm searching." I did a Clint Eastwood pose with an eyebrow twist as I asked, "How about you girls?"

All three responded, "We're LDS."

Dove explained, "The Church of Jesus Christ of Latter Day Saints."

Devyn blurted, "You're Mormons?"

Stormy instantly distanced from him.

Alayna squinted at him.

I said, "I would enjoy learning more about your religion."

Dove said, "I'd love to be your teacher." She poked a howitzer into the crook of my arm.

Had to salute this woman again. It had only been a few weeks since we met but she was already my commander. She was my dream, my queen, and soon – I hoped to cream her.

The clerk asked for money.

Pretending it was no problem, I paid for everything.

As we settled into the car, the radio played, "Oh, my soul has been too long locked inside a stone hermitage. Oh, there's nothing, no song, in the journey of my soul's pilgrimage."

Devyn said, "I'm sorry if it sounded as if I don't like Mormons. I want to show respect for whatever you believe. I'm, well, I'm…" he paused. "I'm curious about the Mormon religion."

I carefully pulled my '56 Cadillac Sedan de Ville back onto Main Street, driving slowly and pretending I was a careful driver. I didn't want Dove to realize the Caddy wouldn't shift into 3rd gear.

The shocks complained when Alayna leaned forward. She asked Big Owl, "Are you interested in learning about The Church too?"

Big Owl dumbly swiveled to check with me.

I nodded he should say yes.

With John Wayne's voice, he said loudly, "Why shore."

Devyn tried to act cool by tapping his knees to the song. "Spread our wings over the rainbow. Link our minds, bodies, and souls."

"It's like the song that's playing," Dove's voice was firm. "We believe life is eternal and love between a man and woman should be everlasting. We marry in the LDS Temple for time and all eternity."

I digested this information.

Devyn nodded, saying, "Time and all eternity. Cool concept. To love and be loved forever – a soul mate."

Stormy stared into his face. Then both smiled and started holding hands. The backseat warmed.

Dove said with zeal, "Our young men go on a mission to convert and save people. Our family believes if a man fights against the communists that military service is equivalent to a church mission. Our brother is doing his duty in Vietnam right now. Don't you agree, Alayna?"

"Yes, the best way to serve God is to stop the communist aggressors." She leaned forward, capturing Owl's eyes. "Like the Crusaders, warriors saved Jerusalem from the Muslim infidels. A warrior's wife is a saint because she supports him. The best way of fighting injustice in the world is through couples fighting together against evil." When she shifted back, the rear shocks complained.

Stormy pulled her glasses off and chimed in, "Dove says it's okay to make love with your soldier if you're engaged." Putting her thick glasses back on to see better, she glanced at Devyn.

Dove flashed a frown. "Shush, Stormy!" She turned to me. "Stormy often speaks before she thinks. But she is correct: Our role in The Church is to do all we can – even giving our bodies to support our warrior who fights for God." Her hand slipped close to my trouser mouser.

I was on fire.

In my mind, I was enlisted in the army, killing Viet Cong, and was also engaged to Dove. My mortar tube spoke loudly in the dark of night, blinding reason. *This is it, love, pure love, no doubt.* Touching her slender hand, I pushed it tight against my manhood while steering the old Cadillac along Main Street toward North Delta.

Big Owl perked up with his most profound thought for the month. *All I got to do is listen to their religion and then I can snuggle my ears between this here gal's huge honkers.*

Alayna let her big breasts touch Owl's big arm when she leaned forward. "If women don't marry by the time we're twenty-one, we are supposed to go on a Church mission ourselves." She sat back in the seat and the shocks squawked.

Owl looked disappointed.

Dove smiled dreamily. "Yes, we've talked about going to Biafra in Africa. They are being starved by the Muslim Nigerian Army. Mother said we would be the Mormon version of Mother Teresa who works with the poor in Calcutta, India."

Stormy interjected, "I have to use the bathroom." She crossed and squeezed her legs together.

Dove asked me to take Stormy home.

"I don't want to go home. I just need to use the restroom."

"No, we'd better take her home."

A few minutes later, I pulled up in front of their house.

Dove said, "We all should go in. We are to come home together."

Despite our protests, the sisters got out.

Dove slid a note into my pocket as she stepped from the Caddie.

Stormy said to Devyn, "I forgive you for saying what you did about my church." She offered her hand, and he took it gently.

"Thank you." His eyes were soft. "I never want to make you feel bad."

Stormy walked to the house with him following. "I like you, Devyn." She offered her hand. The sweet breath of the evening touched their lips.

He took it. "I really like you too. I can tell you're smart." He paused. "Be my friend." His voice was sincere.

Alayna walked to the house with Big Owl. As he opened the storm door for her, she softly brushed her butterballs across the back of his knuckles. Instantly, something went twang!

Dove and I stood by the car wrapped around one another. A tractor beam linked our eyes. She kissed me gently and then touched her lips. "Rowdy, will you do anything for my love?"

I didn't need to think. "Of course."

Back in my car, we watched the girls go into the house. Big Owl slapped the back of the seat. "Geez, Dev, you damn near blew it!"

"Hey, I pulled it out. Did you see? She kissed me."

I razed him as they headed to Cedaredge. "You're always opening your mouth and getting into trouble."

"Can't help it. At least you don't have to guess what I'm thinking, do you? I'm too honest." As second or two later, he said, "The Mormons have a strange view of sex, don't they? It is amoral out of wedlock but fine if the guy is in the Army killing communists."

I grinned. "Like somebody we know, Stormy engages her mouth before her brain."

Devyn started in about me playing the religious theme. "You haven't been to church in…"

I interjected, "God, she squeezed my cock as we got out of the car. I almost had an orgasm!" I checked my pocket and pulled out her note. I hit the overhead light but couldn't read it, so I gave it to Devyn.

He read, "I'm falling in love with you."

I took a big breath. "Hey, I'm in!"

"You're always smooth," Devyn said, "Good for you. She'll lead the way for her sisters."

Big Owl gahuffed. "Yeah, I reckon Al…Ala, what's her name? She drug her boobs across the back of my hand at the door. Man, she got the best of them all."

Arguing about which one was the hottest, we agreed Dove had it all: a perfect body, a beautiful face, and, best of all – she was smart.

"I like Stormy," Devyn said, "She says what she thinks like me. I'll never wonder what's going on."

I said, "Boy, she looks nothing like the others. I met the older brother when he was home on leave. He's blonde with blue eyes like Dove and Alayna."

Big Owl chuckled. "Must have been a Mexican in the woodshed."

Devyn changed the subject. "Hey, I didn't tell my old man that we quit the cherry orchard. I said I'm camping at the orchard so I don't waste time and gas, but I'm camping at Hart's Basin. Why don't you guys come to the lake and we can swim, fish, and catch crawdads?"

"Huh!" Big Owl chuckled. "Now yer talking – let's party!"

I got interested. "Yeah, we can hang around and decide what to do. Hopefully, I can get Dove to come up."

Big Owl said, "Well eat my shorts! We can build a fire."

4. The Green Berets

I took her for a walk in the Delta Park. Dove wore a silky dress that showed off her incredible body. She was ever so sweet and submissive. What luck! The joy of being in her presence, her soft fragrance, and the delight she had in flowers. She bent over in front of me to smell them and looked up in time to see my blushing face.

She asked, "Would you like to see The Green Berets? It's playing at the drive-in."

"It would be my pleasure." When dusk's veil slid over the sky, we took off for the TruVu outdoor theater.

Pulling my old Cadillac onto the drive-in hump, I rolled her power window down so she could get the speaker. She said, "This is a cool car, it has everything."

I said, "Check this out – watch the antenna." I pushed a button and it came down. "Automatic opening truck too." I didn't reveal I always drove slowly because the transmission wouldn't shift to third gear.

"Cool." She hung the speaker on her window and scooted across the worn leopard-patterned seat next to me. I put my arm around her and she snuggled in tight. "I think you'll like this movie. Its exciting and you look like David Janssen who plays a reporter in this film."

We watched the movie unfold. Toward the end when the boy's pet dog died and they lost the grave marker, Dove cried slightly. I gently brushed the tears from her cheeks. We kissed for a few minutes but she insisted we watch the movie.

The reporter said he'd be fired for a story supporting the U.S. involvement in Vietnam. Dove asked, "Do you think we're doing the right thing?"

"Yes, it's like fighting the Nazis in my homeland of Holland."

We started feeling each other up.

"I've never touched someone like this. There's never been a man I respected enough and you are *so* handsome."

One of the heroes in the movie was killed by a booby trap and they had to leave his body behind. She asked, "Will you go fight the Viet Cong for me?"

Breathlessly, I said as I touched her breasts, "Sure, anything you want." Eyes full of desire, we stared into each other's souls.

"If you enlist, I'll give you my virginity. You can teach me how to satisfy you. You'll be the boss and I'll give you as many children as you want."

That was it! A submissive mother of my children and a beauty at that! I'd do anything for this woman's love.

We lay down in the seat to kiss. She moaned so loudly that I put my hand over her mouth. We were the last to pull out of the empty drive-in theater. No problem, I'd kill communists for this woman's love. She was worth it.

The radio music sent us out on moonbeams, "I'm hooked on a feeling. I can't help believing I'm high on believing that you're in love with me."

When I went to the lake, Devyn and Owl were snockered. They laughed and jumped around the campfire. We had lost our jobs and didn't have a clue what we would do for money, and I was in love – time to celebrate!

I said, "I've got it! We ought to join the service!"

Owl said, "Yeah, let's join the Army. My brother just got out. He said it weren't too bad."

"Hey, no way!" Devyn exclaimed. "I can't go with you. I'm sixteen and my parents won't sign for me."

Ignoring him, Owl said, "Hell yes, let's get away from Cedaredge; ain't no point in going back to school."

"Yeah! We're both eighteen so we can enlist without a parent signature."

"Hey, my brother is in California, south of San Francisco." Owl's drunken face was red. "We can go there to join."

"That's it. California Dreaming."

Dev was suddenly sober. "You guys are nuts – the war isn't going good. Martin Luther King Jr and Robert Kennedy both got killed, and they're protesting the Vietnam War all over the world. We can have our jobs back at the cherry orchard."

A song came on, "You say you want a revolution."

I said, "This song says it – the whole world is crazy. If we're not in school, we'll get drafted. Every week or two, somebody gets shot up. Patterson took one in the head and Luna got wounded. If we gotta go, let's do it and get it over with." I paused. "It's clear that the only way I can have Dove is to go to Vietnam and kill commies." In the back of my mind, I was invulnerable. It would be like going rabbit hunting.

Devyn said, "They're supposed to start a lottery for the draft next year. You may get lucky and not get drafted at all. My old man says to join the Navy or the Air Force – at least you'd have a warm bed." He grabbed sticks in each hand as if he had a machine gun. "I want to fly a Cobra helicopter." He stared into the sky, imagining diving and firing rockets at the Viet Cong.

Big Owl said, "My brother drove trucks in the Army. The Air Force and Navy take four years and the Army is two. Now my brother is a truck driver in California."

"Hey, we'll be truck drivers for the U.S. Army." I slapped Big Owl's shoulder. "I'm not going back to high school. There's no point. I have to enlist and fight in Vietnam to marry the most perfect woman I've met. My brother is a driver for a General in San Francisco and Dove's brother is coming back from Vietnam. They're both okay."

We hit the sleeping bags and I dreamed of making love with Dove.

5. For The Love Of A Woman

Two weeks went by and Dove and I spent hours and hours talking, dry humping, and making plans among our many promises. We'd have eight kids or more. Wouldn't they be smart and beautiful? She let me touch everything but her pussy, saying, "It's yours once you enlist."

I was crazy obsessed. Hell, I would have done anything for even *one* night with her.

Devyn went for a swim first thing one morning and afterwards, he turned on his transistor radio and then he let the sun bake the moisture off his hard body. The announcer said, "Scotland Yard recently arrested James Earl Ray, the alleged assassin of Martin Luther King Junior as he attempted to board a flight from London to Rhodesia this morning. In other news, assassinated U.S. Senator Robert F. Kennedy will be laid to rest at Arlington National Cemetery this evening."

I crawled out of the sleeping bag, feeling ragged since I had dreamed of fucking Dove and killing Asians all night. "Yikes, turn that down. Why are you up so early?"

Dev laughed. "It's nine in the morning, my friend." He motioned in a wide arc at the sun, the lake, and Antelope Hill – a fruit-growing mesa. He pointed at the beauty of Grand Mesa and Cedar Mesa escorting the waters of the Surface Creek Valley. It was astounding. "Another shitty day in paradise." He stirred coals in the campfire. Tossing a capful of Everclear grain alcohol onto it, soon he had water boiling for coffee.

Big Owl arrived at the campfire as Dev swung the coffee pot in a fast calf-roping loop to settle the grounds. Devyn turned to me and saw my eyes. "I suppose you laid Dove last night."

I shook my head. "Close, but no cigar."

"So tell me."

The radio played, "Come on baby, light my fire."

Taking evasive action, I left to pee near the lake, but when I returned, Dev persisted.

I said, "Let's say everything but, and it isn't going any further until a key event happens."

"What key event?"

"It's like this song – she lights my fire!" I shook my dark hair as I combed it out with my fingers. "She's a virgin. I have to get baptized and go on a Mormon mission or like she wants – fight the Viet Cong." I shook my head to clear it. "So I'm going to enlist."

"You sure she's worth it?"

I said with awe, "Dove is everything I've ever imagined in a woman. She's smart, funny, kind, and gentle. She loves children. She is so great with my little brothers and sisters, they don't want her to leave." I smiled softly. "Mama thinks the world of her."

"And?" Dev raised an eyebrow.

"Dove is extremely religious yet she is as sensual as a butterfly's silk wings. Man! We dry humped and kissed and hugged half the night until I came in my jeans."

"You sure you're not just in lust? Wanting to get the fire burning in your pants put out?" Dev cupped his mouth at Big Owl. "Call the fire department, quick!"

"Hey, don't talk that way." Transfixed, I stared across the lake. "She also had the big O. She's my soul mate, the mother of my children – everything I could ever want."

"What's the big O?" Big Owl asked.

I laughed. "Orgasm, man. She orgasmed at the same time as me."

Devyn said, "Let me get this straight: You are all but banging your brains out with a pretty girl and you're going to join the Army because she wants you to or she won't fuck you if you don't?" He shook his head. "What's up with that? You're a walking contradiction."

"Well, gosh darn it, we'll get drafted anyway," I said.

"You can't be sure. They may change how it's done. They're talking about a lottery for the draft and you might get lucky." He scratched his head. "You're sure Dove doesn't just want to control you? That's lust, not love." He went on, "You don't need to rush things. My luck, if I left Stormy alone at home while I was off being her hero, she'd find someone else. There I'd be on a Mormon mission or fighting the Viet Cong, and she'd be with some Don Juan. Either way, it would suck."

I was sure Dove would be loyal since she had promised. We had the same vision of a big family; we read the same novels, and enjoyed the same music. I ignored my best friend who was probably smarter than me.

6. Cherry Pie

Saturday rolled around. "No beer or smoking tonight," I warned them. "They aren't allowed by the Mormon Church."

"No beer, that's queer!" Owl's eyes went wide with surprise. "Dang, I'm glad I didn't hook up with Dove's older sister. I'd be up a shit creek without a paddle!"

I laughed, knowing the debt of Owl's thoughts were half the length of his dick.

Dev interjected, "No problem, we'll play tunes for the girls. I have my guitar here. Got your harmonica, Rowdy?"

"Always."

Owl complained, "What about me? I can't bring my drum set to the lake."

"You want to use my Indian drum?" Dev asked.

Off they went to Dev's house to snag the drum while I drove to Delta to pick up the three sisters.

There was a lull in the combat between his parents, so Dev got permission to take the grill, camp plates, and utensils. He also took a black iron kettle to make a deep-dish fruit cobbler on the campfire.

As they drove past his neighbor's house, his neighbor, Cheri, flagged them down. "Take me with you."

"Are you sure?" Knowing her father, Dev cautioned. "Do you have your parent's permission?"

"I'll go ask." She ran back to her house, skipping like a kid with bouncy boobs.

Dev told Owl that her father was more than a little off from being one of the marines who fought in Korea at the Chosin Reservoir. "If he found out you banged Cheri, he'd kill you."

Owl grinned. "I can take care of myself."

"He's got guns."

As the song ended, Cheri jiggled back. She had changed into a tight white T-shirt, painted-on white shorts and no bra. No way her father would let her leave the house dressed like that. "I can go. Mom said its okay."

Devyn was nervous. "Where's your dad?"

Big Owl drooled with a big stupid grin.

"He's in Grand Junction on a job. He won't be home for a few days." She hopped into the back of the old jeep and immediately started singing Beatles tunes.

At the lake, Devyn organized the kitchen gear into a neat setup. He had pork chops, tin-foil-wrapped potatoes, canned veggies, and a loaf of his mother's homemade bread for dinner. After starting a campfire for the coals, he mixed brown sugar, biscuit flour, and fresh-picked pie cherries in the black iron kettle.

While he got things organized for dinner, he wasn't surprised that Cheri and Owl did their thing in the tent, sounding like pigs wrestling in the mud. Owl grunted and Cheri moaned. Dang! He opened Stormy wouldn't demand that he go kill commies to be with her.

Devyn heard voices coming from the cow trail and yelled to Owl and Cheri. "Hey you guys, they're coming. Better stop or you'll be embarrassed."

Muffled moans and a loud grunt and giggling in the tent.

Dev pulled out his guitar and sang to cover up for them. "Eckert, Eckert the place where we belong, but you won't never, ever get it on."

The moment we walked into the area, Big Owl roused out of the canvas Army tent, zipping his pants.

Dove said, "Stormy, you'd have a real catch if you land Devyn. He cooks."

Stormy helped Dev cook as Alayna and Big Owl stood uncomfortably around the fire.

Cheri came from the tent, straightening her micro clothes. Tension redlined as she walked to Owl and snuggled her head under his arm. Nothing like a fresh-sexed girl to bring the group energy to a different level. Her nipples stuck out and her shorts were stained like she wore a sign that you didn't need to know Braille to read.

Devyn tried to break the tension. "Ah, ladies, this is my neighbor, Cheri. I've known her for a long time." Seeing their expressions of dismay, he stumbled on, "She hitched a ride to the lake and wants to hang out."

Alayna had the expression of a deer in headlights. Stormy and Dove stared at her, at Devyn, and then at Big Owl. Disgusted, they turned away.

I grabbed Dove's arm and whispered, "Let's go for a walk."

She hesitated.

I whispered urgently and got her to leave. No way I wanted to be involved with what might happen, and if I could get her alone, we'd soon be making out. I walked her quickly away.

Cheri provocatively put her arms around Big Owl.

Alayna was twice Cheri's size and was nearly as tall and broad as Big Owl. Momentarily, she was angry. She could have lifted one hand and crushed the impish girl like a beetle. But her face went from stunned to addled and upset. Her expression settled as if she was slowly dying. "I'm sorry, I didn't realize...." She scanned the ground. "Oh Lord, this is uncomfortable." She turned to Devyn. "Can you take me home?"

Owl stammered, "Oh, Mam, ah, ah, ah, I ain't wanting ta hurt your feelings. Didn't know you was coming." He spun Cheri away from Alayna as if it might help.

Alayna's face was splotchy as she decided whether to explode or faint from embarrassment. Glancing from Owl and Cheri to Devyn, she pled, "Take me home, please."

He shrugged. "Wish I could but I can't. My jeep doesn't have license plates – we use it on the back roads." He flipped the chops. "Can't we eat first? I made enough for everyone and..."

His voice faded as he saw tears welling up in Alayna's eyes. "I'll check with Rowdy to see if I can borrow his Cadillac."

Owl offered his talon key chain. "You can take my old truck if you don't mind it stalling now and then."

Cheeks in a salt-water flood, Alayna walked away from the camp.

Devyn knelt to push his pork chops to the side of the grill. He bit his lip and asked Owl, "Can you finish cooking these?" His expression was frustrated. "And don't overcook this," pointing at the kettle.

"What is it?" Owl's big dumb face brightened with the thought of food.

"Cherry pie."

He asked Stormy, "Can you come with us?"

She was moving toward her sister who marched firmly down the path to Owl's old grey truck. "This thing overheats and vapor locks. We'll be okay on the way to Delta but its uphill coming back and you can never predict."

Dove and I returned to the camp with the beatific look of saints having seen the Lord. She wasn't upset at her sisters' disappearance since her brain was saturated with neuropeptides.

Everyone was famished. We made the grilled chops, baked potatoes, veggies, and cherry pie disappear.

Devyn returned without Stormy and was pissed because we ate everything. He stomped around the campfire until I said, "Listen, I need to take Dove home. I'll buy you a burger on the way back.

Two hours later, I got back. Devyn had driven Cheri home and he didn't want the cold hamburger since he had loaded up on crawdads and gotten a taste of his cherry cobbler.

Owl said, "Hey, it's time to head to California. We gotta get out of this place. I ain't taking no chances with Cheri's dad coming after me." Devyn had filled him in on Mr. Nelson's temper, saying that's why he hadn't ever done it with Cheri.

I agreed.

Dev announced, "I talked to Jan at the cherry orchard and he's got our jobs back – even you, Rowdy." He said, "Owl, Cheri isn't the girl for you or anyone else. Lots of problems because her daddy messes with her. She wants someone to take care of her and only has one thing to give. She's tried to get me to do her several times."

"Huh," grunted Big Owl.

I stayed quiet, thinking of my promise that I'd go kill communists for the woman I loved.

Owl said, "Hell, let's party."

I grinned, thinking of finally getting between Dove's legs. "We'll make it a big one and then go to California."

Rain began to fall. I tossed grain alcohol onto the smoldering coals. It leaped into the sky.

"Cool!" Owl grabbed the fifth from me, took a chug, and tossed more alcohol on the fire. It followed the stream back to the bottle like lighter fluid but instead of dropping it, Owl took another chug. "Look at me, I'm a fire-eater!" He spit it on the fire and it flamed back at the big dummy.

We broke out laughing.

Dev said, "Don't burn yourself, Owl, you're nuckin' futs!"

We did rounds, chasing shots of grain alcohol with beer as the rain splattered mud around our ankles. Owl said, "I done told my folks I want to see my brother. They don't care."

I agreed. "Yeah. I mentioned I might enlist to my parents and they think it's a great idea."

Devyn tried to convince us to work the cherry harvest, but the idea of enlisting had us amped. Killing Viet Cong wouldn't be much different from elk or bear hunting.

I said, "Man, I've got no future here in this valley. I won't graduate next year and going to 'Nam is the only way Dove will ever make love with me. I've got to go."

"You guys will be back."

"Why?"

"Haven't you heard of The Ute Indian Curse?"

They hadn't so he explained, "Back in the old days after the U.S. Calvary defeated the Ute Indians, they herded them from this area. The feds wanted them on a reservation near what is now Vernal, Utah."

Devyn illustrated with his hands. "Close to Olathe, the young bucks got angry at being treated like cattle, and despite the fact they were outnumbered and they had no weapons, they wanted to attack the Army. The old chiefs got them calmed down, assuring they would get revenge on the white man."

Owl said, "Revenge, my ass. Ain't no Indians around here now."

"The Cloud brothers are Indians who live here," I corrected him. "The oldest brother was an incredible runner and football player."

"Anyway," Dev continued, "The Calvary moved them through this area to the south finger of Grand Mesa to the one called Indian Point. You guys remember where it is?" Seeing uncertainty in our faces, he said, "It's above the Falcon's cattle ranch; remember where we went hunting with Gabe?"

"Oh, yeah," I answered, "It's where the Orchard City water pipeline comes down from the Grand Mesa."

"Yep." Dev nodded. "The young bucks were furious – they wanted to die honorably even if they didn't have weapons; they wanted to fight the whites who herded them like stupid cows. The morning after they reached the top, the old chiefs gathered their people. From there you can see the whole valley from the Lone Cone in the La Plata Mountains to the Uncompahgre Plateau and the Escalante and Dominquez Canyons. You can see Saddle Mountain up the North Fork, and the tips of the Manti-La Salle Mountains in Utah near Moab are also visible." Devyn paused for effect so we could imagine the magnificent views.

Owl guzzled Everclear and passed the bottle.

Dev continued, "The Calvary got scared there'd be an uprising, but an old Indian chief lifted his hands and scattered a gift of tobacco to the four winds. He prayed, 'Great Spirit, Ancestors of our Fathers, these white men force us to leave our home and our valleys. May you bring a great curse upon their heads and the heads of their children and grandchildren down through time.' Everybody expected a devastating curse like Moses brought down on the Egyptians. A plague of locusts, water turning to blood, or your firstborn dying. The old chief closed his eyes and offered a tobacco pipe to the sky. 'May those who are born here never leave.'

Everyone was surprised and confused. How could this be a curse? The young bucks were angry and the US Calvary was relieved. But that was it: Those who are born here can never leave."

Owl said, "Bullshit! Once I leave, I ain't never coming back."

Dev's transistor radio played, "We gotta get outa this place if it's the last thing we ever do."

I said, "I was born in Holland, not here. So it doesn't affect me."

"Seriously, the curse affects everyone who lives here for more than a year. Could be a new awareness or a different phase of life." He looked into my eyes. "You won't ever leave – born here or not. Your heart, mind, and spirit will stay in the valley no matter where your body is. Someday, even if your body is gone, you will come back. The Ute curse says you can never leave."

I thought a minute. "Well, as long as Dove and my family are here, it's a possibility."

The Animals sang, "We gotta get out of this place if it's the last thing we ever do."

Owl said, "Hey! We oughta become blood brothers and cut our palms."

"Now there's an idea!" Devyn agreed.

The next thing, we had a sharp hunting knife, splashed Everclear on our skin and each of us slashed a right forearm and palm. Clasping hands and forearms, we pressed blood to blood.

Whooping drunkenly, we danced around the fire. "We're blood brothers!"

Owl tripped and I ran into him; we fell, spilling beer.

Dev staggered over and fell on top of us, breaking the jug of Everclear as the drops of rain thickened and the mud rose to our ears, soaking our feeble brains.

7. The Ute Curse

We got to the bus stop at noon outside of the Delta Hotel.

Stormy and Dev greeted each other but respectfully stood apart as her emerald eyes blistered into him. *I love you.* I watched my buddy surrender to her energy, her love, and intensity. I realized women were always in control of men and would be forever. Fine with me.

Dove and I started to hug but stopped, inches apart. Something passed between us, a silent, spiritual essence of oneness….an energetic glow surrounding our bodies.

I had no other choice. If a young man wasn't in school, he was expected to find a low-skilled labor job and be happy with it. He would marry one of the homely girls who stayed around instead of going to college and never coming back. She'd get chunky after having a few kids. He would work the harvest, drive tractors or trucks, and maybe they'd buy a used trailer house. He'd drink most nights, trying to avoid her criticism. Not for me. The military was a good way to escape the poverty and small-town boredom of Delta County. It would be a total ADVENTURE in caps.

Despite her pain, Alayna wanted Big Owl to know she would pray for him while he was in Vietnam. Because there was few young men her size, she imagined Alvin could be the one. She wasn't fat, just big and quite good-looking. Reddish hair cut in a short cute pattern framed both sides of her lovely symmetrical face. Alayna had a compassionate smile that made her freckles glow. It made you feel warm inside like grandma saw you at the door and welcomed you in. She generated gentle energy with a sense of home, stability, and responsibility that scared the hell out of guys her age. She would not give up because a confused little girl had sex with Big Owl. He drank, smoked, and wasn't bright, but he could change – she'd convert him to Mormonism and he'd learn what eternal love was. No doubt their kids would be star athletes. "I will pray for you each day you are gone."

Owl blinked. "Okay." His thoughts stopped as soon as he tired of searching the blankness.

Her hand on his monster bicep, they walked into the Delta Hotel. She sat beside him on an old brown leather couch in the hotel lobby.

Dove carried a special energy. When she focused on me, it was like Mother Teresa touched my soul. It was an honor to be in her presence. She kissed me sweetly on the lips and brushed her tongue lightly across my left ear. Her eyes wandered to my groin, and she looked pleased to see my colonel at attention.

I wanted and needed her. I was joining the army to kill communists for her because I wanted her love more than anything in the world.

She pulled me into the old-fashioned solid oak phone booth inside the hotel. "I want to tell you something in private." Once inside, she described the meeting with Bishop Hawkins as she wrapped her legs around my thighs.

The Mormon Bishop had pulled her in to his office for a special meeting this morning. He said, "Your young man is volunteering for Vietnam because of you. He is *not* a church member, therefore you are not obligated to him. Be faithful to him until you meet a man who is LDS. Now, if he converts, it's a different story and you must be loyal to him."

After she told me about this conversations, she asked, "Will you please become a member of my church?" She kissed me passionately.

Although I would do whatever it took to have her, Mormon conversion was a new requirement. "Sure, when I get back from Vietnam." Dove was my vision quest. I looked into her sparkling blue eyes and touched her long blond hair gently. Next I slid my index finger and thumb along a river of golden strands. Softly, I sang to her, "I'll send you all my love, every day in a letter, sealed with a kiss."

"Please consider it. You must be LDS so we can marry for eternity in the temple. It's the only way." She French kissed me and then she looked into my eyes. "I'll write you every single day until you come back home."

Absorbed in one another, we felt invisible. She whispered, "I will make love to you as soon as you get a leave from the Army. I am yours, only yours."

Wait a minute, I thought, *If I have to be a Mormon to marry you, why don't I just do that instead of enlisting?* Unfortunately, the bus tickets were in my back pocket, I had sold my Cadillac to Devyn, and everyone knew my plans. I thought it was too late to switch plans, become a Mormon, and go on one of their silly missions to convert people who were happy with their own religion.

Momentarily, Devyn and Stormy watched us in the phone booth and then she said, "Let's explore this old hotel."

Alayna slid close to Big Owl on the old couch, saying, "We should talk, really talk."

He shrugged and using a Western drawl, said, "I'm all ears, Ma'am."

Alayna knew that Cheri wasn't the one for him. She explained eternal marriage in the Mormon Temple. "I will marry a worthy man and we will raise an army for God."

Owl sat with his mouth open. His thoughts flecked about like fireflies, understanding pieces. He was lost in thought since it was unfamiliar territory. Admiring her Betty Boops, he thought, *She wouldn't be half-bad.* She was offering love and an army of kids but he didn't understand what the big girl meant about being worthy. With two alcoholic parents, he had no experience in the home stability department.

Stormy and Devyn wandered the halls of the hotel until they got bored. She said, "Let's go into the men's restroom." They went into a stall and started making out, their hands everywhere.

A little later, the bus arrived.

After looking everywhere, I knocked on the men's room stall door. "Hey, I don't want to interrupt, but Dove said to find you two. I figured you'd be somewhere private. We gotta get on the bus. I don't care if you come, but Dove might get upset."

Stormy's voice was soft and slightly husky, "We will be together for eternity."

Their noises left little to the imagination. I shook my head as I stood outside the stall door. I heard Devyn take a huge breath and then he groaned.

I yelled as I stomped out, "I'd like to say goodbye." I let the bathroom door slam shut.

Despite the romance, it was a sad day. As in Korea, World War Two, World War One, and every war ever fought in human history, us soon-to-be enlistees bravely yucked it up as if we weren't afraid.

Stormy and Dev stood respectfully holding hands but their eyes blistered into each other, *I will love you forever.*

Devyn pulled himself together. Handing me $350 cash for the keys and title to the '56 Cadillac, he promised I could use it anytime I came home. In 1968, a guy could do a lot with $350. It was a month's pay for a working-class family or a teacher. The wife could stay home with the kids. The bus tickets to San Jose, California cost $25.00 each.

Dev pulled out two 1868 and 1869 silver dollars from his father. "Here," he handed each of us a coin. "My old man wants you to put these in your front pockets and carry them all the time."

We each took one and looked at them curiously.

Reading our expressions, Devyn showed us his father's badly damaged silver dollar. "Dad had this in his shirt pocket at Chosin in Korea. Saved his life. He wants you each to have one for luck. He wants you back alive." No one realized tough old marine McDowell cared.

Without warning, tears ran down Dove's cheeks.

I put my arms around her lovely body as she involuntarily shuddered.

"I promise once you're in the Army, we'll be lovers." But her voice was fragile and lacked conviction. Gone was her assurance that I must go fight communists. Gone was her strength after the Bishop had told her she didn't have to be loyal to me since I wasn't a Mormon. Her faith floated like feathers blown by a light breeze.

Only a few minutes earlier, I had romantically proclaimed, "I will step in front of a bullet for you. I will die for you."

The other two girls teared up for Dove and me.

Big Owl slipped his arm around Alayna to comfort her and was amazed at how her soft energy enfolded him. Briefly, he thought, *Is this love?* But similar to most of his insights, it danced away before he actually grasped it.

There was fear and honor in my face but in Dove's – questions. She was scared because she was making me go, *and* she was afraid of what may happen.

My greatest fear was not dying – it was coming back missing body parts or being paralyzed.

Stormy whispered to Devyn, "This is stupid. Your friends don't need to join the Army. The rules are changing to a lottery next year and they might not get drafted."

Big Owl and Alayna moved like a couple grown comfortable with each other. As he turned to step onto the bus, they shared a kiss, a real kiss, not one of passion, but a kiss of affection and friendship. It was the kiss of a saint on the lips of a sinner. Owl threw his huge arms around her, giving her a teddy bear hug. He brushed her grand boobs with the palms of his hands as they parted.

Alayna announced, "I'm leaving on a Mormon mission for Biafra, Africa the first of July."

Everyone stared at her. It was like drinking at a sports bar and after a touchdown, she said, "Let us pray."

Big Owl broke the tension with a John Wayne impression, "Well, Honey, we'll both be on a mission for the Lord!"

Everybody laughed in relief.

With a swagger and his mouth twisted, he said, "Ma'am, I'll put this here coin in my front pants pocket 'ta save the special things for you.

Everyone laughed again.

Stormy realized why we liked Big Owl. He was dumb but innocently funny – a good guy. She hoped her big sister could have him as her forever husband.

Alayna couldn't have agreed more, and even Dove's attitude toward Owl softened slightly.

The bus driver honked the horn. "Gotta go."

The fateful time to get on the bus could no longer be delayed. Dove and I hugged deliriously.

Devyn said, "Hey, remember you've got the Ute Curse and you gotta come back."

Owl was already in a seat, but I turned on the steps. "I'll be back but not because of the Ute curse. I'll be back because I've been blessed by Dove."

She twittered like a songbird marking territory.

Watching the Greyhound bus pull onto Delta's empty main street, Devyn stood with the forlorn sisters. It looped around the block and turned left, heading west on U.S. Highway 50 to Grand Junction and the California Coast.

Stormy glanced at Devyn, admiring his rugged profile. She decided that no matter how hard Mom pushed, she wouldn't force him to do anything he didn't want to do even if Mom ripped her hair out during one of her psychotic tantrums. The thought made her queasy because she felt like it might happen. She snuggled tight to Devyn who had no clue – just like me and Big Owl – what we were getting into.

8. The Mormon Dance

Alayna and Dove chaperoned Devyn and Stormy to see Doctor Zhivago. They also got to see the new Romeo and Juliet movie while under close observation up f. Both were tearjerkers and they made Devyn and Stormy worry. Were they star-crossed like Romeo and Juliet, or worse, cursed like the lovers in Doctor Zhivago?

Stormy invited him to a Mormon dance at their church. Delighted to see her smile, he didn't mind taking Dove and Alayna along. It was the last party for Alayna because she was leaving next week for the LDS mission in Africa.

He escorted the three girls into their church, and he danced with each sister although Alayna was three times his size. She laughed and felt good to hold as he looked up at her face. When he danced with Dove, her sexual energy gave him an erection. Suddenly, he knew why Rowdy had joined the Army for the love of a woman.

When he danced with Stormy, they sensually touched while doing popular dances like The Monkey, The Jerk, and The Hanky Panky. Other couples artlessly moved around the church gym and stared jealously at Stormy and Devyn who radiated joy.

Bishop Hawkins walked out onto the dance floor, ordering Stormy to his office so Devyn followed. He wouldn't allow Dev in the office. "You are not a church member so I cannot tell you how to act, but Stormy is, and she must be straightened out."

He waited outside the door and periodically knocked politely.

The bishop finally opened the door with a snarl. "What do you want?"

"Sir, I don't mean to be rude, Sir, but Stormy is the girl I want to marry. I will take whatever punishment and do what it takes to be her husband. Please let me come in."

The bishop hesitated and then a clever smile rose on his face. "Come in McDowell. We have many things to talk about."

Bishop Hawkins said the President of BYU, Mr. Wilkinson, had banned all fad dances in 1966, and it was upheld by the LDS Church President, David O McKay. No debate allowed. To the Mormons, a directive from the Church Prophet was a direct order from God.

The bishop launched into a lecture. To be worthy of Stormy, Devyn must join the church and go on a mission to convert others to Mormonism. "This is the true church, the only true church," he exclaimed. Hawkins went into detail about the church mandates. They must be pure and worthy to marry for time and eternity in the LDS Temple. The bishop gave him a long penetrating stare. "Without a doubt, you both must be virgins or your marriage will not be sanctified in the Temple." With a satisfied smile, he said, "It is your responsibility, Devyn McDowell, to protect Stormy's virginity and ensure you are both pure and as white as snow when you enter the Temple or *you* will be condemned to the Telestial level." The bishop described their theology – how God was once a man and He perfected Himself by doing all the right things. "You must be perfect." He quoted their Doctrine and Covenants, "As you are, I once was. As I am, you may become." Hawkins said that only by doing everything according to the Mormon Church, they could be sealed in the temple.

Devyn was stunned. He liked the idea of eternal marriage, but this was strange. He thought that Jesus came to save, not condemn. To Jesus, being saved was to be freed from all the rituals and rules of the Pharisees. Dev fought to keep his mouth shut and his face blank.

Stormy looked down because she was bored, having heard this many times before.

The bishop explained the three Mormon heavens. Once in the Celestial Kingdom as a new God, in addition to Stormy, Devyn would receive a bunch of other wives because men can fertilize more women and thus populate more earths.

It took Devyn every ounce of self-control to avoid busting out with laughter. He asked, "What about men who don't make it to that level?"

"Men are challenged to control their desires. Therefore, most males will be in the Terrestrial and Telestial levels and few will make it up to the Celestial Glory. Millions of women will have no mate. It is only fair they also get to procreate." The bishop smiled, enjoying his sex-in-heaven lecture. "When Jesus returns for the resurrection, our physical bodies will rise. We will have no disease or imperfections."

"Do you mean my body now, my child body, or a future body?"

"If you die as a baby or as an old person, you are resurrected at your perfect age of around twenty. The process will start all over with you, Stormy, and your other wives because you will become Gods, and eons later, other people can also perfect themselves and become Gods. They will procreate and start their own worlds." The bishop gave him a hawk-like look.

He barely kept from saying aloud, *This is crazy*, because Stormy shook her head. Devyn sputtered out, "I don't want a bunch of wives. I only want Stormy." He stuffed his thoughts as you must in Church or a courtroom – same difference.

The dance was over by the time Bishop Hawkins released them. The other Mormon teens snickered when they saw them come from the office with their heads down.

As they walked to the parking lot, Stormy said, "Don't worry – I don't believe most of this because it isn't logical. All I know is that I will love you forever and I want to marry you in the temple."

Dove smiled sweetly when they got in the car. "Devyn, if you want to keep seeing Stormy, you must start taking the LDS missionary discussions. I don't know how much longer Mom will let you two hang out if you don't."

That was the first time my best friend realized he was getting into more than he had imagined, just like me and Big Owl.

At eighteen, I knew little about myself and less about the world. 1968 was a pivotal year for the United States. It was the worst year of violence, political turbulence, civil unrest, and cultural change since the American Civil War over one hundred years ago.

A U.S. athlete raised a black power fist at the summer Olympics in Mexico City. The Soviet Union invaded and crushed Czechoslovakia. Hippies protested the police clashes with the anti-war crowd at the Democratic National Convention. It got ugly when Mayor Daily called out twenty-thousand police and national guardsmen. The young people said, "Don't trust anyone over thirty." China was at the height of its "Cultural Revolution" making Mao into a cult hero while stalling modernization. The War in Vietnam escalated despite the promise of every presidential candidate.

9. Recruited

The day we arrived at Big Owl's brother's house, I got a letter from my girl.

Rowdy my eternal love,
God loves you and He will protect you when you do His will. Jesus will guide you - ask Him. He will bring you back whole and alive. We will have six to ten lovely children. I tremble at the thought of you inside me and can hardly wait. I long for you to complete this mission so we can be together. Please, oh please, tell me you have enlisted. I want to consummate our love!
Yours Forever and Ever,
Dove

A few days later, the Army recruiter, a burley guy who looked like Sergeant Rock, showed us a black and white film showing that the Vietnamese communists were savages.. He shared a news article about the people of Hue, a community slaughtered by the Viet Cong. The Hue intellectuals had disregarded communism as an insignificant concept. A VC squad assassinated their leader and killed everyone, then tossed their bodies into a shallow trench. The photos weren't sad – they were heart-wrenching.

Sergeant Rockbutt proclaimed, "They will stop at nothing. They're butchers worse than the Nazis." He showed us graphic photos of Vietnamese village leaders with their peckers cut off and stuffed into their mouths. Their bodies had signs saying that if you supported the Saigon government and the Americans, it would happen to you.

We got angry and wanted to be heroes – the next Sergeant York or Audie Murphy.

Bruce's wife asked us every day if we had found work.

I replied, "No, sorry. Everywhere we try; the employers ask what our draft status is and then they won't give us an application."

Bruce said, "Yes, if they hire you and you get drafted, they have to keep the position open until you're back."

She shook her head. "You boys need to enlist. We have a new baby and cannot support you."

Dearest Rowdy,

In my prayers, I am so hungry to make love with you, but Jesus said I must wait until you are trained as a warrior to fight for His Just Cause in Vietnam. God will protect you when you do His will. He promised me that He will bring you back whole and alive. We will have at least eight lovely children. I tremble at the thought of you inside me and can hardly wait.

On a serious note, Stormy tried to commit suicide because Mother wouldn't let her see Devyn. Thank God she is home from the hospital. They put her on anti-depressants. I'm worried about her. Enclosed is a Saint George necklace. He is the guardian of warriors and will protect you. Please write and tell me you have enlisted. I want to consummate our love!

Yours Forever and Ever,

Dove

I wondered what the heck was going on. I didn't have the money to make a phone call to Devyn so I wrote him a note, but I didn't have a stamp. I thought, *I'll have money when I'm in the Army.*

I read that during Tet last January 1968, the communists had conscripted every male big enough to plant a mine or carry a weapon. If he refused or ran away, they killed his relatives. America pounded their red asses during Tet but the communist show of force surprised the world. General William

Westmoreland's strategy was to wage a war of attrition. He believed the Communists would eventually surrender if enough of them died. It was the General's only avenue since Congress forbade crossing into North Vietnam. The commanders sent platoons on patrol as bait and when the VC attacked, America blasted them with napalm or artillery. Take ground, then give it up. Hamburger Hill was the norm. Officers asked, "How many communists did you kill today?"

On September 2, 1968, we took a bus to the San Jose Army recruiter's office.

The tough Sergeant said, "The Army needs infantry, that's it. These are the brave guys who fight on foot. They engage the enemy in face-to-face combat, and they win. Their training is more demanding than any other job because it requires sustained aggression. You gotta be brave and you gotta be tough."

He challenged me, "There are no openings for anything else." Pointing out that the Soviets had recently invaded Czechoslovakia, he said, "You boys might end up in Europe the way things are going."

Fueled by passion for my girlfriend, I said, "Let me and Al go in on the buddy system so he can make it through boot camp."

Sergeant Rockhole shook my hand. "You remember the Nazis?"

"Of course, my parents were in the Dutch resistance."

"The only condition for evil to thrive is when good men sit and do nothing. The U.S. Army needs men like you two." He filled us with war stories, the adrenaline rush of killing someone, and the feeling of power when you tossed a grenade or fired a mortar. He described the thrill of jumping from an airplane and gunning from a helicopter. "You boys will do it all!" He added, "If you don't join now, you'll get drafted and they'll do whatever they want with you. You won't have ANY choice." Sergeant Rockdick had been based in Germany, Korea, and around the world. He asked with a big sincere smile, "Where else is there a job that lets you country boys see the world?"

I couldn't argue. The problem was the Army didn't need truck drivers. There was room for just one truck driver in the whole U.S. Army in the entire world. "You can do the buddy system and go through boot camp together, but I can't promise both of you can be truck drivers." Sergeant Rockass asked sarcastically, "You guys aren't like those hippy freaks who raised hell at the Democratic Convention are you?"

"No!" We responded.

Big Owl had to get rid of beer from the night before.

While he was gone, I told the recruiter, "If there's only one opening for a trucker, give it to my buddy Al. What happens to me, I don't care. You don't have any openings for anything else?"

The only thing needed was infantry. "General Westmoreland wants and is getting hundreds of thousands more infantrymen but if you insist, you can give me your three top choices."

"Well, I want truck driving, but being an MP or helicopter mechanic would be great." I worried Rockface would give truck driving to me because I was the leader and the smarter one. Owl's IQ was proof evolution could go in reverse. Big Owl wouldn't know what was going on because no amount of training could fix stupidity.

I hurt inside, *Al's gonna get blown away. He will never survive as a grunt packing a rifle through the jungles. His train of thought doesn't have a caboose and sometimes, no engine. He'll step on a mine or a pudgy stick and be killed right away.* I had to make sure Big Owl was safe. Left to his own, he would have hung around Bruce's house drinking beer until he was drafted. *He's joining because of me.*

I said to Boulderbutt, "Let us go in on the buddy system so my big friend can make it through boot camp. I'll take whatever you have, just give the truck driver job to Al." I thought,

I'll do it all in one big bang. Shoot 'em up. Bang, bang, and if I die – who cares? I imagined that was the attitude in World War II.

Sergeant Rockcock said, "Okay, because I'm giving truck driving school to Al, I can't guarantee you anything." He repeated, "Rowdy, you do *not* have a guarantee, but I'll put you down for those other three choices." Rockface seemed to care about big dumb Al. He had a crafty look on his chiseled face. "To put you in the buddy system, you have to sign up for three years – that's the rule."

I didn't realize the recruiter was lying his ass off. "Fine as long as you promise that Al gets truck driving school."

Sergeant Rocknuts suppressed a smile. "I can guarantee Al gets truck driving only if you *both* sign up right now, today, for three years. Might not be another opening for a truck driver for a long while."

"Okay, good enough for me."

10. Ain't No Point In Looking Back

On September 2, 1968, I proudly wrote Dove, "I am officially in the Army." I had enlisted for the love of a woman. We received as the enlistment prize an all-expense paid trip on a Greyhound bus to Fort Lewis, Washington.

I began reading the war story the hippy chick gave me when we went looking for Cheri around Haight and Ashbury. *Johnny Got His Gun* quickly captured my attention. Joe Bonham was a young American soldier from Western Colorado who served during World War One. He woke up in a hospital bed after being hit by an artillery shell.

Fort Lewis is one of the largest military reservations in the world with 87,000 acres cut from the Nisqually Tribe's reservation. Ninety percent of the men at Fort Lewis were from the Bay Area of California. Men from Colorado usually went to Fort Bliss, Texas. The Army sent draftees out of State so they weren't tempted to make a trip home. Neither place was anything like Vietnam. In the summer, that Texas base was hot and dry, but the idea that Fort Lewis was a jungle training place was an example of Army intelligence.

It started raining in Washington State in late August. One recruit joked, "Maybe that's why they call this *washing* - ton since it rains a ton and washes everything down, every single day." It never stopped. Ninety inches of rain a year. It was wet, cold, muddy, and moldy… and fucking cold as a brass bra on a witch. Very tall and straight evergreen trees grew everywhere. You couldn't see shit. The rain ain't warm like in New Orleans or for that matter – Vietnam.

We went through the usual humiliation bullshit, getting shaved bald, uniforms, and shots. We pretended we didn't care. We acted brave to cover our fear. Had we hung around San Jose a short while longer, we may have tried the new Big Mac at McDonald's – on sale for forty-nine cents. Instead, we ate Army grub. Fat, greasy, carbo-loaded, foul-tasting mass-produced stuff. Not much difference when it came down to it.

The Army listed assignments on a big blackboard. Mine was Olive and Bravo, meaning infantry. The numbers correspond to your MOS (Military Occupation Specialty).

We double-time marched to our assigned company area. Because of our enlistment agreement on the buddy system, we got the same barracks in the same platoon, but Big Owl and I were on opposite ends of the ground level. It was a message.

Rayferd was this short black guy from Oakland who was married with a kid. He was in the same platoon as us. Older than the rest of the guys, he had long arms, hard bulging muscles, and was tougher than a big black anvil. Drafted once before, he had enlisted and spent four years in the Marine Corps. After he did his duty, he was supposed to attend reserve meetings. He thought, *You can kiss my ass. I'm not going to your goddam reserve meetings after serving four long years.*

Turns out that if you didn't go to reserve meetings, the Army could draft you even if you already served. Rayferd was a sergeant in the Marines but because he didn't go to the reserve meetings, he lost everything. The Army drafted him as a witless cherry, making him go through damned boot camp again.

The D.I.s knew he was a sergeant in the Marines so they gave Rayferd a ration of shit. He dealt with it by cracking jokes. "This Drill Instructor says to the draftee, 'I suppose that after you get discharged, you'll be waiting for me to die so you can piss on my grave.'

'Not me, Sir!' The draftee replied. 'Once I get out, I'll never stand in line again!'"

I glommed onto Rayferd because he had been through this before and knew the game. We stood at attention in front of our bunks while the drill sergeants dressed us down. The DIs cursed, called us pussies, hairballs, wimp-asses, mommy's babies – anything to make a guy realize he had lost all rights. So much for freedom of choice, dignity, and respect. The DIs told us what, when, and how to do everything, and especially what to think. The military was an instrument, not a shaper of national policy.

They conditioned us Army life through cadences, "There ain't no use in lookin' back Jody's got your Cadillac. Ain't no point in feeling blue. Jody's got your woman too." It was a ball-busting song to make us feel there was nothing at home, and we were now owned by the Army.

The Drill Sergeant lived in a private room at the end of the barracks with an orderly and supply room nearby. Squads were controlled by a lieutenant who was the platoon leader. We never saw the lazy sucker. Four platoons were in a company commanded by a captain who was also rarely seen by us recruits.

Rayferd said, "I pretend to work. They pretend to pay me."

I got into the spirit of it. "Yeah, and a pat on the back is a few centimeters from a kick in the pants."

The DI said, "Pain is temporary, pride is forever."

I worked hard. I'd be a hero for Dove – live with honor and die with dignity. Nobody wanted to die, but I wasn't afraid of it. Dove said if I was killed, she would have me baptized by proxy in the Salt Lake temple, and then she'd be sealed to me for time and all eternity. We'd be in the celestial glory and spawn millions of children. I couldn't wait. I wacked off every night thinking of her creamy hot body.

The day shot out like a cannonball into the stratosphere at the crack of dawn and it didn't land until late at night. We lined up and got eight minutes to eat. I wolfed down breakfast, lunch, and dinner. Lunch was "C" rations – some from World War Two.

At chow, we laughed about the guys who messed up. "Did you see the kid from New Mexico on the obstacle course? The DI made him low crawl for a hundred yards because he didn't do it fast enough." Low crawling was a favorite punishment. The soldier got on his belly with his rifle cradled in his arms in front of him and wiggled up the field. It was difficult and draining, especially in the cold mud of Washington State.

The DI roared, "Kill!"

A hundred men yelled, "KILL," in response.

Rayferd told me while we marched, "Ever notice, no matter which way we march, it's always uphill?" Humor kept us going. "Can I trade this job for what's behind door number one?" Rayferd said. Everyone within earshot laughed under their breath. He constantly talked and joked.

The pay phones were on a different part of the post from our barracks. We could call home only if the whole platoon earned the privilege to leave the company area. No one got a pass, instead, we chanted, "Ain't no use in calling home – Jody's got your girl and gone. I wanna go to Vietnam, I wanna kill a Vietcong."

The purpose of basic was to teach us how to clean and use light infantry weapons like the M-1, M-14, and M-16 rifles. Because me and Owl were farm boys who had hunted since boyhood, we became mentors to the city boys. We were also good with the M-79 rocket launchers, and we loved firing the M-60 and .50 caliber machine guns.

Rayferd had this irreverent way of dealing with the whole thing. When we took a water break, he whispered to me, "Sarge must be an experiment in artificial stupidity." It was hard not to laugh, but if you did, it was pushup time. Rayferd said, "When do you kick a midget in the gonads? When he is standing next to your girlfriend saying her hair smells nice."

I imagined the army was my path to heroism. I was only there to please Dove. In a letter, she quoted the New Testament, "For whoever wishes to save his life will lose it, but whoever loses his life for my sake will save it." I was her brave young man fighting for liberty and freedom of religion against the devil communists. If I gave my life for the cause, I'd have eternal life with her. I got an erection every time I thought about being married to this lovely creature.

I was a toy soldier defending her God to death. I wondered, *If God is all-powerful, why does He need me to go defend him? Why doesn't he just swat the commies and end the whole thing?* Patriotism was nothing but a type of blind faith. Reality was *not* romantic.

Rayferd said, "An Army grunt and a Marine were walking down the street. They saw a kid working with a ball of shit. The Army grunt says to the kid, 'What are you making?' The kid says, 'An Army Grunt.' The grunt asked, 'Why aren't you making a drill sergeant?' The kid said, 'I don't have enough shit.'"

Devyn wrote, saying he blew his knee out in football and was in a walking cast. He was also depressed because he couldn't see Stormy. "Mrs. Knutson won't let me see her because I'm not a Mormon. I'm thinking about taking the missionary lessons so I can date her. You better start taking them and get baptized a Mormon or Dove might break it off. Think you could have their missionaries come to boot camp and give you the lessons?"

Fat chance, I thought, *I can't even use a phone to call her.*

Day after day the weather report was, "Chance of scattered sun breaks, otherwise, expect an overcast sky and drizzling rain turning heavy."

Rayferd cracked, "We ought to change the motto on our money from "In God, We Trust" to "In War, We Trust."

"Ain't it the truth," I agreed.

We hated the forced marches while wearing rain gear. And we chanted, "Got a letter in the mail. Go to war or go to jail. Sat me in a barber's chair, spun me 'round and I had no hair. I'm gonna go to Vietnam and kill some commies for my mom."

The DIs pitted us against other platoons at every chance. Which platoon had the best shooters? Which had the strongest men? Which group ran the obstacle course the quickest? Training to become a cog in the Army's machine, I was surprised the trainers didn't have the men do a shitting contest. Beat the others and your platoon got rewarded...less duty, passes to use the phone, better food, and more time to rest. Our platoon was punished day after day, and night after night because a few guys kept messing up.

At lunch after a fifteen-mile run, Rayferd said, "This drill instructor says to the new recruits: 'Today, pea brains, I have good news and bad news. First, the good news: Private Peters will set the pace on our morning run.' The whole platoon was happy because Private Peters was a fat guy who was always last. The drill sergeant says, 'Now the bad news – Private Peters will be driving the truck."

11. Who's Jody?

As I ran and chanted the Jody songs, I distracted myself by recalling how Dove's cheeks glowed when we talked about Vietnam. Her moonstone eyes had sparkled, then she got horny, squeezing my pump shotgun and rubbing her pink derringer against my thigh. I remembered the envy in men's eyes when they saw us together. I still couldn't believe she chose me – I was the lucky guy out of all those who wanted her.

Big Owl, me, and Rayferd got to shoot the .50 caliber BMG sniper rifles because of our marksmanship. For an unknown reason, we weren't offered sniper school. Rayferd explained it, "These officers couldn't pour water out of a boot if the instructions were on the heel. Tell yourself it don't matter or it will get to you."

According to the Army entrance exams, Rayferd and I were the highest-scoring men in the entire company. While others were on evening KP, we were pulled to take tests like how to imagine folded drawings of paper into different shapes; and how to make symbol-number associations. Could we visualize a battlefield and strategize how to win? How quickly could we learn a foreign language? Could we enact multiple-step directions without error?

I was excited to make Officer Candidate School (OCS) until Rayferd said it meant a four-year commitment. To be on the buddy system, me and Owl had signed for three instead of the typical two years. *Another* year commitment to be an officer. Rayferd said officers were the number one target for the Viet Cong. We began intentionally flunking the officer screening tests.

It seldom snowed but Washington *enjoyed* periodic black ice. When fog and rain off the ocean met the cold air coming down from Mount Rainier, it froze quickly. They called it black ice because it was so clear you saw through it to the asphalt. It was hard to walk on this stuff, especially on asphalt or concrete. The men came out from the barracks and several guys fell on the ice.

Drill Sergeant Wilson was black and he gave Rayferd a ration of horsepucky. However, Rayferd was unbreakable, fought and survived Vietnam tough, and he was more leathery than Sergeant Wilson. The drill sergeant had rank and he glared at Rayferd as if he made the guys fall. For no reason, he said, "You black son-of-a-bitch, get down on your hands and knees!"

Everybody respected Rayferd because he was so frigging tough. We were surprised that after a slight hesitation, Rayferd got on his hands and knees.

Sergeant Wilson said, "Now you crawl here, boy! And you say, 'Drill Sergeant Wilson, I apologize for these men falling.'" He stared and Rayferd didn't move. Wilson yelled, "Now *Boy*! You crawl over here right now."

It was cold, wet and icy. Calling Rayferd boy made steam boil off his head. The grunts couldn't believe Sergeant Wilson was making him crawl to apologize for other men falling. He sweated with rage but made a little scoot toward the sergeant. Rayferd debated a moment, and then he low crawled, enraged vapor rising from his neck.

I thought, *Ah oh, this isn't good. He's a short guy, but he has those long muscular arms hanging down to his ankles. He will smack the sergeant and it will be one hell of a fight. Rayferd will be busted and tossed in the brig.*

"Crawl over here!"

Rayferd belly-crawled to the feet of Sergeant Wilson but said nothing. Instead, he stared at the ground with steam boiling off. It was clear he wouldn't say a word.

Wilson said, "Now Rayferd, you apologize, don't ya?"

Rayferd nodded his head.

Sergeant Wilson said, "You jump up and get back in formation."

So Rayferd did.

Everyone was shocked because Sergeant Wilson let him off the hook. Wilson often laid into other guys for nothing and he never let them off, but he was smart to let it go with Rayferd. He must have sensed if he pushed Rayferd one inch further, the guy would explode and punch him out.

Standing in the icy mist, the men stared at the Sergeant. I was suddenly aware that I had surrendered all personal freedom. I decided I would not see myself as a victim. There was no point in being sorry and I wanted no pity. Choice was part of life – sometimes you correctly anticipated the outcome and sometimes you didn't.

Rayferd returned in line and whispered, "His mother never saw the irony in calling him a bastard."

Nearby grunts suppressed laughter.

Everything was okay.

As we took the morning fifteen-mile run, Rayferd cracked, "It's not necessary to be an idiot to be a drill sergeant but it sure helps."

I thought of one. "What's six inches long, two inches wide, and drives women wild?" Nobody knew so I said, "A hundred dollar bill."

Behind my façade of being tough, I was an idealist. I'd make the world safe from communism; I'd stop the Viet Cong from brutalizing villagers. I wouldn't be one of those REMF's – a Rear Echelon Mother-Fuckers.

The Jody chants were the most popular. They reinforced that we had nothing at home and the Army was our family. We double-timed and chanted, "Ain't no use in lookin' back, Jody's got your Cadillac. Ain't no use in going home, Jody's got your girl and gone."

At night, the men talked about Jody before dropping off to nether land. Most figured he was the rich kid who avoided the draft, went to college, and got your girl after you left.

After several nights of listening to different theories, Rayferd said loudly, "You grunts don't know shit. Jody ain't a person – it's the damn government that sends us off to a no-count war to make the rich even richer and let the college boys bang your girl."

I wondered, *To have a Jody who stole your girl, doesn't she also have to be a Jodie?*

12. Mighty Marty

To motivate us, the drill instructors told stories about the Vietnam War. The D.I. yelled as the men stood in formation, "The Viet Cong hate the Montagnards because they don't take to Communism. On December 5, 1967, two battalions of Viet Cong burned to death 250 civilians in the hamlet of Đắk Sơn." Sarge said, "Bunch of chicken shits – they attacked the village with flame-throwers in the middle of the night. Flame lashed from every direction, scorching everything. These people only recently discovered matches and were terrified to see fire coming at them out of the night."

He went on, "This wasn't a military victory. The Viet Cong wanted to send the message they'd wipe out resistance. Women and children were burned inside their houses; those who got into dog holes beneath their houses were asphyxiated. The Viet Cong set fire to everything: trees, fences, gardens, chickens, and grain from the annual harvest. Huts that survived the fire were leveled with grenades."

Such stories pissed us off, making us want to kill the commies. "I wanna go to Vietnam – I wanna kill a Viet Cong. I'll pay him back for the blood he's shed."

My company had some real dufus-heads. One was this really skinny guy assigned to the top bunk across from mine. Private Martin Moya was a gangly eighteen-year-old Hispanic kid as green as the corn stalks on the farm where he was born. He was a non-entity with brownish hair, dark empty eyes, and a few pimples here and there. He was the distant cousin you never talk to. He wasn't repulsive and had nothing remarkable. Martin was just there.

He failed to react when guys sang, in reference to the TV cartoon, *Mighty Mouse*, "Here he comes to save the day, Mighty

Marty will find the way." They ragged him mercilessly when he fell off the obstacle wall. "Where's your cape, Mighty Marty?"

The DI had us chant, "They took away my faded jeans. Now I'm wearing Army green. Ain't no use in lookin' down. Ain't no discharge on the ground."

Nothing moved Marty – neither praise nor punishment. He played no musical instruments or sports and had few interests – not even girls. His strongest preference was for Marvel Comic books, but he wasn't a collector. They were just something to look at.

"Where're you from?" I asked.

"New Mexico."

"I'm from Colorado. Makes us neighbors. Did you sign up or get drafted?"

"Drafted."

"I thought you got a deferment if you lived on a farm."

"Nope. Never heard of no deferments. The letter from the draft board said to get a physical."

I considered letting it drop. "Trying to get to know my bunkmate." I pushed on, "You figure we're all going to 'Nam?"

Marty said with a touch of irritation in his voice, "We ain't got a say in it."

"Just trying to make small talk. Are you scared?"

"No, I ain't scared a nothing," trying to sound grown-up. "Damn, you're a nosy cuss. I'm writing a letter here."

"Sorry, I didn't mean to offend you, go ahead and write. If you're interested in me, I'll tell you whatever you want. My point is, I'm trying to make friends." Private Moya was a hard read – as if his pages were out of focus.

Turned out he was from Aztec, New Mexico – a small town just south of the Colorado border near Durango. Marty was as bony as a stalk of dried corn. He had deep, dark eyes and he slouched. He wrote letters home every day although he didn't have a girlfriend.

"Hey, Marty, who are you writing to, man?" I asked.

"Betty, she's a family friend." Once in a while, Marty gave the name of a family member – Aunt Judy, his sister Linda, or his mom, Mary.

"You got a picture of Betty?"

"Nope."

"Hey, you wanna see a picture of my girl? I got it at mail call today."

"Sure."

From my upper bunk, I handed it across, expecting the usual, "Wow, she's beautiful, how'd you snag her?"

"Blond hair and blue eyes," he said without enthusiasm and handed it back.

Private Moya's lack of interest translated into no energy and even less motivation in the field. Marty said, "I went through this once at Fort Bliss, Texas. I'm doing basic a second time."

Private Moya wasn't doing much better this time; he was too thin, weak, and defeated. The Drill Sergeant punished the whole platoon for Moya's failures. It did not endear him when we did a hundred pushups in the mud while Marty stood and counted.

When the guys short-sheeted his bunk, Marty crawled under the scratchy blanket without saying a word. There was talk of a blanket party – where a group of men wait until the victim is asleep and then they pulled his blanket tight so the guy couldn't move. They punched the slacker so he understood the men were sick of him blowing it.

We chanted, "Mama, Mama can't you see what Ole Jody's done to me. If I die in a combat zone, box me up and send me home. Pin my medals on my chest and tell my mom I did my best."

The low crawl pit taught you to keep your head down under live ammunition. The sign said, "More Sweat Here, Less Blood There."

Owl complained, "I wish the sign said 'more beer here.' I could sure use one. I got the shakes!"

The only way we'd get a pass was if everybody in the whole platoon did everything perfectly. No phone calls because of Marty.

That's when Owl disappeared.

13. More Beer Here

Big Owl showed up a day later. I asked, "Where were you the last two days?"

Although exhausted, Big Owl laughed and told his story.

Along the fifteen-mile running trail, we had often crossed an old country road and Owl eyed it. He wanted to get drunk and party. Owl couldn't get that dirt road from his head. One night after lights out, he quietly slipped from his bunk.

He found the old lane using the skills he had picked up while hunting in the woods around Cedaredge. Despite the darkness and misting rain, he walked the road to the highway where he hitchhiked to Olympia.

Spotting a 7-11, he asked to be let off at the exit ramp and ran into the store. It was minutes before midnight, just before liquor sales were cut off. He picked up a case of Olympia beer and sat it on the checkout counter.

The older clerk recognized he was a grunt in basic training. "Man, you better go back before they catch you. You'll have hell to pay if you don't."

"I don't care, I'm gonna get drunk!" Big Owl exclaimed as he pulled out Army script.

"I gotta see your I.D."

Big Owl shrugged and said, "I ain't got one, they took it the first day."

"To buy alcohol in the State of Washington, you must be twenty-one and have a photo I.D. Also, we don't accept Army script here – sorry man."

Big Owl was stunned. "Aw, come on, I can drink in Colorado. I just hiked two hours to get here."

"No can do, Big Guy. I'd lose my job and get fined. They could pull the store's liquor license. No can do."

Big Owl got mad. He lifted the case of beer, stuck it under one arm, and walked to the door.

"Ain't worth it man, I was a grunt too. Been there, done that. Not only will they get you for theft but the Army will throw the book at you. Don't ruin your life over a few beers."

Owl stopped with the door half open. He turned to the clerk and connected that the clerk was like me, giving him good advice. "Son of a bucket!" With a shit-eating grin, he walked back to the cooler and put it away. On the way out, Owl waved to the clerk, saying, "Thanks."

Walking the road to the interstate, he was surprised that a state patrolman pulled up beside him. "What are you doing out here soldier?"

Soon, Big Owl was cuffed and in the back seat. MP's at the main gate pulled him from the squad car. They made him stand in the thickening rain at attention outside the DI's office until morning.

They read him the riot and charged him with being absent without leave, or AWOL, and gave him an Article 15. They restricted him and docked his pay. Owl washed greasy cooking pots in the kitchen all day and then he'd do it every night for the next three weeks after working his arse off all day.

Big Owl laughed. "Well, I done learned there ain't no drinking in this puke state 'til you're twenty-one."

We marched in double time, jogging with a full pack and rifle in hand. If any man didn't do it right, Drill Sergeant Williams yelled, "Charlie will get you and you will die!" Charlie was what they called the Viet Cong. It came from when the Americans used the Vietnamese to wage guerrilla war on the Japanese. They were called the Victor Charlies, our allies.

Rayferd told Owl, "Hey listen, this is an Army Intelligence test. Sergeant Williams has three girlfriends. Their names are Doe, Ray, and Me. The girls wanted to give him something special for his birthday so they set up three dates in a row. So, three days ago, Doe kissed every part of Sergeant William's body. Two days ago, Ray had wild and crazy sex with him. Yesterday, who sucked his dick?"

Owl thought a minute, then said, "Me."

Everybody in the barracks burst out laughing.

Owl had a confused expression.

I explained why the men had laughed and Owl's face turned bright red with anger and embarrassment. I thought, *I'm sure glad Owl is gonna be a trucker. A platoon leader would put him on point in 'Nam and he'd lose his legs the first day.*

Coming in from marching through muddy fields one late afternoon, Marty lagged far behind.

Sarge screamed, "You lady-boys ain't going into MY clean barracks. You are to crawl because you are slow maggots!" From then on, we slithered in the mud each time Marty was late.

Exhausted, the men were beaten down and enraged. "Let's kill him to put him out of our misery."

Privately, I talked to Marty about his problems. He said he wanted to pass basic. Being dishonorably discharged from the Army was a huge black mark on a guy's record. It was almost as bad as getting a felony. Marty's prospects were trashed if he didn't make it the second time.

Marty's eyes spit fire. "I've been through a blanket party and it ain't fun." He apologized. "I'm a skinny wimp and I can't help it." He jumped from his bunk and spoke directly in my face. "I know the game this time. They humiliate and demoralize you. They try to scare you and they make you hate them – it's brainwashing to become an attack dog – ready to take orders without question – its do or die."

His voice was low and tight. "The first time through boot camp I failed most of the PT tests but I thought, 'Up yours, you can't break me.' After basic, they put me through two weeks of motivation camp. You think this is tough! Hell, I did push-ups and sit-ups and ran 'til I puked. And I did it all over again. I ate and ate and ate. It don't work. I can't put on weight and I can't get strong." His voice turned into a shout, his red face inches from mine, "I AIN'T SCARED OF ANYTHING. I'LL GOUGE THE EYES OF THE GOD-DAM COMMIES. I'LL DIE FOR THIS FUCKING ARMY BUT I STILL CAN'T PASS THEIR P.T. TESTS!"

I realized, *He's been mentally raped – he's become an Army puke but physically, he can't do it!*

Everyone stared at Private Moya. He slumped back into his Sad Sack form.

Marty fell into line when the trainer barked, "Shut your mugs and get back in line you lazy maggots!" The DI walked beside him talking in his ear, "I'm doing this because I care. I don't want you to die for your country. I want the enemy to die for his. You gotta be the tougher one, the stronger one, and the smarter one or it's you who will die."

I continued reading "Johnny Got a Gun." Gradually, Joe realized he lost not just his arms, legs, and his face; he also lost his eyes, ears, teeth, and even his tongue. Only his hearing and mind worked. He was a prisoner in his own body. I considered the predicament. Joe Bonham didn't choose to have an artillery shell hit him but he chose to go to war. He could have run to Mexico or claimed to be a conscientious objector. It was more honorable to take responsibility instead of blaming others for your misfortune. There was no respect in pointing fingers and playing the victim; Joe had exercised his free will and here he was with his body busted up lying in a hospital. *I won't focus on fault, only solutions.*

Anticipating something funny, I opened a letter from Devyn.

"Hey, I'm seeing Stormy since I'm attending their church. You talk about a strange religion. Prepare yourself. If you want to marry Dove in their temple, you have to become one. Not sure I can force myself to pretend I believe this drivel.

Hey, I'm surrounded by queers. Remember Lloyd McPecker who tried to seduce us a couple of years back? The guy was married with two kids so we never guessed. He went after you, but you told him to take a hike; so he tried to get me in the sack. Claimed he had a job for me in Gunnison and I went up with him. All we did was walk around. He took me to dinner and said we'll spend the night and then start tomorrow. That night in the motel, he tried to talk me into sucking him. I told him to fuck himself and slept in the car. Pedophile city – we should cut his winky off.

Anyway, I moved back home because I've got to have knee surgery. I'd be walking along and bam, out of nowhere, I'm on the floor. Mom negotiated a cease-fire between Dad and me. We don't talk. Now and then, he explodes, "What you got a head for, nothing but a hat rack?" Heard it so many times that I ignore him.

Mom took me to Saint Mary's Hospital in Grand Junction and this guy in his twenties came to shave my leg for surgery. He pushed my horned toad to the side to shave around my nuts.

I said, "Why are you shaving so high? They're operating on my knee, not my groin."

The Mcfagget grinned, "Got to, doctor's orders."

"You touch my balls again and I'll break your fingers then shove 'em up your nose!"

He packed his little shaver kit and left.

A female nurse came in and finished the job. She didn't know why he was shaving so high for a knee operation.

I laughed loudly and a guy asked what was funny. I read the paragraph aloud and everyone laughed. "Wait, it gets better." I read the next paragraph to the men.

After surgery, this cute candy striper named Albie came into my room. Big blue eyes, short dark brown hair, and a pretty smile that lit up the room. Late one evening, she gave me a sponge bath. She wiped my good leg, then my bad leg. I made a tent out of the sheets so she wrapped her fingers around it. I was slowly considering stopping her because of my promise to Stormy, but I didn't have to worry because this older nurse came in. Nurse Ratchet saw the sheets jumping up and down. "What are you doing?" She yelled.

Albie jerked her hand away and ran from the room.

I didn't see her again until I checked out. I asked where she had been.

They had ordered her to stay away from me. Turns out, she wasn't a nurse, instead, she was a volunteer, which is what a candy striper is. She was sixteen and from Grand Junction High School. Had I known, I might have stopped her.

Just kidding.

Other guys wanted read the letter. This one was going to make the rounds.

Dev continued, "Listen Rowdy, you have to get baptized to marry in the Mormon temple and they will try to force you to go on one of their missions to convert people. It's the only way. You should have done that instead of joining the Army. Plan on it."

I felt misled by Dove. Had she been upfront, I might have gone on a mission for their church instead of enlisting. I had no interest in killing any Vietnamese. I was Dutch and they weren't involved in the Vietnam War, but it was too late.

Me and Rayferd talked to the other guys about Marty. "Guys, we either keep ragging Marty and losing any possibility of privileges during basic training, or we figure out how to cover for him. We live or die as a team."

From then on, the platoon worked to get Private Moya's record up to speed, regardless of his actual performance. I handed Marty's card to the observer on the obstacle course. Big Owl gave Marty's card for check-off at the bayonet station. Somebody else took the hit on the two-mile run. Everyone who could afford it, took one for Moya. At times, men supported him by the armpits and others hauled his gear so he could keep up. Suffering together, we became a mentally and physically tough team of killers. We finally won passes to call home.

It was wonderful to hear her voice. Dove said, "You don't know how much I love you, or how often I think of you. You're my crusader for Christ."

I felt her sure and strong faith. I tried to believe I was a soldier for God. Mostly, I wanted to be loved by her. I was going overseas to kill for the love of a woman.

We double-time marched in the rain, "See a V.C. in the grass 50-cal will bust his ass. Killing gooks is lots of fun. Knock one up and it's two for one."

What the hell? I asked myself. *What are they telling us to do? Knock one up and it's two for one?* Maybe, as Rayferd said, the Army was the only Jody who mattered.

14. The Numburger Picnic

One Friday evening, buses took us to the dense forest in the foothills of Mt. Rainier near Seattle for an escape and evasion exercise. It was early November and getting dark earlier each day. After a siege of unusually cold weather, the ground froze solid and six inches of crusty snow lay on it.

Officers dropped the platoon on an icy road and we stood at parade rest with an open field to our backs. A thick stand of evergreens loomed in front of the men, boughs pushed near the ground by clumps of snow as thick as pillows.

Sergeant Williams stood in front of the formation. Usually, he boasted at each opportunity, reminding us of how he had lived up to everything the army put before him with honor and toughness. He was a lifetime subscriber to the macho law prohibiting him from admitting he could be wrong.

Today, however, the boasting stopped. D.I. Williams explained that this exercise would sharpen our survival skills and sculpt us into effective soldiers. "Listen up, men," he barked. He strutted as stiff and erect as a wood plank – prancing back and forth in front of the company, his arms clasped behind his back. He stopped to stare into the darkening sky. "You are to enter the forest and come out twenty-two miles on the other side. You will have no compass, map, or lighting. It might take the whole night to complete the course. On the other side, you will locate the railroad tracks – that is your final destination, your safety zone. There for your comfort, you will find a mess tent where you will receive donuts, coffee, or hot chocolate along with breakfast. Buses will be warm and waiting to take you back to the barracks as soon as everyone is accounted for. Do not waste time." He looked from side to side of the company. "Do I make myself clear?"

"YES SIR." We shouted in unison, filling the crisp damp air with the combined breaths of two hundred men. The effect created an eerie white mist rising from the formation as if men's souls suddenly deserted them.

He stared at the men. "Now a warning, so pay close attention: Straight ahead is a prisoner of war camp. Assume it is real. Do you understand?"

"YES SIR." A fog of breaths rose.

Sergeant Williams paced from one side of the formation to the other. He turned to face the men. His voice rose a louder octave as he moved to the center of the company. With relish,

Sergeant Williams explained what lay ahead, "The prisoner of war is a compound surrounded by fences, barbed wire and has locked gates. Armed commando units patrol its perimeter. They are your enemy. If captured, you will be taken prisoner."

He grinned. "Remember, the enemy doesn't notice until you make a mistake." His voice became shrill, "Listen closely: Do not resist or you *will* be hurt. You *will* be interrogated, and men – you *will* be humiliated."

He spun sideways and froze like a statue, except for puffs of vapor. He exhaled with a sinister chuckle. "Give only your name, rank, and serial number, and nothing more. Do I make myself clear?"

"YES SIR." White steam rose from two hundred voices.

Sergeant Williams continued, "One more thing: do not get lost. If we waste a single day looking for you pussies," he paused, "When I find you, I'll put a boot up your ass so far your breath will smell like boot polish for a month."

The sky was clear and bright with the early evening stars beginning to show. A run through the trees might be an adventure, except for the darkness, snow, freezing temperatures, and twenty-two miles of an unknown forest. To our horror, canisters sailed hissing into their midst, sputtering and spewing tear gas.

Sergeant Williams yelled above the gasping and coughing, "The tear gas is to motivate you to enter the forest without delay. So get going!"

It worked and we rushed into the woods like spooked cats trying to avoid a pack of dogs.

As instructed, most men paired up with a buddy or bunkmate, but Marty took off on his own. I saw his skinny frame plunging into the thickets as if he knew where he was going. He moved clumsily, pulling his knees up high with the right knee crossing over the left, and the left knee crossing over the right.

Walking quietly through the forest, my mind wandered back to Delta, lingering on Dove. She always showed caring for others. I recalled how she had shared the plot of movies we saw with my younger siblings. She carried small treats to give to the children. She giggled or laughed like a happy child, never showing sorrow or sadness for herself. Dove believed my mission in Vietnam was the best way to show love for mankind. As I struggled through the snow with Rayferd and Big Owl, I wanted to believe there was no Jody to betray me. I especially hoped Dove was not a Jodie and she would love me forever as she had promised.

Rayferd couldn't keep from telling jokes as we snuck through the tall dark pines. "Do you know how to save a drowning drill instructor?"

I answered, "No."

"Take your foot off his head."

A little later, he said, "How do you circumcise a hillbilly?"

Owl laughed. "Tell us."

"Kick his sister in the jaw."

After a half hour of Rayferd cracking jokes, I said, "Hey, we better be quiet, we might be getting close to the prisoner of war compound."

We came to an eight-foot-wide canal covered with a thin layer of ice. It looked deep and cold, so we decided to walk around. We hoped to find a bridge or log to cross. We headed to the right, along the bank for half a mile, calculating distance by cupping a match near Rayford's watch and blowing it out quickly. We estimated we covered a mile every ten to twelve minutes. It didn't occur to us that striking a match could get us caught.

We found no bridge and followed our tracks back. In a short while, we saw tracks in the snow leading into the canal. There was broken ice where someone had crossed. "Do you want to jump in and cross here?" I asked.

Rayferd said, "Hell no, man! It's too deep and cold. Let's keep going."

We heard rustling to the right, near the edge of the canal. We moved closer. "Sounds like somebody is crying, don't it?" Whispered Big Owl.

Sneaking along behind brush and tree limbs, we moved quietly to within a few feet of the weeping sounds. We hid behind a large tree with long, snow-covered branches. It was hard to see without being seen. It was Marty. He sat in the snow with his back against a tree trunk.

"Can you believe that?" Rayferd whispered. "He's sobbing like a baby calling for his momma."

On our hands and knees, we crawled closer. I whispered, "Crap, I better go get him." I started to stand up.

"Naw, leave him." Big Owl pulled me back.

"Why?" I whispered. Marty was pathetic, sitting with his legs stretched out and his helmet upside down on the snow. "He's in our platoon."

Private Moya pulled up his knees and put both hands over his face. "Oh, Momma, what'll I do?" He cried with hiccup sounds and more sobs.

Rayferd argued quietly, "If this was a real war, I'd get him but it ain't. We were supposed to buddy up, but the dummy went by himself."

"What's wrong with that?" I said in a low voice.

"He should'a got a partner like they told us. They're trying to teach us to work together," Rayferd whispered as he gestured to leave.

"You're right, he should have partnered up. He'd be embarrassed if he knew we heard him crying."

We followed the canal for another two miles. Dim lights shined through the trees. Owl whispered, "Listen, do you hear people hollering?"

"Yeah, I can hear it. This must be the prison camp." We stood silently, ears up like Doberman dogs.

"Sounds like somebody is pounding nails," Owl whispered hoarsely.

Rayferd added quietly, "I hear guys groaning."

"They're getting tortured," I whispered, "Oh damn, it's a trap. The canal's a trap, see? You walk along the canal expecting to find a bridge or somewhere to cross but there's no bridge, and you run into the compound. Hurry, we gotta get outta here."

Following our old tracks in the snow, we trotted along for twenty minutes and heard something ahead. "Do you hear that, Big Owl?"

"Quiet, man, it might be a patrol," Rayferd whispered as he grabbed Owl's sleeve.

It was too late. The patrol had spotted us. Four dark figures ran straight at us.

We split up – Big Owl in one direction, Rayferd in another.

I headed into the forest and dove under a big pine tree. Sliding underneath the boughs, I rolled up against the trunk.

Two pairs of legs ran past, followed by two more sets of legs. They huffed, trying to keep their breath. The men ran so close they kicked up snow that dampened my cheeks. I heard the fading sound of their hard breathing as their boots crushed through crisp snow. I peeked from under the limbs as two of the patrol tackled someone.

I quietly snuck over to them. It was Big Owl. They were in for a fight. My big buddy tossed them in the air. I grinned. It was like when Owl used to toss me and Dev around when we wrestled in the orchards during lunch.

The other two men on patrol turned around to help – it was four-on-one and Big Owl was going down.

A new figure appeared. It was Marty! What the heck is he doing?

Private Moya tackled one of the MPs, allowing Big Owl to take on only three guys. Rayferd dropped on and it was a pile-up, three on four.

What the hell, if I go in, it's four on four and with Big Owl, we'll kick butt.

I bailed out from under my hiding place and bowled into the group like a defensive end taking on a football sweep. I knocked the whole group off their feet. Someone tumbled into the canal.

Whistles and other guards appeared. Suddenly, I was on the ground with my arms pinned. Big Owl tossed one into the air and he kicked off the soldier who held Marty. The distraction affected the guard who wrestled with Rayferd. He sprung free. Big Owl picked up Marty by the back of his Army jacket and ran into the woods at full speed.

The guards started to give chase, but I went into a wild, bucking, crazy fight to draw their attention. All the guards dog-piled me and soon had me in handcuffs. An MP I had made fall into the water crawled from the canal. He was the one in charge and Man, was he pissed.

"Is that you, Big Owl?" Marty whispered when he sat down by the big guy. "Damn, you choked the crap outta me!"

"Sorry," Big Owl said, breathing hard. "But hey, we got away."

"Yeah, but they got Rowdy." Marty stood on his tiptoes staring into the darkness, listening. "Where's Rayferd?"

The patrol leader yelled, "Take this asshole to the stockade and torture him!"

Marty asked, "Did you hear that?"

"Yeah, they got Rowdy alright. Shit!" Owl shook his freckled head. "We can't help him now. We gotta get away from here."

The guards took me to the prison compound and made me lean face down against a piece of angled plywood. They tied my arms and legs and pounded on the other side of the flat board with baseball bats. After pounding, guards stood me at attention to recite the Army Code of Conduct from memory. They swatted my face with a rolled-up newspaper each time I forgot a part of it.

"I am an American fighting man. I serve in the forces which guard my country and our way of life. I am prepared to give my life in their defense. I will never surrender of my own free will. "

I missed parts of the code so back to the plywood board. After three treatments, they realized I'd never get it. "Okay soldier, recite The First Nuremberg Principle."

I had that one memorized. "Any person who commits a crime is liable to punishment. War crimes are murder, slave labor, mistreating prisoners of war, forcing persons to serve in the forces of a hostile power, killing hostages, killing or punishing spies or other persons without a fair trial, wantonly destroying cities, towns, villages, or any object not warranted by military necessity."

I got it right so the guards let me wander around because they had more prisoners to torment. I hung out near the gate and when a patrol brought in more guys, I slipped away.

Later in the morning, I caught up with Big Owl, Rayferd, and Marty who had already eaten breakfast. They held cups of steaming hot coffee. I asked Marty, "Why did you jump in when the patrol captured Big Owl?"

Marty explained, "I followed these three guys along the bank of a frozen canal. One was a tall guy so he was easy to see. This squad of goons ran past me from the shadows and you split up, but they had Big Owl just like that." Snapping his fingers. "He threw those guys around like rag dolls so I thought, what the heck if I can distract them, he'll get away, and maybe I will too." He shrugged. "You guys are in my platoon and I wasn't scared they would torture us."

Owl chimed in, "I thought you was Rowdy at first, but they got you down and I saw your skinny ass. Rowdy has big bones. I was thinking we're fucked, but Rayferd piled in and it was a cluster bang. All of a sudden, here came this cannonball from the woods. He knocked everybody down like a bunch of bowling pins!"

"You see the MP fly into the canal?" Marty asked, and we laughed loudly.

I explained, "He was the patrol leader and he was pissed as hell when he came out of the canal. He ordered me to be tortured." I described what they did to me.

Owl exclaimed, "Shit, they'd still be torturing me. Ain't no way I could recite the frigging Code of the Numburger Picnic!"

Courtesy of Rayferd, the night before graduation from basic as Sergeant Wilson walked across the field to the barracks, we quickly threw a heavy green blanket over his head. Pulling off his boots, we used them to beat the snot out of him.

Sergeant Wilson was a big man, and he fought like a hellcat but was no match for a dozen toughened boot camp graduates. Every time Rayferd swung the boot, Sergeant Wilson grunted, "Arggh!"

To the amazement and respect of the troops, the next morning, a bruised Sergeant Wilson led the graduation parade without limping.

15. An Evening Like This

After graduation from basic training, Owl was assigned to truck driving school in Fort Wachuka, Arizona. I'd stay at Ft. Lewis in Washington State for Advanced Infantry Training (AIT).

We got a two-week leave starting Veteran's Day weekend. Me and Big Owl caught a plane from Seattle to Denver and on to Montrose. It was Saturday noon in early November.

Big Owl's mother waited with Dove who came to Montrose from Western State in Gunnison for the long weekend. We would have three days together at home and then I'd hang out with her in Gunnison.

There was a lot of freedom in 1968. No airport security, no high-jacking a plane for a ransom, and no one crashed a jet into building to make a political statement. No IDs were required to buy a ticket. You could swap airline tickets or give them to someone else. A person could walk onto the tarmac if you didn't mind the heat or cold, and noise.

Al's mom and Dove stood at the door to the tarmac of the Montrose airport where the planes parked fifty yards away.

I walked down the movable stair ramp in my formal military hat and Army uniform.

Dove got so excited she darned near wet her pants. As we embraced, she put my Army hat on her head and hugging tightly, we walked out to her 1961 gray Rambler with a three-speed push-button transmission. She offered to let me drive.

I said, "Whatever you want."

She took the wheel.

On the highway to Delta, Dove said, "Can you stay at my house tonight?"

I was surprised. "Where's your family?"

"Mom and Stormy went up to our mountain sawmill to see my brother and Daddy. Then, they're going to the Mormon Stake Conference tomorrow in Grand Junction. David O'Mckay, the Church Prophet is to speak."

"So you have the house to yourself?"

"Isn't it great! I have everything planned. I want to cook you a special dinner and," she winked and flipped her long blonde hair. "I have special treats for you." She gave that beautiful cheerleader smile like a toothpaste commercial.

"Sounds delicious. So you're keeping your promise?"

"Oh Rowdy, I've been dreaming of this for months!" She grabbed my hand and tucked it between her legs.

I pressed her hand onto Mr. Happy. Small talk underscored the coming deal.

Arriving at her house, we carried in the bags of food and drink. As soon as possible, we embraced passionately, but she stopped me. "Wait. I have a romantic dinner planned. This will be our first time and we have the whole night. No need to rush because they won't be home until Sunday afternoon after the church conference." She pushed me back. "I want this to be memorable." She said, "You take a shower while I cook. And put your uniform back on – you are so handsome and sexy in it."

I headed for the shower.

Dove prepared oysters on a half shell and made a delicate ginger mignonette sauce. She arranged half figs in a semi-circle inside avocado halves. She put bread sticks in a container for dipping, setting it at the open V of her dish. Closing the window curtains, she lit candles around the house, then started work on the main menu and dessert.

Her eyes lit up when I came into the kitchen. She grabbed me and wrapped a leg around one of mine. "I love you so much." She handed me the Army hat. "Please wear it for me."

"Fine with me. It hides my big ears."

Lifting chilled martini glasses from the freezer, Dove turned to me. "I love your big ears. More for me to chew on." Pouring a red-hot martini, she said, *"The Word of Wisdom* from the Prophet Joseph Smith says to use everything with wisdom. Tonight is special. Cheers."

I was astounded because Dove never drank. I took the martini and we hooked arms to sip from our glasses. "Here is to lifelong love."

"To eternal love, Rowdy. I will love you forever."

We slurped raw oysters and enjoyed the figs and avocados. Dove teased by licking a bread stick up and down its length.

"Be careful. I won't make it through dinner."

Laughing, she rose to tend to the main course. The red-pepper vodka warmed our insides.

Sitting at the table, I watched her tight butt as she moved around the kitchen. Much to admire. Her perfect breasts jiggled slightly and the curve of her waist was something to behold. Amazingly, tonight I would make love to this beautiful, blonde-haired, blue-eyed angel – my future wife.

Dove had stacked romantic albums on the stereo and out came, "Oh, love, I need you now. I need your strength to face the day."

We chatted happily.

She started with one whole boiled artichoke and a side of small boiled and shaved carrots she had etched into erotic forms. Pouring another red-hot martini, she leaned to nibble my ears, running her tongue inside. It made me shiver.

Candles flickered, giving off a soft, waxy aroma.

We shared the artichoke, peeling leaves, dipping them in the garlic-onion butter, and feeding each other, scraping the meat with their teeth. "Does this look like a vagina?" She giggled.

I licked my lips. "Wouldn't know – I've only seen yours in the dark."

"You will very soon." She laughed.

"Your wish is my command."

Finishing the artichoke, Dove presented a sizzling seared Porterhouse steak soaked in beer butter with mushrooms, basil, and a hint of cayenne pepper. Grilled asparagus graced the side. It smelled incredible.

"Oh, my favorite! I haven't had a decent meal since leaving home. How did you know?"

"You told me last summer and I remembered."

"Dove, I love you so much."

We tore into the juicy seared meat with its pink, slightly bloody center. The album changed to The Moody Blues, *On the Threshold of a Dream.*

As we ate, she put one leg over mine and twisted her foot around my ankle. We toasted one another:

"Here's to love."

"To children, many children."

"To delicious sex!"

She stood. "Time for dessert?" A bubbling hot cup of chocolate dipping fudge, fresh Bing cherries, and vanilla ice cream with a cinnamon stick arrived in front of me.

As we savored the fudge-dipped cherries and vanilla, Dove asked, "Can I read you a poem?"

I was in heaven. Anything she wanted, anything. "Sure." His eyes were warm and slightly glazed from food, vodka, and romance.

"It's by Elizabeth Barret Browning. "How do I love thee? Let me count the ways…."

By the time she finished reading – despite my fight to hold back, tears were in my eyes. Dove sensually licked them from my cheeks and nuzzled her breasts back and forth across my nose.

She moved the dishes to the sink and pulled a bottle of red wine from a lower cabinet. Pouring each of us a glass, she said, "Come, I want to play the piano for you."

In the living room, Dove sat gracefully erect at the piano bench as I perched on the arm of a nearby couch. "My cousin wrote this for us."

She had never played piano for me before. I was amazed she played with a concert pianist posture and sang first soprano.

Dove had the song memorized and looked at me, her eyes soft. "I don't give to receive, I just give 'cause I choose, and most of all in this life, I choose to give to you."

This woman! I experienced a blend of exhaustion and relief to be away from the Army. It could be the martini, food, music, and atmosphere, but to me, it was love – pure, unadulterated love.

Wrapping her arms around me, we kissed. I tried to pull her onto the couch but she resisted. "Wait. I need to shower and change for you."

"No, no you don't. You're fine, I want you now!"

Grinning mischievously, she pulled from my grasp. "No, we have ALL night. Let's stretch this out. This is our first time." She headed for the shower.

Fifteen minutes of restless anticipation passed. My erection faded but it was instantly back when, dressed in a white, filmy robe, Dove came into the living room steaming from the shower and sat on the arm of their couch.

Removing my military hat, I watched her as I straddled a wooden chair.

Dove's hair was in a bun to emphasize the femininity of her lovely neck. She twisted slightly, emphasizing her shapely breasts.

Awed, yet apprehensive, I was quiet. My left arm dangled from the back of my wooden chair. Staring at one another, the air was thick with sexual tension.

She asked, "Do you want me?"

"Absolutely."

Dove stepped from her transparent gown, revealing a centerfold body. As she kissed me, I turned to putty. Turning me in the chair to face her, she unzipped my olive-drab pants and pulled them to my ankles and began doing oral. I was Sergeant Rock, D.I. Hard, The Six Million Dollar Man. I was a mortar-launching stud. I groaned. "Stop, stop, I'm gonna…"

On her knees, Dove looked up into my face. "Go ahead! I want you to – again and again. We have all night."

I arched and vibrated as I held her silky yellow hair in my hands and gave her face a string of pearls. *Wow!*

Unbuttoning my shirt, she pushed it and my military coat open. Using her heavenly spheres to caress me, she slowly massaged from my hard tummy up to my chin. As she did so, she slipped my shirt and Army coat over my relaxed shoulders, pinning my arms behind my back. I was helpless and didn't mind. I was in love, doing everything for the love of this woman.

She went crazy wild for the next half hour. We French kissed, our tongues wrestling as we made love. Peaking, Dove quaked with an oscillating squeal as the front door opened.

Stormy yelled, "Hey you guys! We're home. Mom is right behind me!" In the direct line of sight, Dove's back was to the front door.

My arms were pinned behind my back. I leaned out from Dove's trembling shoulders to see who was there.

Stormy tried to block her mother from entering, but the little woman pushed through.

Mrs. Knutson yelled, "What are you doing!?" She let out a string of obscenities and rushed us. She slapped Dove's butt and screamed like a mashed cat, "You evil scum! I command you in the name of Jesus Christ – stop fornicating in my house!"

Falling sideways, I slammed to the floor, unable to buffer Dove due to my bound arms. My breath exploded, "Ugh!"

Her mother slapped me across the face as she yelled, "Stop @%!&) screwing my daughter, you !&@!"

I let out, "Ye-owh!"

That broke the spell.

Dove came to and pushed away from me. She jumped up, her tummy muscles contracting. She yelled viciously, "You have no right to judge us. You got pregnant with Stormy by having sex with Bishop Falcon right here in the living room. I walked in on you!"

Stunned, Roberta looked back and forth at everyone's faces. Her toothpaste commercial smile appeared, disappeared, and reappeared.

Stormy froze in place and stared blankly.

Dove's eyes blazed fire.

My eyes were wide open. Rolling sideways, I got the Army jacket back over my shoulders so I could use my arms. I pulled up my pants and had my hat on before you can say 'chicken farts' and skedaddled out of the house like a greased pig.

Tearing at her hair, Roberta ran to her bedroom, slamming the door so hard that a framed picture of the family fell off the wall, shattering its glass.

Shaking, Dove said to Stormy, "I'm sorry you found out this way. We need to talk later." She glanced at the bedroom. "You have to help Mother come back to earth." Dressing, she said, "Call Devyn, he'll help you work through this." She left to find me. It was dark at 5:30 on this cold winter evening.

16. We Belong In Love

We got a motel and tried to make love again but the mood was broken, and she needed to get back to the college for final exams tomorrow.

Rather than distract Dove from her finals, I spent the next four days reconnecting with family and friends. My mother said, "I have something precious for you and Dove." She handed me a time-weathered ring box, "This engagement ring was my mother's,– your Grandma Oma's. We hid it from the Nazis."

Dumbfounded, I took it with trembling fingers. All the kids wanted this ring. "Thank you, Momma, thank you so much."

"The whole family decided. We love Dove too. We want her to be part of our family."

A couple of days later, I called Devyn from my parent's house. We talked for half an hour about the recent events, then I asked, "Tell me what you know about the Knutson family."

Their mother had a major mental illness. She believed angels talked to her. She had often had wild mood swings and was periodically physically and mentally abusive to Stormy. We talked about the shock of learning Stormy was the result of an affair. She was badly traumatized.

"Now I understand why Dove feels guilty about leaving Stormy home alone. It's making sense."

Devyn laughed sardonically. "We're involved with the Munsters. No wait, Stormy calls them the Adams Family."

"You going to hang in there with Stormy?"

"No question – she's my best friend. I can tell her anything, and she's straight-up with me. How about you with Dove?"

"We're engaged and we've made love."

"Good for you! Way to go. I'm jealous."

"I hope I come back from Vietnam in one piece."

"Me too, my friend, me too."

That Friday, Dove and I drove up Highway 65 through Eckert and Cedaredge following the main road. Ascending the south side of Grand Mesa, our favorite pullover was behind a low hill. I coasted in and shut off the engine as the radio played, "I belong to you, you belong to me and together we see, a life that is free. We belong in love."

We kissed and looked at the lights of the valley. I asked if she heard the story of the Ute curse – if you're born here, you can never leave.

Dove heard the curse was that no one born in the valley may leave unless they collect sand from junctions of the Umphaghre, Gunnison, and Colorado Rivers.

"Should I try to collect sand so I won't return?"

"You better not! I want you back in one whole piece," Dove exclaimed. "Another version is the Utes bewitched the land so the white man will never be happy here."

"Sounds like the curse of America." I chuckled. "I'm from Holland, so it doesn't apply." I nibbled her left ear. "Dove, I've never been this happy." I added, "Even in boot camp I was happy because I knew your spirit was with me."

"Me too. Each time I write, I light a candle for you. I'm sorry I pushed you to join the Army because of the danger. I wish you were on a Mormon mission instead. I've missed you so much."

The outlines of Grand Mesa's arms cupped the hazy valley below. Her tone was challenging, "Would you marry me today, right now?"

"Yes, of course, but our marriage may not be best for you, " my voice trailed away. "I go back next week to Fort Lewis for Advance Infantry Training, then I'll be in Vietnam for a year. I may never come back."

"What's your wish?" Her blue eyes twinkled.

"I want to be married and sitting beside you forever."

Dove laughed. "So, do you want me right now, Rowdy?"

Confused, I stared.

"Well, do you?"

"Yes, yes, of course I do." Blinded by her beauty, I didn't recognize her insecurity. "I'm going to Vietnam because I'm willing to take a bullet for you."

"Oh, Rowdy!" She threw her arms around my neck. As I leaned in for a kiss, she said, "Rowdy Jaeger, I want you so much that I want you to penetrate my very core." She lay back in the seat, pulling me with her. She peeled open her blouse, revealing firm nineteen-year-old centerfold breasts. A song came on the radio, "The look of love is in your eyes. A look your smile can't disguise."

I was so excited, I had trouble getting the condom on. Soon, Popeye went dancing with Miss Olive. It was rock and roll time. The old station wagon with worn-out shocks moved with our boogie-woogie. I thumped her like a rabbit on a hollow log. Her soprano scream that stopped beasts in the night burst forth and she flailed my back with small fists. Suddenly, she was gone.

I freaked, thinking I was too rough. *I've offed her.* I moved her head back and forth but she was limp, flaccid, and dead gone.

I wilted. *They'll think I raped and murdered her.* How could I have zapped her? It's not like I snapped her neck. "Dove, are you okay?" My voice was tight.

She failed to stir.

For sure, I did her in. My fiancé just died on me. How do you treat a heart attack? Did she have a stroke? Panicking, I took her chin and moved her head back and forth, "Dove, Dove, wake up, please wake up." Elvis Presley came on the radio, "I'll have a blue Christmas without you."

I put my mouth over hers and tried to give her artificial respiration. After a minute, she came to. "Wow! Now that was a fuck!"

I was shocked. She had never cussed in front of me. I grinned. "Have to agree."

Most men might not have thought it was satisfying to have sex in the cramped quarters of a car seat on a cold November day, but for me, it was more. I was going to war for the love of this woman.

I suggested we step out to enjoy the fresh air.

Dove slipped on her sweater, but I didn't want a jacket. "It's nice out, almost warm."

She walked to the edge overlooking the sparkling valley underneath the bright moon and stars.

I took her hand and with a graceful movement dropped to one knee.

Her eyes opened wide.

"Dove, you are my life's inspiration. Before I met you, I was a lost and blind time traveler like the words in one of Dev's songs. You've given me purpose, meaning, and direction. I want you to be the mother of my children. I want to live my whole life being and doing for you."

Tears of happiness ran down her ivory cheeks. She brushed a wisp of blonde hair from her beautiful blue eyes.

Pulling the old ring box from my pocket, I opened it to reveal a gorgeous antique blue, green, and fiery red opal ring. Oval in shape, it sat in a 24-carat gold band. The opal was surrounded by a ring of brilliant diamonds. "This was my great-grandmother's. It came down through my mother. They hid it from the Nazis during the occupation of Holland. It holds a fortune in luck and perseverance. All of us kids wanted it but Mama gave it to me because she loves you." I let it sink in. "Please, will you marry me?"

Dove wept softly. With both hands in mine, her tears ran gently in the night. "Yes, oh, YES!" She trembled as I slipped the ring onto her finger.

It was too big and could easily slide off.

95

17. Drill Sergeant Hard

Join the Army. Visit exotic places, meet strange people, and *kill* them. Advanced Infantry Training (AIT) taught us how. I felt great since Dove had honored her promise to give me her virginity if I enlisted to fight the Viet Cong. We were deeply in love, but I wasn't looking forward to AIT. I had no desire to kill anyone, communist or not.

Rayferd went to helicopter mechanic school and Big Al to Arizona to learn truck driving. The lucky ones, ha-ha – Marty and me, walked across the street from Alpha Company to Bravo Company for two challenging months of infantry school.

"Gentlemen, my name is Drill Sergeant Hard. Did you hear me, gentlemen? My name is Drill Sergeant Hard!"

"Sir, Yes Sir!" Three hundred graduates of basic training answered in unison.

I stood at attention, my gear in a big green duffle bag. Here's this monster in a Smokey Bear hat and he referred to us as gentlemen. It was a surprise because so far, the DIs called us wimps, girls, assholes, or dick-heads.

"And believe me, gentlemen, I live up to my name!"

Our eyes were the size of oranges. This man was at least three hundred pounds of solid muscle. He looked like a pro football lineman or a pro wrestler. *Oh shit, we've had it now.*

"It is H.A.R.D!" He spelled it to make sure no one misunderstood. "And you thought boot camp was a challenge, well, it ain't nothing compared to AIT. You men gonna wish you were back at the beginning!" Hard pounded on his chest and bellowed like a bull. It was clear he got more miles out of his nametag than his meager rank. "Welcome to Advanced Infantry Training and our fine facility."

We were transformed. It was the first time we were called gentlemen, instead of one of the five Ps. "Come here Piss-ant," "Go over there Puke." "Stand at attention Prick," or, "You Pussy! You ain't no soldier, you're a Pud!" Those endearments were replaced with trainee, men, or our favorite – gentlemen.

Sergeant Hard kicked butt in training and pushed the men to their limits. He made it tolerable with jokes and stories. "What do Hanoi and Hiroshima have in common? Nothing – yet."

We learned rules of thumb: "If the enemy is in range, so are you. There is never a convenient foxhole." According to D.I. Hard, "Courage is being the only one who knows you're afraid."

Or was it Die Hard? The son of a motherless goat kept going and going like an Energizer battery-operated rabbit. He never stopped. We didn't realize that the D.I.s dropped out for a rest as another one took the lead. Later, the original D.I. returned, running without appearing winded.

We chanted, "See that enemy on the hill – he's the one I got to kill. And if my M60 won't do – I'll smoke him with my M2."

"The enemy diversion you are ignoring is the main attack. Incoming fire has the right of way. Ammo is cheap, but life is expensive. The enemy attacks on two occasions: a. When they're ready, and b. When you're not."

Big Owl couldn't understand how he got into truck driving school while I went into the infantry. His school was in Ft. Wachuka, Arizona, south of Tucson. In the winter, snowbirds in travel trailers enjoyed the perfect weather. Life was good.

Owl was introduced to pills: Reds, whites, pink ladies, ludes, barbs, and yellow jackets. He tried them all. Occasionally, Owl wrote weird letters with FTA written all over the paper. FTA replaced 'Eat My Shorts.' I worried Owl would get stoned, run off a road and kill himself.

In AIT, we ran before breakfast, after breakfast, and to every area. We got three to four hours of sleep. Using strategies from World War 2 and Korea, we assaulted hills with fire teams.

The first team put out rifle fire while the second team advanced and dropped to lay down bullets for the first team to advance. We practiced it over and over. The Army used these tactics at Hamburger Hill in Vietnam. The plan was to kill more enemies than we lost. We gave it back to the VC, then did it again. It was digging a hole and filling it with dead grunts.

Sergeant Hard asked, "What do you call a Roman warrior after oral sex?" He grinned. "Gladiator."

The training assumed massed tanks and infantry in conventional warfare with two sides coming at each other. Not much use in a guerrilla war with no fronts fought in deep and congested jungles. Sgt. Hard gave lots of tips. "The enemy never monitors your radio frequency until you broadcast on an unsecured channel. Tracers work both ways. Friendly fire – isn't. Any order that can be misunderstood has been misunderstood. If your sergeant can see you, so can the enemy."

During breaks and just before lights out, the guys cracked jokes about the Army and the drill instructors: One grunt said, "I wouldn't say that DI Hard was unpopular as a child, but his parents had to tie a lamb chop to his leg so the dog would play with him."

As the laughter died done, another guy cracked, "How do they say 'fuck you' in the Army?" He slapped his leg. "Trust me, I won't cum in your mouth."

Marty and I were bunkmates again. Marty was a likable person, but he seldom spoke. If you asked him a question, you got 'yep' or 'nope.' Prying anything from him was worse than pulling weeds. I pushed Marty to talk about his family because it reminded me of Cedaredge.

Marty hesitated but to my surprise, he answered, "I'd rather be home in New Mexico hanging out with my grandfather."

It was a start. The question left Marty open like an ear of shucked corn, so I prodded, "So how is it in New Mexico?"

"Life was good most of the time." Marty told about his mom and two sisters, one of whom was married. He grew up on a farm near a small town called Aztec just south of the Colorado border. "We grew hay, barley, and oats," he said, clearing his dry throat. "But Dad sold half the farm to pay taxes after Grandpa Moya passed away."

I looked down from my bunk in time to see Marty roll onto his back and put his writing aside. Our eyes met. Aware there may not be another opportunity, I asked, "What do you remember about your grandpa?"

"I was ten when we moved to the farm. Before my dad died, we visited on weekends on account that we lived in town. It was a lot of fun. Gramps showed me this huge old tree stump in the backyard. The tree once shaded the house and barn in summer. Lightning killed it and Gramps cut it down. He said it was over three hundred years old, and he showed me how to count the rings."

"The exposed tree rings?"

"Yeah, Gramps hammered in a nail to show the year he was born. He drove in another nail for when Grandma was born, one for Dad as a baby, and one for Ma, which was right near the edge. There weren't nails for me or my sisters 'cause the tree died before we were born." Marty paused for a minute: "I wish I was back there right now, sitting on the ole stump."

18. Surrounded

I called Dove, "Why don't you enlist in the Army nursing corps and volunteer for Vietnam since that's what you want to be? They would train you and we'd be closer. We might be able to see each other."

Dove said that first she wanted to finish her bachelors degree at Western State.

I didn't question her logic. The kind of love I was suffering from is definitely blind.

AIT training was seldom boring and routine. We learned about new weapons and forest tactics. We were taken deep into the cold, wet, and dark Northwest forests for two weeks of bivouac and war games. They ordered us to set an ambush using camouflage techniques. It was important to do a good job because our opponents had one week before leaving for Vietnam.

My company planned to be extremely quiet and stealthy. We snickered as we put on grease paint, stuffing sticks in helmets and arranging ferns and branches on their backpacks. We would become one with the forest, invisible to the human eye.

D.I. Hard placed a man every twenty feet on a narrow trail overgrown with dripping ferns, shrubs, and giant slugs. Huge Ponderosa pines towered above. A drizzle fell throughout the day.

Our ambush was shaped like the letter L. I hid among the roots of a large tree. There were grunts to my left and Marty was to my right. Although hidden among the overgrowth, Marty and I could see each other through the roots.

We waited thirty minutes, staying silent enough to hear the beating of our hearts. Anxiously, I watched fog rise from Marty's breath. I motioned at my mouth.

He used a cloth to cover his steaming breath so it wouldn't give him away.

Walking slowly and deliberately, a line of troops entered my field of vision. They knew rookies were planning an ambush. Watching every direction, they tried to spot us first. They were spaced ten feet apart, trying to be quiet, but there was a snap of a limb and rustling of equipment. Someone suppressed a cough. Marty was to initiate the ambush when the last man passed him.

The troops entered the foot of the trap, walking into the coming fire from the front and right.

Periodically, the opponent platoon paused and crouched. Cautiously, they moved at a slow, steady pace. One of the soldiers stood for a minute next to me; another passed so close I thought I was spotted. Nothing! I could have untied the man's boot laces. A soldier stood near Marty and scratched his knee as he looked toward me without seeing.

As if blind, the passing soldiers didn't see anything amiss. As the last man passed Marty, it struck me how vulnerable those guys were. Marty returned a shocked gaze. Our eyes locked. Fear. Passing in front of us were not cherries but trained infantrymen shipping to Vietnam this week.

It was a play ambush, but they had blindly walked into a trap to their fictitious deaths. The best-trained soldiers in the world had entered the Twilight Zone. They would be sent to their graves by a barrage of lead and mortar shells that if real, would have shredded their limbs like fresh-mowed grass.

I saw myself in the faces of these men. The impact of being surrounded by the Viet Cong was real. The stakes were the critical point between life and death.

The message was crystal clear – a patrol was extremely vulnerable. A guy's destiny may be an ambush without seeing his end coming.

On signal, my platoon opened up with blank bullets and firecrackers, yelling and screaming. The ambushed men twisted and turned in confusion. If real, all of the enemy was dead. I wanted to puke and run away.

When the exercise terminated, I realized that awareness is essential for survival. I must learn to stay calm and be brave for no other reason than to save my neck.

Because I loved a woman, I was going to kill or be killed.

19. Blue Christmas

Halfway through infantry school, my unit was given two weeks leave for the holidays. I flew from Seattle to Denver and on to Gunnison where Dove was in college.

Landing there, I hiked from the airport to Western State College. I was high would do anything she wanted as if I was a stoned Zombie.

Opening the door, she stood quietly as if I were an apparition. She wavered, but as her eyes adjusted to my image in a dress Army uniform, she flashed her sweet pouty lips.

I dropped my green Army duffle bag at the door. We slammed together like snooker balls hit hard, inhibitions scattering into the table pockets. On her single bed, we sank into each other's arms, melting as one. No more separation, no more loneliness, no fear or alienation. I was her king and she was my queen. Call it lust or love – it didn't matter.

Afterward, we lay panting on the sheets.

I realized the dorm room door was propped open by my Army duffle bag. I jumped up and ran to shut the door as giggling girls ducked away. My face was hot, and I apologized to Dove, "Sorry 'bout that." I meekly slipped back to her side.

She grinned. "Don't worry, they probably got an education." She touched my chest. "Wow, your body is so hard." She reached down. "Just like your baby maker."

We did it again and again. We couldn't get enough of each other. There was no doubt that she loved me and would be a perfect wife.

For three days, I distracted her from final exams by following her around like a puppy dog. She showed me off, taking me around Western's small campus. I was her soldier going to Vietnam to save Christians from the godless communists.

Dove's girlfriends fawned and her roommate insisted on staying in the room despite other girls offering her a place to sleep. It was 1969, Woodstock Nation, naked and sexual in its yearning for freedom.

Initially confused over the roommate's noises, I decided it was interesting to hear the girl take care of herself while we were intertwined a few feet away.

I was in extraordinary hard-body condition and when Dove took me around, girls brushed their hands against my steel butt, pressed a boob onto my muscled arms, and unknown feminine fingers ran across my chest. At a bar, the girl sitting next to me started fondling my crotch. Dang, it was exciting to have Dove move her fingers away. I asked her about the girls touching me.

"I know who you love. Let them fantasize."

This was the era of free love and I was confused – *am I supposed to be religious or liberal?* I'd do anything to please Dove. I considered attending her Mormon Church. Had I not enlisted, a mission would have been a better choice.

We went home to Delta for the holiday. I talked with her sister, Stormy, my buddy's girlfriend. She said things were going better since Devyn was going to the Mormon Church with her. "Mom's rules, you know."

On Christmas Eve, I picked up Dove in Poppa's blue and white station wagon. She grabbed blankets and pillows, then we drove up to Grand Mesa. Parking in our special spot overlooking the Surface Creek Valley, we looked out at the holiday lights of Cedaredge, Delta, Olathe, and Montrose.

The earth was dusted with snow and it was cold. I started the car to stay warm. The radio played Christmas music, "Sleigh bells ring, are you listening?"

We cuddled. Periodically, I turned off the motor until it got cold again. We talked about people, infantry training, and her friends at Western State. I asked about her mother.

Dove said, "She's been off since Tommy died. Our father left and has yet to come back."

"What do you mean; he has yet to come back? Please go on."

"Mom went into a deep depression. She'd lie on the bed with the curtains closed for days, and then she'd jump up, clean everything, and run all over town acting as if she was on top of the world. Without warning, she'd crash and not talk to us." Dove took a breath. "Dad works above Glade Park in the sawmill and doesn't come home unless he has to. That's what I mean by he never came back."

"Must have been rough for you kids."

"It was. Mom went off the deep end and hasn't been the same." Dove bit her lip. "I'm taking abnormal psychology next semester. I need to understand what her problem is."

"What about her affair with Joe Falcon that produced Stormy?"

"Let's talk about something else. The situation gives me a headache." She nibbled my ear, then rested her cheek against mine.

The sky was clear and speckled with stars from one end of the horizon to the other, stretching for miles. Raising her head from my shoulder, she asked, "Do you have a Christmas wish?"

"Yes, to be married to you."

The radio played a gentle waltz, "I'm grateful for knowing you. I'm grateful for love that's true."

She looked up into the clear mountain sky. The outlines of Grand Mesa's arms cupped the valley below. "Would you marry me right now?"

"Yes of course. You're the woman of my dreams." Foreseeing death, I said, "Our marriage may not be wise for your sake." My voice trailed away.

We faced the Valley of the Ute Curse where the lights from Cedaredge, Eckert, Delta, Olathe, and Montrose twinkled in the crisp night.

"I leave next week for Fort Lewis for another month of training, and then I'll be in Vietnam for a year. I may never come back." I hoped to change the mood by asking lightly, "What is your Christmas wish?"

She smiled and her sapphire eyes responded with a silent laugh of their own. "The same as you. I want to be married and sitting beside you next Christmas Eve." Dove look me in the eyes. "So – do you want me right now, Rowdy?"

She had raised the same question the night she gave me her virginity. It was confusing that she was so unsure of herself.

"Of course, I want you. Do you want me?"

Her blue eyes twinkled. "More importantly, do you love me?"

It sounded like an order.

"Yes, I do," I whispered. Blinded by her beauty, I didn't see any trouble coming. "I love you, Dove; I love you more than anything in the whole world. I'm going to Vietnam because I'm willing to do anything for your love."

"Oh, Rowdy!" She threw her arms around my neck. As I leaned to kiss her lips, she said, "Rowdy Jaeger, I want you so much, I want you to penetrate to my very core."

A holiday song from World War Two came on, "I'll be home for Christmas. You can plan on me."

Once we had our clothes off, she welcomed me home. We bounced the springs of the car until suddenly, she let out a scream and collapsed.

Although this was her way when she orgasmed, I was still frightened when she passed out. I sat holding her, my ears ringing.

Her listless legs lay on top of my hips and I gently pushed them off to look at her face. "Dove, are you okay?" My voice was tight.

She didn't stir.

For sure, I did her in this time. Panicking, I took her chin in my hand and gently shook her head back and forth, saying, "Dove, wake up, please wake up."

Elvis Presley came on the radio, "I'll have a blue Christmas without you."

I kissed her softly and her eyes fluttered open. She exclaimed, "Wow, now that was a fuck!"

Shocked because she had never cussed, I couldn't speak for a moment. Time ticked past. I said, "Yeah, I'd have to agree."

20. Worm in a Hole

Big Owl's letter was a challenge to read because FTA and Fuk The Army, were written everywhere and some words were scratched out. Worse, the sentences ran in all directions. The Army truck driving school was in Ft. Wachuka, Arizona, south of Tucson, where snowbirds in travel trailers enjoyed the warm weather. He and I had enlisted in the Army on the buddy system for three years for the privilege of being together during basic. I thought it was ironic that I didn't get truck driving school along with him. As Rayferd liked to say, "The military is anything but logical."

FTA Hey fudge nuggets, this here ain't bad in ft Cuca. But it's hot no air condition in truks. Fuk The Army There's fun pills – red and pink and gray. Get Laid. Yellow ones makes time go fast FTA i got colors ya ain't never FTA seed. you oght to be ere. motherucker rat it. Eat my sorts rite ya from Nam.

I wondered, What happened? Big Owl never had an interest in drugs, just alcohol. His idea of a seven-course meal was a burger and a six-pack. Owl was shy because he wasn't good with words. If Big Owl had an idea, it died of loneliness.

When we were freshmen in high school, we rode the pep bus to a basketball game and this red-headed senior, Rachel, stretched her ravishing legs on the seat across from us.

Rachel was giving us a panty flash. I whispered, "Hey Owl, you're getting your picture taken."

He gawked at the space between her legs. "Hey, she got on black underwear."

"Not so loud." I grinned. "At first I thought she didn't have any panties on."

Big Owl laughed, "Yuck, yuck."

She caught us staring and said to Owl, "Like what you see?"

Owl's freckles went scarlet.

Seductively, Rachel stretched her long pale legs. "You want to sit with me and touch them?"

Owl didn't know whether to check his ass or scratch his watch. Dumber than a coal bucket, he replied, "Well, eat my shorts!"

In a huff, Rachel put her legs down and tucked her feet under the seat.

If there were twelve kinds of stupid, Owl had eleven of them. "Eat my Shorts" was now "FTA." I worried that Owl would get drunk and stoned, run off a road, and kill himself before getting to Vietnam. Enemy not needed. Where does innocence go when it's gone?

Maybe it's like trying to put an earthworm back into its hole after a rainstorm.

21. Last Chance

Moments before leaving Delta to enlist, Dove had begged me to join the Mormon Church. "It's the only way we can be married in the temple."

"Okay, if they have any Mormon missionaries in Vietnam, I'll take the lessons." I knew they didn't so I was safe for a while.

At the end of ten weeks of AIT, I graduated and called Dove, "Why don't you enlist in the Army nursing corps now? If you volunteered for Vietnam duty, we'd be closer and might be able to see each other." I was thinking about making love with her and sensed she was having the same idea

"That's a good idea. Why didn't I think of that?"

"Dove, I have a three-day layover in San Francisco before shipping out to Vietnam. Is there any way you could meet me there? I'll send you a ticket and we can see the city. It's our last chance to be together."

"When?"

"I get to Oakland Army Terminal at noon on January 24, but it will take a couple of hours to process through and get to where I could meet you. I already called Owl's brother in San Jose. Bruce said we could stay with him, and he'll also pick us up."

She gasped. "Three days?" There was silence. "I'll have to miss classes, but yes. Yes, send me a ticket. I so much want to see you."

Translation, *We're going to fuck our brains out for three days and nights.*

Four hundred troops flew from SeaTac in Seattle to the Oakland Army Terminal at noon on Thursday, January 28, 1969. We'd ship to Vietnam at eight AM on Sunday the 31st. We disembarked in San Francisco to wait for buses heading for the Oakland Army Terminal, or OAT.

Some guys said, "To hell with the Army, I want to see my girlfriend." They'd get an Article 15 if they were late, but it wasn't a big deal until a guy was gone more than thirty days.

After an hour of standing around with our thumbs up our…, the Army loaded us onto a bus to OAT where we were herded into more lines. I lost track of Marty, my bunkmate in AIT.

OAT was the location for troop transfers to the entire Pacific region. There were thousands of men from different parts of the country. I was awed by the huge warehouse. It was bigger than a professional basketball stadium. The main floor had bleachers on one side.

Men stood in long lines so I joined one. I scanned the room for my buddies during basic training. I wondered if by chance Big Owl or Rayferd might be processing through OAT at the same time.

The lines drove me crazy. There are three types of intelligence: Animal, man, and Army – the latter an oxymoron. I eventually processed through and was assigned to a barracks where I was to be inanely bored with the other hairy legs for the next three days. I headed for the bus station immediately.

I didn't spot her and Bruce at the station so I wandered around, watching for a big red-headed man with a petite long-haired blonde.

I happened to run into another GI who was just back from the war so I stopped to talk to him. He seemed distant and detached. There was something vacant in his eyes. I said, "I'm shipping out in three days. Tell me about it. Were you in combat?"

"Yeah, it's hard to avoid if you're infantry."

"Did you get wounded?"

His face colored. "Yeah."

"So?" He didn't want to tell me, but I pushed on, oblivious to his discomfort. "Where'd you get hit?"

"I was riding in a Slick on the way to a hot LZ."

"Did they get you in the helicopter?"

He tried to turn away, but I stayed with him. He wouldn't meet my eyes. "Come on man, I'm headed over there, I'm trying to learn how to keep my balls."

He slowly shook his head. "Good luck. I was sitting on my helmet and they still got me." He rushed away, his face bright red.

I realized that he had lost his nuts sitting in a helicopter. I was suddenly worried. Fuck, the hell if I wanted to lose mine.

I walked up to this long-haired blonde woman and touched her shoulder, "Dove, it's me, I'm here for you."

He turned around. He was carrying an anti-war sign and seeing my uniform, he lit into me, "You fucking baby killer, you ought to be hung."

I thought about punching him but right then, Dove walked up with Bruce behind her.

She threw her arms around my neck. "Oh, you're so handsome in your uniform and you're going to kill communists for me!"

The hippy dude looked like he wanted to slap her with his peace sign.

We stayed in Bruce's camp trailer in the backyard. Everyone thought I'd be dead soon. *This was it. If you're gonna die, you have to live while you can - make a party of it.*

We ate in the best places I could afford. I took her to a strip show and although we were underage, they let us in since I was in uniform. I was surprised that Dove's face flushed, and it wasn't from embarrassment. She was excited and even more so when a gorgeous stripper sat down and talked to her. "So, honey, would you like to strip like me?"

"It's a thought," Dove replied.

I was shocked. *Miss Mormon?* My eyes opened wide.

The woman with only a G strap on kissed her lips while rubbing her bare nipples against my lady's chest.

Dove opened her mouth and their tongues danced.

Watching them make out gave me an intense erection.

The stripper asked if she could meet us after her shift. Dove was about say yes when I spoke up, "We're newly engaged and I'm shipping out in three days."

The stripper was disappointed and continued looking into Dove's eyes who stared back.

My pants were about to burst.

The woman said without breaking eye contact, "Well, maybe when you come back home, we can hook up." She wrote her phone number down and gave it to Dove.

She carefully folded it and put the number into her purse.

As we walked out, I asked, "What was that? Do you want to be with a woman?"

Dove shrugged and winked at me. "I was thinking you would enjoy it."

I took a deep breath. She saw the fear and wonder in my eyes. "Well, sure, if that's what you want. We'll call her when I'm back from 'Nam."

With the passion of lovers who knew it may be our last hurrah, we rocked the camp trailer morning and night, swimming in ecstasy. I took her out dancing but avoided strip clubs. I had no desire to share the luxury of this incredible woman, a woman who, when I returned, would share me with a big titted stripper. In the back of my mind, I started wondering if she was a jack Mormon – someone who believed, but didn't follow the rules about drinking, smoking, or sex.

By Saturday afternoon, our private parts were sore. Lying naked by each other, I said, "Being loved by you gives me the strength and courage to go to Vietnam."

Dove responded, "I'm wearing your grandmother's engagement ring. We should tell everyone."

We called home to announce our engagement. My best friend was at Stormy's so I asked to say hello to him.

Devyn said that for the second year, he was the sixth man on the basketball team because Head Coach Winehead played his cousins and his wife's two brothers. "Dad said I didn't raise you to be a quitter, so I have to stick it out." He went on, "After Christmas break, Mr. Vandick, the new high school principal, pulled me into his office because of a twelve-foot-tall snowman on the front steps. I had nothing to do with it, but as usual, he blamed me. Vandick was upset because somebody moved the carrot from his nose to his groin and stuck straw around to make it a snow MAN."

It was funny but trivial. I was going to war.

Sunday morning, I was halfway around the world and mentally distant.

Dove pulled off my condom.

I looked at her with questions in my eyes.

She said, "I will carry your seed and you'll be a father when you return."

Ordered to report at eight Sunday morning, I didn't care if I was a few hours late. I didn't want to miss a fraction of a minute with her.

It was noon when we took Dove to the airport. She asked again, "Rowdy please take the missionary lessons so we can marry in the temple when you return." There was guilt and fear in her blue eyes.

"I'll look into it, but I doubt they have Mormon missionaries over in Vietnam."

Turning away, she walked to the airline gate with tears streaming down her face.

Watching her plane take off for Denver, I thought about escaping from the Army. But where? Canada, Holland, or on the run in the U.S.? Every alternative meant I lost Dove. She would never accept me for failing to be *her* warrior for Christ. The silver plane became a dot in the sky.

A hundred buses pulled through the main San Francisco bus station. Once on a bus, my heart raced with fear. *I am a living, breathing man who wants only what all men want – Love, not death.* This was a date with destiny, and I was filled with dread.

It was late afternoon, but the sun was bright. A slight breeze cooled my skin as I got off the bus. I walked through the entrance to the OAT building into a long hallway filled with soldiers, and into the massive warehouse.

As always, troops stood in long lines – a few sat on the bleachers nearby. My heart pounded. I took deep breaths to clear my head, then walked from the monstrous warehouse and down a long hallway filled with men. Outside, I breathed fresh air. Buses and taxis came with more soldiers. It'd be easy to jump into one. Dire thoughts of impending doom. *All my options are bad.*

Back inside the building, I spotted a row of pay telephones. She may be back at college by now. With an overwhelming urge, I called to say goodbye.

A sweet voice answered, "Hello."

"It's me, Dove, it's Rowdy." It was hard to contain myself. "I'm calling from the Oakland Army Terminal and we're about to ship out."

"Oh, Rowdy, I've been thinking of you. It's wonderful to hear your voice. I'm so glad you called."

"Listen, I want you to know I wasn't just having sex with you. Sex for the sake of sex is the mentality of a cancer cell. I was making love with you. I love you Dove."

"I know. I will never forget how you made me feel this weekend. I already miss you so much! You're constantly in my prayers and dreams. Don't worry, Darling. I love you with all my heart and soul. You'll be home soon."

"I will use my last breathe to say I love you."

Dove sobbed. "Oh, please do whatever it takes to stay safe and alive. You *must* come home to me." She hung up and wept uncontrollably.

I was confused, sad, and angry. I was angry at the Army, angry at the United States, at Dove, and especially at myself. Anger made me feel brave again, and it turned on the communists. If they weren't causing this war, I wouldn't be in this situation.

The Sergeant at OAT was pissed since I was hours late. Defiantly, I said, "Do what you will, but send me to 'Nam so I can kill some gooks!"

His face turned from an angry snarl into a smile, "You're there." He stamped the shit out of my papers.

February 1969

22. Into the Heat

The North Vietnamese honored international laws against shooting down commercial jets so the U.S. flew its military personnel on them. I boarded Continental Airlines flight 690 from San Francisco to Saigon at ten at night. There were two hundred nineteen other servicemen and one hundred civilians on the flight.

I stared through the window at the lights of the San Francisco Bay, seeing ships steaming under the Golden Gate Bridge. I watched until clouds took away the view. As the bay disappeared, I spent the long flight thinking of friends, family, and Dove.

I remembered last June 1968, the first time we were alone together. We drove to the top of Grand Mesa and parked on an isolated turnout. The lights of Cedaredge were three thousand feet below. The radio played, "Nights in white satin, never reaching the end."

Dove explained Mormon theology, "Love for all eternity is what I want with you."

The other stuff struck me as religious drivel, which was why, when given the choice of Vietnam or a Mormon mission, I chose the Army.

Sitting among soldiers packed on the commercial jet on the way to Vietnam, I stared into space, thinking, *I am Dutch! How did I end up as a U.S. soldier going to fight in Vietnam?*

When the Second World War ended, my parents married and began having children. The U.S. government had a program where American towns could sponsor families from war-torn Europe whose breadwinners needed a job. The Delta Presbyterian

Church offered to help us make the journey from Holland to Delta, Colorado to become the town barber.

We had boarded the Groote Beer, a converted troop transport ship, on January 27, 1957, headed to New York City via Halifax, Nova Scotia. I was six years old and in the 2nd grade. I didn't want to leave my friends and particularly, Grandma Oma Wijnands, Mom's mother. Oma loved me, and I had given my heart to her. Losing her made me chronically sad. I didn't understand – why leave our country you fought so hard to free? Again, I was leaving my country, going halfway around the world, and losing Dove as I had lost Grandma Oma.

Because of my blank staring eyes, a stewardess touched my shoulder. "Are you Okay?"

Imagining she offered a drink, I shook my head no.

She rushed away.

It struck me: I was on this plane to Vietnam, not only because of Dove, but also because of my parent's absolute conviction: "You must fight against oppression even to death."

Yes, that was it! Jody was the oppressor – the one who stole and lied and took away your freedom like Hitler. Everyone said the communists were oppressing the Vietnamese people like the Nazis had terrorized the Dutch people. I'm going over there to kill Jody.

I closed my eyes and in my mind, it was snowing lightly. The scent of a Colorado blue spruce with Christmas lights in Dove's living room, Silent Night played softly on the stereo. We laughed and talked.

A touch on my shoulder startled me awake. "Do you need me to find a doctor for you?" It was another stewardess. The first one stood behind her. Their faces were concerned.

"No, no, I'm okay. I was thinking of home."

"You worried us, your eyes are glazed and we thought you had a heart attack."

I smiled weakly and waved them off. *Wow, they've already*

got me dead and I haven't even made it to 'Nam.

Landing at the Saigon airport was risky because the Viet Cong took potshots at airplanes. Periodically, someone was wounded or killed so the planes landed and took off as quickly as possible.

When the jet rolled to a stop at Tan Son Nhut Airbase, a Army colonel boarded the plane. He directed everyone to remain seated. "I want all infantry troops to the front of the plane. Pronto!" The colonel was smartly dressed in olive drab jungle fatigues with clean, pressed seams.

I thought, *Oh shit, we're under siege, and they'll give us rifles to fight. I ain't gonna live but hours.* Half a dozen grunts moved to the front. *Who are these other slugs?* I looked around the plane. They said it took eight people to support one grunt in the field.

The officer ordered infantrymen down the ramp. I feared the worst and the only thing I carried was a green duffle bag. *Have to throw it at the Viet Cong, I guess.* Stepping from the air-conditioned plane, hot humidity smacked me in the face. It was like being pushed into a steam sauna, or more accurately, through the gates of hell. I said to the officer, "Okay, give me a rifle."

The colonel laughed and pointed at a jeep.

Jet exhaust rankled my nose. The unbelievable heat made me break into a sweat. It was early afternoon and oppressive humidity waifed over like a steam clothes iron, knocking my energy flat. The dank, heavy heat fed dire thoughts.

Eyes wide with fear, one teen asked, "Is there an enemy assault on the airfield?"

The colonel suppressed a grin and again pointed to a long jeep parked on the tarmac. I realized an immediate firefight was not the plan and breathed a sigh of relief.

Vets shuffled past, making cracks, "It's a lick on you dumb fuckers." The air smelled of rotten vegetation, dust, diesel, and aviation fuel. "More cannon fodder." There were no smiles.

What could they say? Have a nice war?

I had made a serious mistake. I walked along with the other men, lost and dazed, hoping to wake up from this nightmare.

The colonel drove us through a gate in a twelve-foot-high fence. Tents and Quonset huts, a few trees, and jungle trees were scattered haphazardly. It was dusty, causing me to cough and hack.

The officer pulled into a large airplane hangar and stood us in a circle in the middle of the big domed building. The stinking aroma of burning human shit was indescribable.

Speaking loudly, he explained, "The Army is looking for helicopter gunners. We have more birds than men." He paced. "You gentlemen have the right training to join us. You are qualified on the M60 machine gun, and you have specialized jungle survival skills."

Colonel Ballbreaker walked straight up to me, face to face. "Gunners are in big demand. You got what it takes?" He moved around the circle, singling out a different man. "It's your choice," he said, "Volunteer for helicopters or be a ground trooper." He smirked. "Grunts pack 60 pounds plus your rifle, and you'll be wading through mud and rice paddies. You'll sleep in the jungle at night with mosquitos and poisonous snakes, waiting for the Viet Cong to attack." He turned to a new man. "And you cherries always get the worst jobs. You'll be burning shit… you smell it?"

We did. How do you describe the odor of burning diesel and human shit? It permeated the moist hot air. The Vietnamese said Americans smelled like shit and they were correct. Who would deal with human excrement by burning it with diesel? Oh yeah – the U.S. Army and Marines.

"Because you are NFG, new fucking guys, you'll also carry the radio or the med kit, adding another twenty pounds." He swung back to me. "Sleeping in the rain with a poncho for your only shelter, or be an aircraft weapons specialist? Helicopter gunners get a dry bunk at night at the base camp."

He backed up and pushed through the group so we formed a U in front of him. Gesturing with his arms as if he could fly, he said, "You guys are lucky. You've got a choice – either you're up in the sky looking down at the beautiful scenery, dropping troops off and firing your machine gun at gooks, or you're crawling in the mud, dodging AK-47 rounds."

He made it sound like riding shotgun on an old west stagecoach. As he fidgeted with his watch, the colonel said, "Grunts spend most of their time in the swamp." He shoved his left hand into a trouser pocket. "Here in South Vietnam, you get six months of sweltering heat and another six months of unrelenting rain."

He waved an arm. "They tell you about the fat disgusting leeches which hang off bushes and live in the mud? A soldier had a leech crawl up inside his penis. It sucked itself full of blood and blocked his piss. Painful as hell. Took surgery to get it out. Permanently scarred." He waited for our shocked expressions to fade. "And there are snipers, booby traps, and mines."

He slapped his leg for effect. "I'll bet you've never seen what a bouncing Betty does to a man's legs. You won't be getting any pussy after one of those takes your nuts and pecker off for damn sure." He paced. "A grunt's survival rate is a little better than a door gunner but not by much."

He smiled behind a pair of gold-rimmed sunglasses. The nut-cracking colonel went on, "The infantry has about ten percent of the people in country but they take 80 percent of the casualties. You got a choice – it's a matter of where you sleep at night."

I didn't understand what he talked about, but he had my attention.

"If you aren't killed by a bullet or booby trap, your chances are good for catching a disease like malaria or jungle rot – either of which can send you home in a body bag." He slapped his chest. "The gook sores aren't anything to write home about. You'll have them because you can't clean up. You'll get them on your face, in your hair, and under your balls."

He shook his head. "You guys are fortunate because you have a great opportunity. In the past, the policy was you couldn't be a helicopter door gunner until after you served at least six months in the field, but your group is lucky. I'm authorized to offer six men a chance to volunteer without doing time in the mud with the snakes and slugs."

Was he telling the truth or simply a superb recruiter? Sergeant Hard told me about the dangers of being a door gunner. Half got killed. More were wounded. The U.S. lost fifty helicopters a day, not counting the ones salvageable.

"I ain't got time to waste, you got to decide now! How many want to be door gunners with a dry bed at night? Or you can be in the jungle, sleeping in defoliated swamps that smell like puke."

The officer was correct – if you're gonna be shot up, you might as well have a warm bed. The grunts rode in helicopters too, but they slept in the mud. I raised my hand. "That's what I want."

"Sign your name and come with me. I'll start you processing." Following my example, all but one of the newbies signed as door gunners. The officer put us on a C130 with a bunch of other cherries.

We sat strapped to the walls in the plane's big belly and flew north to Bien Hoa airbase north of Saigon. Trucks took us on to a sprawling camp. Everyone went through there when you first came in country. Bien Hoa was where they took your files and assigned you to a unit.

Landing at Bien Hoa, I thought, *This is my first step to death.* I didn't know what was happening, but a Spec 4 took me with a small group of other cherries through the huge camp. It was in a ravine with high razor wire fences encircling it. Looked like a prison camp.

Someone said I'd spend a night or two here, and then take a helicopter elsewhere after I got my orders. Herded around, ordered here and there. I was used to the army way and if they said jump, you said how high? You waited until somebody came along and yelled, "How come you're not jumping?"

While standing in lines, the guys joked to pass the time; one said, "Why is being in the military like a blow-job? Because when you discharge, it feels great."

I went from place to place processing through various tents, Quonset huts, and tables where I signed this, filled out a form, and stood in more lines.

I reminded myself of my commitment to fighting oppression to the death as a warrior for my beautiful fiancé. *I'm doing this for her*. I received a couple of letters she had written before meeting me in San Francisco. She said, "I love you, I love you," over and over.

From Bien Hoa, men were sent to bases all over South Vietnam. I got orders to the 162nd assault helicopter company, the Vultures. I'd be a gunner on a Huey transport helicopter. They called them slicks because their only protection were the door gunners on each side.

I was to report to a little olive-painted trailer house with TWA painted on it, the initials for Trans World Airlines – a joke for Teeny Weeny Airlines. I passed the time by copying funny sayings on the helmets of Veterans on their way somewhere.

Guns don't kill people. I do.

All things being equal, you lose.

Recoilless rifles – aren't.

Tracers work - both ways

Friendly fire – isn't

Don't steal. That's the government's job.

Sure enough in two days, a slick helicopter was on the flight line kicking up dust and a man waved, so I grabbed my duffle bag and ran out. I threw my bag in and away we went. I sat on my helmet, thinking about that guy at the station who got his nuts shot off in a helicopter. I wondered when I'd get a weapon.

Five troopers were on board, all cherries – NFG, new fucking guys, likely to get our asses shot off because we didn't know what was happening. It was exciting to look out the doors as we flew for forty-five minutes. Below rice paddies were everywhere. We flew south to Dong Tam. The 162nd Assault Helicopter Company was stationed in one of the most VC-infested areas of the Mekong River Delta region.

23. Company Clerk at Dong Tam

Dong Tam was in the center of Viet Cong operations with one of the highest casualty rates in the war. It was four miles west of My Tho in the Dinh Tuong Province. It was also the nerve center for the 9th Infantry Division operations, the 162nd Assault Helicopter Company, and home to the 3rd Surgical Hospital. It was intended to be a statement to the Viet Cong, "We are here to stay and we're united in hearts and minds."

The Viet Cong had other ideas. Three to five times per night, they mortared and rocketed the base to say, "No you aren't."

Major Kenneth Loveless was the commander on the day I arrived. The name seemed fitting.

Dong Tam was built in the center of Vietnam's rice breadbasket, using sand dredged from the river. It was supposed to be a showplace of American life. Eight to ten thousand people lived inside its three rings of defenses. It had churches and a golf course. An Olympic-sized pool and athletic field were under construction. It had stores, barbers, and an airport with a 1000-foot runway. Its man-made harbor was one of the largest U.S. Navy bases in the world where John Kerry, who would later become a Senator and the Secretary of State, was stationed on a swift boat.

Dong Tam also had the largest helipad in the world. It was horseshoe shaped with a two-mile-long flight line. The VC sometimes got lucky and took out a bunch of helicopters with one rocket because the exploding metal hit others even though each ship was half surrounded by a four-foot-high stand of sandbags. If shrapnel hit a rotor blade, they cost $6,000 and took time to replace.

I landed and walked past Quonset huts to a building with a tin roof and several flagpoles. It had the U.S. Flag, the South V.N. flag, and the U.S. 9th Army flag. A guy pointed. "You're to process through here."

I checked in through battalion headquarters. Dispatch was also there because the helicopters needed centralized communication functions similar to emergency services in the States. Each infantry platoon was assigned to one or two barracks.

A clerk gave me a company number and said, then check in at this other building." A company had around one hundred men. It had an orderly room where the commanding officer, the XO, the company clerk, the assistant company clerk, and the first sergeant had offices.

I walked to the orderly room where a guy named Bill Gordy was the assistant clerk, temporarily acting as the company clerk. A hippy type, he was from Southern California. Bill asked, "Can you type? Truthfully, can you type?"

"Well, I took typing in high school."

"We need a company clerk, and we need a clerk real bad. Our company clerk checked outta here two weeks ago, and we're constipated with paperwork. Nothing is going right. We gotta have somebody who types. I'm an assistant company clerk but I'm not THE company clerk. I can't type."

By the time I arrived, the U.S. was approaching 47,000 casualties and the anti-war movement was running full steam around the world. Servicemen said if you could get any job other than combat, go for it. "I can type thirty words a minute with a bunch of errors, but I can type."

Bill hunted and pecked on the typewriter. Anyone who could type, no matter how slow, sounded good to him. As the acting company clerk, Bill had the power to appoint a new company clerk. Normally, the training to be a company clerk was three months. Bill said, "You take the job and I can get you a promotion to Private First Class with an immediate pay raise."

"I can't promise how good I'll be, but for a promotion and a pay raise, sign me up!"

In one minute, I had gone from a soon-to-be-dead or wounded helicopter door gunner to an eight-to-five clerk-typist puttering away in an air-conditioned office. I had to be dreaming.

I had no idea what I had agreed to. *This is great, I'm gonna live as Dove said. I'll pull through this and everything will be okay. Boy, she sure knew what she was saying.* I came back to life.

"I got your name here, you're checked in." Bill was excited. "I tell you what – because you're the company clerk, you'll have a promotion to PFC, and I'm also giving you a three-day pass for whatever the hell you want to do. Go to the PX, get an S & C, and do whatever you want."

"What's an S & C?"

Bill grinned. "An S & C is a steam and cream – a sauna bath where cute Vietnamese women give a rub down and whatever else a guy needs." He winked, but seeing the hesitation on my face, said, "Whatever – you take it easy and come back in three days. I'll help you learn to be the company clerk."

The other guys arriving with me were immediately sent on combat missions while I got three days off. Talk about good luck! I wrote everyone at home about how I got a promotion and a raise, and was assigned a safe job in an air-conditioned office.

Dove thanked God as did my mother, but Devyn was in typing class and knew how crappy a typist I was. I had passed the final test by typing "THAT" repeatedly.

He wrote, "Hey, how's it hanging? I'm Mr. Elk's assistant in his 7th-grade science class. He's encouraging me to major in science in college. Hey, what's the real reason Santa is jolly? Because he knows where all the bad girls live.

Got a haircut from your dad. He is sure proud of you. He's telling everybody in Cedaredge you're a helicopter door gunner in

Vietnam, and you're kicking ass on the communists. Guess he doesn't want to tell people you're a clerk.

Gabe Falcon transferred to Western since Dove is there. He comes home every weekend to hang around with Mrs. Knutson. Kinda strange since he's a half brother to Stormy. Like they say, 'Incest is best.'

Anyway, that was lucky for you getting the clerk job. Maybe your typing will improve. Keep your head down and don't volunteer.

Three days after I arrived at Dong Tam, the Tet offensive of 1969 started. A hundred cities and all U.S. bases were attacked all the way from the Demilitarized Zone (DMZ) to the tip of South Vietnam. The assaults were beaten back, but there were four hundred-fifty Americans dead during the first week. Like the 1968 TET, the offensive caused fear the communists could attack whenever they wanted. No one realized the enemy took terrible losses. If the U.S. had gone on the offensive, they may have overrun all of the enemy positions, possibly ending the war.

I wondered when I'd get a rifle, but a company clerk wasn't expected to fight. I heard stories about TET 1968. It worried me to learn the North Vietnamese Army (NVA) had massacred six thousand civilians at Hue.

"They're brutes, man." This assistant supply clerk named Willy was a short-timer. "The NVA piled them in trenches. I've seen the photos with my own eyes, it was gruesome! They wired people together or tied them up with bamboo strips behind their backs. They stuffed rags in their mouths or tied plastic bags over their heads. The people's bodies were twisted and contorted but there weren't any wounds. They were buried alive!" Willy's face was distorted with anger. "The commies buried them alive to make them examples. The villagers want to help us, but they're scared out of their minds and don't dare."

"Why do they mutilate them?" I asked.

"Because they're animals."

The VC hit Dong Tam night and day with mortars, rockets, and artillery. Everyone feared being overrun. "When in doubt – empty your clip." I didn't have a rifle or a clip to empty because I was a friggin' clerk.

Dong Tam was made by dredging silt from the My Tho River and the soil was fine and soft. The VC rockets left craters three to four feet deep. If a guy wasn't careful, you'd stumble into one. Drunks often fell into one when they staggered back to their barracks at night, breaking an arm or twisting an ankle. The road graders constantly worked to smooth the grounds. Sandy dust blew into my eyes, nose, ears, clothes, and bedding. I felt grimy even after stepping from a shower.

With TET raging, I was super happy to be assigned as company clerk. But the minute I arrived at the office, there was a huge backed-up workload. Not only must I type mounds of letters the company commander wrote on a yellow notepad, but I was supposed to do this complicated *Morning Report* that identified the status of every man in the company.

In theory, I was in charge of one hundred eighty-five men's files, including all enlisted soldiers and officers. Papers were stacked everywhere in the office. No idea where to start. If ignorance was bliss, I'd be the happiest guy in Vietnam, but I was the dumbest guy in the Army.

Captain Badwin expected me to make coffee and serve him. Revelry was at six in the morning and I went straight to the typewriter. The captain hand-wrote reports, memos, orders, and letters, and I was supposed to type them correctly. Typing, typing, and typing all day long. I got hand cramps.

Men were killed and Captain Badwin wrote letters to parents. "I'm sorry to inform you…" He wrote them in long hand on yellow-lined tablet paper. I typed them with a high error rate and many spelling flubs.

Half of being smart was knowing what you're not good at. I was a dummy as a company clerk, but I didn't want to give up because door gunners were the most frequently killed or wounded in this war. They were out in the open and the Viet Cong targeted the flash of their M60 machine guns.

The next highest causality rates were grunts in the field – especially the new guys who made stupid mistakes. Cherries got stuck on point or carrying the radio. The antenna was a flag saying "KILL ME" because he was close to the patrol leader. The point man got sawed down in an ambush or he stepped on an equal opportunity mine, and BOOM – off went his legs.

Bill was fun to work with, cracking jokes all day. "This brown water Navy guy goes for an S&C, and a skinny Vietnamese girl takes him back to the massage table. While testing her tunnel, this river rat looks down at her and asks, 'How am I doing?'

The girl says, 'Three knots.'

Confused, the seaman asked, 'What you mean?'

She said, 'You not hard, you not good boom-boom, and you not getting money back."

One joke after the other. Gordy shoulda been a stand-up on the Bob Hope Show.

Now and then, a sniper climbed a tree and put rounds into the base, making everyone nervous. Incoming fire has the right of way. Trotting between buildings, I kept thinking, *Should I hit the dirt or keep going?* Periodically, someone took a bullet – enough to make you double-time between locations. It was oddly satisfying when a sniper took a shot and missed.

The supply depot, motor pool, and the enlisted men's club were in tents. The officer's club had a wood frame, picnic tables, and garbage cans filled with ice and beer. It had hardwood floors, hardwood paneling, air conditioning, a wet bar, a jukebox, and TVs along with nice tables, stools, and even an overstuffed couch set.

The enlisted men's shower was windy since it was in the open beneath a tank filled with water. It had globe valves for showerheads and wood pallets for a floor. The officer's showers were enclosed and tiled. Who says America is the land of equality?

The enlisted men slept in a long wooden bunkhouse with twenty men on each floor. Double bunker cots lined both walls with a small footlocker in front of each bunk. It smelled of decayed rat carcasses. The first floor was protected by layers of sandbags stacked twelve feet high. The second floor was exposed to whatever shrapnel or mortars came at them, but received a slight breeze at night, making it less stinky and more tolerable than the first floor.

They segregated men based on their MOS or occupational status – clerks were in one barracks, door gunners in another, pilots in another, artillerymen, and so on. Each bunkhouse got a hooch maid as their cleaning lady.

Every night, the Viet Cong fired mortars and rockets into the Dong Tam flight line, hoping to destroy a million-dollar helicopter. Occasionally, they got lucky and fire trucks ran with their sirens. Not exactly a vacation resort.

When mortars or rockets started coming in, we were ordered into semi-buried bunkers, but a rocket could blast an enlisted man's bunker to pieces. The officer's bunkers were buried deeper and had encasements of concrete and dirt that were strong enough to take a direct rocket hit. They had wooden floors, finished walls, pool tables, refrigerators, and couches. The enlisted men's bunkers were a hole in the ground with steel planking and sandbags on the roof. We had one naked light bulb, and the dirt floors were damp.

The guys put down wood pallets but the air space between the pallet boards was the perfect home for rodents and bugs that drew snakes. If you wanted something to sit on, you grabbed a folding lawn chair from your hooch on the way. It was better than sitting on a rough board while a poisonous snake slithered underneath your butt.

One night, we were stuck in a bunker and Bill said, "When I was having sex over at the S&C, she was wondering when this guy will be done, and I'm thinking twenty bucks? I can't afford this."

Men laughed and it encouraged him. "What do the Mekong River, the Bermuda Triangle, and a Vietnamese whore have in common?"

Everyone waited.

"They all swallow seamen."

Everyone liked jokester Bill.

My company was on a bend in the river. Near my hooch, a U.S. artillery battery fired shells twenty-four hours a day. Often, up to thirty big guns went off. The building shook and dust floated down. The big artillery pieces shattered the sound barrier, punishing our ears. "How do you sleep?" I asked Bill.

"Try sleeping on one side. Eventually, your exposed ear will stop hearing so you can sleep." Bill shrugged. "Otherwise, you'll lose hearing in both ears."

I gave it a try. During the next weeks, I stayed on my right side, and gradually my left ear went numb to the artillery booms. I didn't sleep – it was a trance where a guy was frozen in place with eyes closed. After several tense nights, I could distinguish incoming from outgoing rounds. Incoming was a muffled explosion as if it were inside a box. When they got close to my barracks, it was a ripping and tearing sound. Gravel rattled on the tin roof like a hailstorm back home in Cedaredge.

The VC weren't well trained and they walked mortars in a straight line. A guy just moved to get off the line of fire. Had they dropped them randomly, they might get more hits. But I couldn't tell where a rocket might land – it came in from nowhere with a crack of lightning.

Dong Tam was hit so often the base commander ordered us to wear helmets and flak jackets anytime we were outside. I took it seriously. When the rockets or mortars hit the base, alarms went off. Every night, the enemy fired at different parts of the base. The commies aimed at helicopters, the navy ships, and our barracks. They lobbed from one to a dozen rockets or mortars. By the time our guys figured out where they were coming from, the VC had taken off into the rice paddies. Impossible to nail them.

24. A Cup Of Cheese Macaroni

One night a lone Viet Cong crawled under the wires, through minefields, and tossed a satchel loaded with explosives at my office building. It landed fifty feet short but was enough to blow the windows. I walked into a total mess of papers. I had barely gotten them organized so I could figure out where to begin. "Jeez oh man, dad-gum it – now I got to start over!"

Bill shrugged. "At least we weren't working when the VC threw the satchel. There are two kinds of soldiers here in Dong Tam – the alert and the dead."

An officer asked me to volunteer as a replacement door gunner because so many were getting killed or wounded. "I'm staying with this job as long as I can."

"What the hell is wrong with you?" A pilot ranted, "A douche-bag Viet Cong tried to kill you with a satchel charge." He spat on the floor. "You're a chicken-ass clerk! How can you look in the mirror?"

A few days later, a door gunner shoved a copy of a *Time* magazine story in my face. "Read this and tell me you don't care!"

I read that when the communists overran North Vietnam the squads forced villagers to witness confessions from landowners, businessmen, intellectuals, and leaders who had thought errors. They were beheaded or beaten to death; others were tied, thrown into open graves, and covered with stones until they were crushed to death. The communists rammed bamboo lances into the villagers and disemboweled random civilians, then draped their mutilated bodies on fences. They hacked men and women to pieces and cut off the fingers of children who tried to go to school.

A door gunner came in to sign some form. He frowned at me. "You're about as useless as an asshole with taste buds."

Bill glanced up. "I love what you've done with your mustache. How do you get it to come out of your nostrils like that?"

I felt guilty. Should I go out as a door gunner? But more than anything, I wanted to live and return to Dove in one piece, so I hung in as a clerk.

The worst thing was the morning report. It was complicated with codes for a thousand different events. If someone was on leave and coming back, he got one code dash number. In case he left and wasn't coming back, it was a different code. If he was wounded, he got an unrelated code – blah, blah, blah. I was supposed to code promotions, discharges, battles, decorations, and demotions. I coded everyone in the company, every day. If a guy was on his third day of leave, or if a trooper took a dump, I was supposed to code the damn thing.

The codebook was as thick as a New York City phone book, full of undecipherable number codes, and I had to research each one. Even if I had a photographic memory, I was out of film. Occasionally, I put something in the space just to get the damn thing done.

Bill tried to lighten things up. "If four out of five people suffer from diarrhea, does it mean one enjoys it?"

The report had to pass inspections up the chain of command. It went through headquarters to post command, past army command, and clear to the Pentagon in Washington.

One morning, an officer came in with yesterday's morning report and slammed it on my desk. "Pal, you don't have the dashes and numbers in the right place."

"I have no training as a company clerk, but I'll do better tomorrow."

"You better get it correct or your ass is had, buddy."

The Vietnam War was unlike any previous war. There were no enemy lines, and the American strategy was to get casualties to accumulate dead communist bodies. A war of attrition was the idea that if enough commies were killed, they'd give up. Platoons dropped in as bait, hoping the enemy would show himself. It was my job to code every ass-bite action, no matter how insignificant.

Like many other company clerks, I struggled with the Morning Report. It was the single most important document in the whole U.S. of A. Army because it showed statistically what happened all over the world. It was how the Army monitored each man and woman – AWOL, WIA, MIA, KIA, whatever. I had to list everyone's rank, race, birthdate, occupational status, and rank every frickin' day. I coded what each of the 185 people in the company did yesterday and last night.

Bill said, "The Army is like a septic tank – the biggest lumps rise to the top. That's why they need your data, they can't think without it."

The reports were transmitted back to the States and somebody in the Pentagon fed this massive data into a mainframe computer to generate huge reports for policymakers and generals. With 543,000 Americans in Vietnam, it had more people than the State of Wyoming. Vietnam military strategy was based on this statistical data. If they got junk reports with typos and blank spots on a form, it messed up decision-making along the entire chain of command.

Bill said, "You're never too old to learn something stupid."

Every day, volunteers were solicited to replace door gunners who dropped like flies off a bull's ass. I sweated. I wasn't dumb, but I had no control over this nonsensical information. Bill helped, but he had never been a company clerk, and he couldn't type any better than a duck. Nobody knew what to do.

Bill said, "I, you are such a good friend, if we were on a sinking ship and there was one life jacket, I'd think of you after I got home."

No one knew when a real company clerk might report. Bill thought he could make a company clerk out of me because the regulations said he could. *I'm gotta learn this as quick as I can, I'm gonna do my best.* I told Bill, "Give me that manual."

I studied it at night until my eyes were so blurry I couldn't see, but there were just too many different codes, it was miles long. *Oh no, how am I going to do this by morning?* The Army codes had no logic or patterns. You had to memorize them.

I stayed up late, studying with a flashlight. I took the monster code manual to the bunker as I waited for the Viet Cong mortars and rockets to stop. I was lucky to get two or three hours of sleep.

I heard from Mama that my younger sister and her best friend were again cheerleading for the Cedaredge basketball team that beat Gunnison High by a huge margin. The children were doing well in school except for one younger brother. Momma asked, "How would I know if he is using drugs?"

My brother, Mark, was still driving a jeep for a four-star General in San Francisco, and my older brother and sister were married and doing fine. No grandkids, but Mama was hopeful. Dove had not come to visit. She asked, "Is she okay? Have you heard from her?"

Her letter made me homesick. However, I didn't worry about Dove. She wrote encouraging letters every day, citing Bible verses. "Joshua 1:9: Have I not commanded you? Be strong and courageous. Do not be frightened, and do not be dismayed, for the LORD your God is with you wherever you go."

In one letter after a Book of Mormon verse, she wrote, "I'm looking forward to being with you and the San Francisco stripper."

Gave me an erection.

Devyn's letter said the basketball team morale sucked the big one because the coach only played his relatives. The Cedaredge wrestling team was also in sad shape, and they sure could use both me and Big Owl if we had stayed in school and been eligible.

Don't I wish.

The Enemy Casualty Reports were another nightmare. Each helicopter crew, platoon, and even the little five-man LRP squads called in their kills for the day. I recorded where the enemy was killed, who killed them, and what the enemy was suspected to be – such as a village leader, a Viet Cong commander or grunt, NVA, whatever.

Half the time my commander, Captain Badwin, made up numbers based on fragmented reports. I signed that the reports were the whole truth under penalty of perjury.

I heard the Korean Army (ROKs) razed the countryside and brutalized people to pacify them, resulting in more Viet Cong than they killed.

The Vietnamese people paid bribes for medical care, to get their kids into school, and for a job. The people who could least afford it suffered the most.

Bill made it hard to focus. "A girl's virginity is like a soap bubble, one prick and it's gone."

Every so often at night, enemy ground forces tried to overrun Dong Tam. I wasn't mentally prepared and still didn't have a rifle. My head was in a time warp. A short while ago, I was a teenage muff diver with a beauty queen playing with my one-eyed wonder. Now, I was filling out forms. I felt about as useful as tits on a bull. The irritating smell of chemical defoliant from leaking tanks made me cough and hack.

Many days, Dove's letters were nothing more than a Bible verse as if she couldn't think of anything else. "Isaiah 43:1-2 – But now thus says the LORD, he who created you, O Jacob, he who formed you, O Israel: Fear not, for I have redeemed you; I have called you by name, you are mine…"

If in the remotest recesses of my mind, I believed the biblical snickerdoodle, it might be easier. I wondered why she didn't tell how her day went and what she was doing. Because she was a good Mormon girl and had been a virgin, I was sure she was faithful.

Inexperience made me miserable. The Red Legs, as artillery grunts were called, broke the monotony with crump, crump-crump every minute of every day. The artillery guys must be deaf because the Army didn't issue earplugs.

The Vietnamese on the base kept poker faces. Everyone knew they spied for the Vietcong because the VC knew where our guys were headed before the patrol leader got his orders. Vietnamese and Americans smiled at each other during the day, and at night, tried to kill each other. It was impossible to tell friends from foes. Kids might walk up to a helicopter to beg, and as they left, toss a grenade and run like hell. An old man looked weak and helpless but pulled a pistol and blew away a soldier before dying in a hail of M16 gunfire. Everybody at Dong Tam pretended Americans and the South Vietnamese were on the same side.

Bill said, "A cannibal is someone who is fed up with people." He waited a minute. "A mosquito is an insect that makes you like flies better."

I couldn't figure out any pattern to the codes. There were simply too many. I never got enough sleep, and my eyes were blurry as I struggled to do the cursed Morning Report. I felt about as effective as scratching my butt with a cup of cheese macaroni.

25. Chicken-Ass Clerk

Although a war of attrition strategy hadn't worked for years, the generals demanded high casualty counts because they couldn't think of another strategy (like just going home). The troops killed any Vietnamese who might be an enemy. Top military brass were too concerned with advancing their careers to do an honest assessment of what might work in Vietnam. Grunts and gunners were killed left and right. The captain wrote letters to each dead man's parents, and I was supposed to correct his mistakes. Neither of us could spell. Combined with typos, the letters looked like a kid wrote them.

"Hey Rowdy," Bill said.

"What?"

"You should take life with a grain of salt. Plus a slice of lime and a shot of tequila."

I looked with awe at the pilots, door gunners, and crew chiefs for what they did. I knew their casualty rates.

They gave a shit less about me – I was a clerk – a guy in the rear with the gear. They laughed at me. "You clerks are bisexual. You get it twice a year."

I felt stupid and incompetent. Replacements were constantly solicited for dead or wounded door gunners. A pilot came into the office. He shook his head as he looked at me. "You're about as useful as a bucket with holes in the bottom."

Bill snapped back, "If I wanted to hear from an asshole, I'd fart."

After he left, I said, "What a beautiful day to hate on myself."

"Man, don't let them get to you. I used to catch shit too, that's why I became a jokester."

Two weeks went by and the company's first sergeant said, "You're not good at this. We're getting too many complaints from those up above about your Morning Reports."

Bill tried to console me. "He may look like an idiot and talk like an idiot. Don't let that fool you, the guy really is an idiot." He took a breath. "Listen, you start with a bag full of luck and an empty bag of experience. The trick is to fill the bag of experience before your bag of luck runs out."

"Man, I'm doing my best, but I have no training." I wanted to hang onto being a clerk so I didn't have to be a door gunner. I learned more each day, but it was overwhelming.

A few more days went by, and the first sergeant came back. "We're supposed to get a real company clerk soon, and you'll be gone."

Instead of drinking at the fountain of knowledge, I had gargled. Lost in the logic of Army codes, they wanted three left turns to make one right turn. It spun into unfathomable territory. *How am I losing a battle of wits to an unarmed opponent?*

One evening parachute flares popped on the east perimeter and soon the whole area glowed with flares. The East section was being overrun by VC sappers – men who carried bags of explosives. These fearless guys crawled under three rings of barbed wire and through a patchwork of claymore mines to toss explosives at us.

I was freaked because I didn't have weapon. The southwest corner of Dong Tam burned like a forest fire with evergreen trees exploding from dry heat or lightning strikes. The concussions from rockets made guys think their hooch was hit as they ran to the closest bunker. To my surprise, I was no more scared or confused than the others.

As things settled down, an MP said the Viet Cong had put a 122mm rocket into a fuel storage tank near the fixed-wing airfield. The burning tank was so hot it ignited other tanks. A brilliant decision by the planners: Put them near each other so the whole fuel storage area could go up from one lousy rocket!

Bill whispered in the dark, "Ours is not to question why, ours is but to do or die."

]Dove wrote,

My sister, Alayna, is struggling with her mission. The conditions in Africa are appalling. There is starvation and disease, and the people she tries to convert are pitiful. Biafra is a violent country with many robberies. Alayna wants to teach in Colorado and be married to a nice man in the temple. By the way, how is Big Al doing? Who knows? Maybe he'll become a Mormon along with you. Tell him Alayna wants his address so she can write.

And how are you doing? I think about you so much. I regret that I had not thought about how challenging and threatening war could be. I have some growing up to do. Wish I talked to the bishop long before you left because if you went on a church mission, it would be safer. We must be strong.

Rowdy, you are so courageous. How dedicated and honorable you are fighting the communists in Vietnam. I feel guilty because you joined for me. I pray daily that you will be in the arms of angels throughout these trying times. The war news isn't good. There are peace protests around the country. But you are in Vietnam to fight for God and for me. We will prove those hippy communists wrong. I cannot wait to surrender again to your strong arms.

Always and forever yours,
Dove

Reading it over for the third time, I felt bad that I wasn't out fighting. I only dozed at night because I worried about the Morning Report. Another monster explosion went off and we all sat up. It was a personal nightmare because in the morning I'd be coding the carnage.

At six in the morning, I walked a narrow path to the showers. As usual, there was no warm water. The guys were quiet. The showers were underneath a water tank with wood pallets for a floor. There was little talking until a door gunner said as he dried off, "You hide behind a desk. You're a chicken-ass clerk. Why don't you go fight the dinks like the rest of us?"

Saying nothing, I finished showering and headed for the office. I was as tired of being called a chicken-ass clerk as I was frustrated with hellish reports. *Does any of this matter?*

It was a relief when Bill said, "Well, Merlin's jockstrap – an honest-to-goodness company clerk is checking in. He has a MOS as a company clerk."

Captain Badwin got wind there was a real company clerk on the way and was happy to have someone who knew paperwork. A company clerk couldn't shoot a weapon but he knew codes, reports, and documents inside and out.

I checked in the new clerk, and the guy showed me what to do. "You're supposed to fill in this; no, you ain't got it right, scratch that out and put it in here."

"Well, you're supposed to be doing what I am, and I'm supposed to be elsewhere." I was happy until it dawned on me, *If I'm not the company clerk, what am I?*

Well, I was a helicopter gunner and I'd been typing letters to parents about destroyed helicopters and dead door gunners. Some days more than three helicopters got blown to smithereens, and they couldn't find the bodies. "We got a torso and fingers and a leg, who does this body part belong to?"

"Your son was in such and such a place and the helicopter did not report back, therefore, we must report him missing in action." I typed dozens of We're sorry to report letters to parents.

Bill shook my hand farewell. "Be careful – it turns out that helicopters can't fly; they're so ugly the earth repels them."

"Dang it Bill, I'm gonna miss you."

Late February 1969

26. The Supply Audit

I was fired as the company clerk, but because I was working as a clerk, they assumed I was a genuine clerk. The Army sent me to the main Dong Tam supply depot as an assistant clerk.

I was as happy as could be. *I'm gonna survive this war!*

Within a few days, I realized that everyone at the depot had his wallet stuffed with thousands of dollars. I watched the supply sergeant do an exchange for cash and realized they were dealing in the black market.

Ships unloaded at the Dong Tam Navy port, things went through supply and then disappeared. The scale was massive. The influx of American money and material drove inflation, and Vietnamese women complained to their husbands about the cost of things. There was no system of checks and balances, and government officials moonlighted as black marketers. The Vietnamese were not constrained by the rule of law. The incentive was to steal to sell, trade, or use material as bribes. Corruption was rampant.

Ernie, the other supply clerk, asked, "You want a cut of the action? It's the only way you'll get something good from this war. You can mail the cash home in bundles paid for by the U.S. Army."

He explained that the South Vietnamese government was a network of clans and gangs held together by American subsidies. Everybody was concerned only about survival. Materials seldom reached where it should. Thousands of Vietnamese officials and upper military officers lived like kings. They ate exotic food, had boy or girl prostitutes, maid service, and drove highly polished American jeeps.

It was tempting to take advantage of the opportunity, but I was scared to get involved. I wanted no trouble, just to be a supply clerk for the rest of my tour. I swore I'd wear blinders and keep my mouth shut. "Don't worry, my lips are sealed."

Up to twenty-five percent of the ARVN's military payroll was in the name of dead or deserted soldiers kept on the roll so officers could collect their salaries. Bribes were common. Enough concrete was earmarked to pave half the country, but it never arrived where it was supposed to go. Vietnamese officers claimed materials for housing, medical supplies, and even food belonged to them.

I now understood why the grunts complained they couldn't get jungle boots and uniforms. The supply officers traded them off. Dong Tam Supply Depot was a hub of nefarious activity.

My chief supply officer got wind of an upcoming inspection, an Inspector General (IG) audit. Documentation in the whole base would be investigated. He said, "Everything has got to match. If I go down, you and everybody else are going with me. I don't care if you just started. We gotta get rid of this extra stuff."

An IG was similar to a company inventory at its stores but a lot more complicated and serious. You aren't fired – you're court-martialed and thrown in the brig. All paperwork must line up perfectly with the supplies on hand. IG Inspections were conducted annually throughout every branch of the service and for each unit. It was a critical function and things better check out or heads would roll.

The Dong Tam supply depot had no records for stuff stored to the ceiling in various buildings and annexes. They had an abundance of footlockers, 14K-gold aviation sunglasses, leather gloves, survival K-Bar knives, .38 caliber pistols, aviator survival packs, gas masks, irrigation pumps, concrete, roofing materials, and on and on. The extras were improperly requisitioned for trading material on the black market. Air conditioners were in short supply and brought a premium in trade. They also had thousands of captured enemy weapons in storage because guys snagged them during combat missions. They weren't supposed to keep them, but men wanted to send them home. Maintenance, cooks, accountants, clerks – everyone had war souvenirs they left with the supply sergeant until they could ship them home.

The chief supply officer and sergeant knew the shit would hit the fan, and they'd be busted by the IG Inspector. They had a big, ugly problem – what to do with all this off-record equipment?

For the next week, we created phony requisition papers for as much as we could justify but lots couldn't be explained away – why did we have six dozen .38 caliber pistols? Many conundrums.

We traded the extra pistols for a future exchange. Me and Ernie delivered them with ammo by driving a three-quarter-ton truck to a firebase camp fifty miles into the jungle. It was a narrow dirt road with deep, water-filled ruts and a canopy of jungle growth overhead. A sniper shot several rounds through the green canvas top and shattered several wooden stays.

Smoking grass on the way back, Ernie got stoned and had his arm hanging out the open window. The passenger side mirror was smashed by the same sniper. Glass shards splattered, hitting his forearm. He shouted, "I'm hit!" He might have gotten a purple heart for the injury but was too scared to turn it in – what mission was he on? Running guns?

The clock was ticking down for the IG inspection. By the time we returned to base, only twenty-four hours were left. We still had hundreds of items to get rid of.

The four of us held a skull session. We came up with a plan – a crazy one – but it might work. We agreed if it's stupid but works, it ain't stupid.

The sergeant checked out a deuce-and-a-half (a two-and-a-half-ton truck) from the motor pool at the five PM closing time. He drove it to the supply buildings and parked it around back.

Problem was, we were exhausted since we hadn't slept for the last twenty-some hours. Ernie had a wonderful idea. He knew about the aviator survival packs and the little packs of drugs. We opened the survival packs and found foil pouches containing white or yellow pills called dextroamphetamine sulfate.

I had never heard of dexies. They were intended for an aircraft crash in a combat zone. What was special about these little white pills was they kept you awake and boosted your energy level. Second, the drug lasted up to forty-eight hours and killed pain from injuries sustained in the crash. It was a perfect drug for a situation where your life depended on evading the enemy. Doctors back home use it to treat children with attention and hyperactivity problems. This stuff was pharmaceutical-grade speed with a high street value.

I was a green kid right off a Colorado farm and knew nothing about drugs. We each popped two of these little pills, and wow, we worked fast. Man, oh, man! Soon, we talked rapid-fire like auctioneers.

At dark, we loaded the big truck until shit fell off the sides. The chief supply officer and sergeant sweated, swore, and petered out halfway through. The jokers sat on footlockers and opened cold beers from a washtub filled with ice.

Ernie and me grabbed a beer, but we were full of energy and continued to load the truck without so much as a bead of sweat. We cracked up like lunatics.

The supply sergeant and officer glanced at each other and shook their heads, wondering what the hell got into these two crazy enlisted men. Sitting on their fat arses, they snickered, chugged beer, farted, and slapped their thighs.

There were side effects to the pills. For example, you might chuckle uncontrollably, giving away your position in the thickets. Your attitude became so carefree you no longer felt anxiety or fear, thus again risking your neck as you went off dancing through the tulips. You may develop a peculiar fondness for everything, including even your own freaking Army. It was downright embarrassing and dangerous because you didn't give thought to what direction to escape.

We stirred clouds of dust as we loaded stuff. Whooping with fun, we opened a fifth of whiskey Ernie had stashed for a special occasion. We drank the whole bottle in under an hour, and it didn't faze our work. We filled the big truck until the bed was packed ten feet high.

The supply officer and sergeant were spooked. "What the heck is going on with those two?" The jerks smelled whiskey and shook their heads. "Look at those two crazy idiots go. You'd think they're packing for a whore party."

The truck was loaded by nine P.M. at mandatory lights-out. Things fell off the sides so we packed stuff in the cab. It got confusing at this point since the "Plan" didn't specify what we were to do with this stuff once it was on the truck. The supply officer said, "Bury it in the ground."

Okay, but where and how?

We threw shovels into the cab. I drove, and off we went across Dong Tam. We couldn't turn on the headlights or go fast because it was as dark as night can be. The grounds were pocked with rocket and mortar holes that pounded the tires as the boys ran into them.

Dong Tam ain't your average U.S. Base. American engineers dredged eight million cubic meters of sand to create an area over one square mile in size. Engineers had raised the land between five and ten feet to prevent flooding during the rainy season. It was constantly under construction, partially because the Viet Cong kept blowing parts of it away.

Crawling along, the left front of the truck rose in the air. I stepped on the fuel and it went higher. I let up on the gas pedal and the front came back down. I thought I was hallucinating because we weren't making forward progress. "Are we zonked by these drugs?"

Ernie opened the door and walked around the truck. Feeling around in the blackness, he discovered that I was driving straight up a steel cable guy-wire from an electrical pole directly in front of the left tire. Luckily, I had stopped because it might have knocked out electricity on the entire base if I kept trying.

I backed and turned to the right. We bumped around searching for a place to bury three tons of contraband. I couldn't drive off base because gates were locked with guards in the towers. Watching for mortar strikes, I ground slowly away from the main part of the base.

As luck would have it, we ended at a closed sand pit area where the Army once got their road-building material. There were shallow pits everywhere. Some were filled with water and others, too narrow to back into. We got out of the truck and explored, but couldn't find anything suitable. After an hour, we found a big hole about twenty feet across in both directions, but it was only three feet deep.

We looked at each other, wondering what to do. "It's time to dig." I declared.

We ran to the truck for shovels. Sucking down more little white pills along with another bottle of hooch, we shoveled, dredged, and excavated. It wasn't long the hole was as deep as we were tall. But was it enough? Oh, hell no. So we dug and scooped. Not stopping, we spaded, unearthed, gouged, deepened, and dug.

We took a breather to assess progress. We were sopping wet. The hole was now nine feet deep and twenty feet square. The sun started rising so we got moving again.

Although we downed the second bottle of whiskey, we began to sober up. We still ran hot on those wacky adrenalin-induced survival drugs – compliments of the U.S. Army. Digging like insane badgers, shoveling deeper and deeper, we exhumed rocks, sand, and soil. Soon we couldn't go any further, not because we hit bedrock or the water table, but because it was so deep we couldn't toss the sand up without it sliding back into the great hole from where it came.

We helped each other climb out of the depths and stood on a fresh mound of dirt surrounding the entire pit. It was impressive. We were proud and elated. "Hell yeah, man!" We slapped each other's backs. But the sense of accomplishment didn't last because we had to clear a path for the truck. We popped one more survival pill and shovels flew – Ernie on one side of the path and me on the other. Without slowing, sand slung as if the clods had wings. We finished as daylight creased the horizon like a rising theater curtain.

The job of shoveling was not the same as unloading. Unloading was a lot easier and faster. Psyched and sopped with sweat, we got with the program. Two stoned maniacs broke the law at the break of dawn. It didn't take long to dump the crap. We moved the truck out of the way and jumped on each side of the mound to bury the contraband. With each heave, we covered our skinny asses with sandy dust.

Having finished the job, we stood on the mound without pangs of guilt. In any other war, the victors got the loot. Today, hundreds of thousands of dollars worth of equipment was buried in a pit. We said a word or two about government waste and the futility of it all. Burying this stuff meant we were out of trouble with the IG authorities. We pledged to never say a word. No one would be the wiser.

It was now half-light and we made out the tops of buildings silhouetted against the brightening horizon. The mound was three feet higher than the surrounding ground so we crawled the deuce and a half truck back and forth to compact the sand.

After our crime was hidden, we drove away in silence, the inglorious job complete.

We arrived at the supply warehouse as the IG inspectors showed up. The audit lasted a week while the entire company was given a going over with white silky gloves. The team of speckled, sharp-nosed examiners peeked into the wrong places. As expected, there were a few demerits but nothing to write home about.

Everything seemed fine, but after the IG inspectors left, I was told to report to the orderly room to see the Company Commander.

Standing before his desk at parade rest, Captain Badwin had bad news and good news. I couldn't imagine what since no way he knew of our night burying party.

"The good news," he said, "Is you're promoted. You'll get a little more pay at the end of the month and another stripe. Congratulations, corporal." He handed me the promotion papers.

"Thank you, Sir." A lump formed in my throat. "So what's the bad news?"

"The IG inspectors went through all company records, including personnel files. They found a few discrepancies here and there but nothing serious. I might add the morning reports are in good order now that we have a well-trained company clerk."

He lit a cigarette and continued, "However, they discovered you're misassigned. You're a door gunner, not a clerk, and we're short door-gunners. You're to report for flight duty first thing in the morning."

March 1969

27. First Assault Missions

I was moved from the clerk hooch to the door gunners' barracks. Most gunners were poor whites, Hispanics, or blacks. We are dispensable. If killed, our parents didn't have the education or the political connections to question why.

No words can describe how young and inexperienced I felt. The pilots and crew chiefs were far above me – a different species. I wasn't angry and did not need to kill. I was a shy kid from Cedaredge, Colorado, what's happening, Que Pasa? As they said, ignorance will take a guy to a lot more interesting places than knowledge.

I felt an unexpected pride as part of a combat team. I was to do what I spent months preparing for – kill communists for Dove. A training chant bubbled up, "I'm gonna go to Vietnam – I gonna kill a Viet Cong."

The 162nd was assigned to the 214th CAB as the aviation battalion for the 9th Infantry Division. There was a large open front hangar with machine shops on the lower level and air-conditioned offices on the second floor. I was with the Vultures, the transport ships.

The Copperheads were heavily armed Cobra attack helicopters and gunships, escorting the troop helicopters. They zoomed in with rockets and mini-guns to protect the slicks as we dropped or picked up ground troops.

"Here's your M60 – keep it working." I received an asbestos glove to pull off a red hot barrel and replace it. I stored the M60 on the flight line in a padlocked olive green box; I laughed at myself: *If ignorance is bliss, I must be orgasmic.*

The sun hadn't poked its golden head above the horizon when a lone barracks window spilled yellow light across the gravel path. Teenage boys trembled with nerves, rising from bunks, shivering as bare feet slapped the floor. Cold hands reached for shoes and boots. I hadn't had enough sleep since arriving at Dong Tam because the Viet Cong wanted it that way. An edgy, tired soldier made errors and got demoralized. My arms fumbled to pull on my trousers. I stretched to crack my back and shoulders.

Thrilled to be going out, I wondered if it would be a rescue or a troop insertion. I hoped it would be a rescue mission. When a helicopter was shot down, emergency scrambles were initiated, and everybody available jumped into the ships to help their buddies. I had fantasies I'd be remembered as a hero after I died. I didn't grasp that a hero was also a martyr, a sacrificial victim.

I headed to the operations center where my name was posted on the assignment board. On the caulk board, it showed the pilot, copilot, and which helicopter to report to. Assignments changed daily regarding which pilots and door gunners were on a helicopter. Door gunners and pilots were with disparate crews on different choppers each day. The crew chief was a gunner who stayed with a helicopter throughout his tour unless it was shot up – in which case, he got another one. Door gunners took the opposite side of the crew chief.

Rotating crews made little sense because you couldn't get to know the other crew members. Unlike grunts in the field, we couldn't develop comradery and a desire to fight for our buddies. Vietnam military strategists had little understanding of combat psychology. It was all based on statistics and bureaucratic needs.

A crew chief was the maintenance manager of the helicopter. He kept records of oil changes, hydraulic fluid, how old the blades were, bolt checks, and so on. As enlisted men, the crew chief and door gunner had the unpleasant task of cleaning blood, vomit, guts, shit, and oil from the bird. The pilots were officers who went to the bar or took a shower.

After checking the day's assignment, I retrieved my M60 from the padlocked green box and went to the assigned helicopter with an intense mix of awe and fear.

This crew chief was a jokester, "Hey, Corporal, what three words ruin a man's ego?"

I shrugged. "What?"

"Is it in?"

The slick helicopter was the pack horse, cavalry, and jeep of the Vietnam War because it was the only way to get men and materials to places. In the jungle or rice paddies, there was often nowhere to land, so we hovered off the ground or above a triple canopy of hundred-fifty-foot tall trees. The rainy season in the Mekong Delta caused a shortage of dry land with swamp or rice paddies and dikes scattered in between.

The crew chief showed me how to hang the machine gun with a bungee cord. "I use a monkey harness instead of a lap belt because it gives freedom of movement. What do you want?"

Eager to ensure nobody ever called me a chicken-ass again, I intended to prove I'd be among the best. "The same as you."

A strap held a gunner tight and made you less likely to get thrown out. Marines mounted their M60s on posts, but Army gunners held them in their laps. A monkey harness went around a gunner's torso and was anchored to the aircraft floor or cabin wall so a gunner could get better firing angles. A guy could even hang over the skids to shoot underneath the helicopter.

Once I was set up, the crew chief patted me on the shoulder. "So what do the Mafia and pussy have in common?"

I grinned.

"One slip of the tongue and you're in deep shit."

A group of six grunts hopped in and settled on the floor. No one spoke or gave direct eye contact to avoid caring about the other men. I wore a flight helmet and dark shades, wondering if anyone besides the crew chief detected this was my virgin flight.

The thrilling sounds and sensations of a helicopter coming to life hit me. I smelled jet fuel exhaust as the rotor blades turned.

We flew off the ground on the way to something dangerously important. No clue what the mission was but my job was to defend the chopper and soldiers.

Six helicopters left the flight deck at Dong Tam in a cloud of dust, one behind the other. Flying in formation, gave a better chance since the enemy had someone else to shoot at. To the VC, it was more efficient to shoot helicopters than to let them land and let the infantry off. The downing of one helicopter meant six to twelve men were out of action, plus a million dollar aircraft.

We were the lead ship with five aircraft close behind. There was a sense of freedom as I looked out the open door. I saw Navy patrol boats speed upriver and silently wished them good hunting.

Doing a gun check, I inspected the M60. I didn't realize it, but after periods of fire, the M60 didn't produce enough gas to operate because of carbon build-up. The gunner must do a full field strip and thorough cleaning which was all but impossible in an airborne helicopter. The barrel change procedure was a pain in the ass. You lay the weapon on the helicopter floor and put on a large asbestos glove before you touched the red-hot barrel. The problems were a reminder every weapon was made by the lowest bidder.

I opened the breach of the machine gun and snapped in a new belt of 308 ammunition, 7.62×51mm NATO. I grinned at the writing on a grunt's helmet: Draft Beer, Not Men. Must be a draftee, most were. What idiot would volunteer to fight over here? Oh, that's right, me.

I was elated to be flying. Two thousand feet below was the shining Mekong River, a squashed snake making its way to the South China Sea. Far to my right, the sea was a dirty green blanket dotted with black boats. Later, I learned that behind the foothills were deep valleys, ridges, and mountains covered with tall trees that canopied the jungle below.

Freddie, the slick gunner I replaced, was killed when he took a round in the forehead. The crew chief said a guy grows to love the excitement, the adrenalin, and the afterglow of survival.

The pilot kicked on the radio and into my headphones came, "Born on the bayou. Born on the bayou."

The song popped memories. I flashed on skiing behind a snowcat run by the Frosts. Holding onto a rope, my sister, along with Devyn, Big Owl, and others were pulled up the pipeline road on the south side of Grand Mesa. That in turn, brought up a memory of my Dutch relatives walking rows of cherry trees. They came to see me at Tongue Creek Orchard. I was stacking cherry lugs and could talk for only a few minutes, but they made me feel special and loved. They were against the Vietnam War and said to come back to Holland if I was drafted. Suddenly Dove's face loomed. *She's why I'm here.*

Shifting back to reality, I was filled with fear and wonder at heavily overgrown hills peeking between clouds and sheets of rain. Like the grunts sitting on the floor, I'd never admit I was scared. Worse than death was the humiliation of being thought a coward. Having a fifty percent chance of being shot down, acting brave was all that mattered. At least I wouldn't be taking flak from the fighters for being 'an ass in the back with the trash.'

Seeing the other helicopters, I realized we had targets painted on us. ARMY in big white letters and a huge white star with U.S. flag stripes along the fuselage along with teeth painted on the front of gunships. Yeah, right! We aren't sharks; we're a flock of ducks floating down for guys in a blind to blast us. We'll flop down in a boiling pot of rockets and rounds will bubble around us.

As we flew past an island of trees, RPGs rose up at us. The crew chief opened up, but it was hard to tell if he hit anything. Last week we had lost ten helicopters and thirty came back full of holes and wounded men. With an eighteen-year-old's magical thinking, I wouldn't get shot down. A chant ran through my head, "See that commie on the hill – he's the one I got to kill."

The pilot radioed, "Lock and load, fire at will." I opened up at running figures. No idea if they were enemies or farmers. Firing the loud machine gun caused an uncontrollable adrenalin rush like shooting deer in the field, but I was up above them and saw where they ran. My knees bounced around as if I was Elvis Presley. *Ain't nothing but a hound dog, rocking all the time.*

"Cease fire."

Surprised that I missed, I had a shit-eating grin. The crew chief gave me a thumbs up and mouthed with a huge smile, "Exciting ain't it?"

The pilot radioed me, "Enemy fire will be on your side and the LZ is hot."

I saw a Red Cross helicopter on its side and realized we were on a rescue mission. *What the hell,* I thought, *Why did they shoot a medevac chopper?* Pissed, I fired the M60 at the tree line. I couldn't tell if the crew was still in the bird, or if they were already picked up. It was a challenge to shoot because I could possibly hit our troopers or helicopters. Watching for sparkling muzzle flashes from enemy guns, I sweated as my trigger finger squeezed. *Breathe, shoot on the out-breath and aim, don't spray,* I heard my range instructor's voice. *Imagine you're about to stick your prick in a girl, aim carefully and control your fire. Don't want to miss her do you?*

The flight of six slicks organized into a staggered line behind one another. We circled the downed medevac helicopter.

Suddenly, a group of black-clad figures jumped up from a nearby dike. They raked us with automatic weapons fire.

My first burst knocked down three of the VC and the rest scattered. The Cobras would clean them up. I smiled to myself. I did it! I had proved I wouldn't falter and break. *Son of a gun, I can do this! I can kill a man.*

We dropped a platoon to guard the downed helicopter and within seconds, were back in the air. A subtle sense of well-being caused by endorphins soaked through me.

Flying high on the way back to the base, I felt wonderful.

28. What Was I Thinking?

In April, Vietnam shifted to the hot rainy season, and despite the wet heat, mosquitoes, and greasy Army chow, I settled in as door gunner. It was nowhere as safe as the gung-ho colonel made it out to be.

Devyn wrote,

Dove hasn't been home so I can't tell you much. Slinky-butt Gabe Falcon hangs around and talks to their mom at the kitchen table. As you know, he's now at Western. Mrs. Knutson and he act like they are best friends. I know he's after Dove. They have money and it's creepy. You heard from her?

Anyway, write and tell me what it's like as a door gunner. Sounds darned exciting. I want to be a Cobra pilot. Wish I were there but only if I could bring Stormy.

I was irritated that Gabe had transferred to Dove's college, but thought, *He's an oddball. Dove will be nice, but she wouldn't date him, and I'll tell Devyn to do whatever it takes to avoid this war.*

The only armor on a Huey was under the pilot's seats and doors. Remembering that guy in the bus station in San Francisco, I sat on a flak jacket and carried a semi-auto pistol in a holster over my groin. I already escaped several near misses; it was common for bullets to smash into the wall above my head or bounce off my chicken plate. The plate was a thick ceramic, fiberglass, and steel plate hanging like a heavy garbage pail lid over the front of my chest.

Seven grunts from the 9th infantry division crawled in, decked out in ammo belts, grenades, and M-16 rifles in a ride to destiny – a cool LZ at 0900 hours. A hot LZ was a landing zone in suspected enemy territory where a firefight was in progress. Our mission was to search the area and take prisoners for interrogation. Six helicopters left the tarmac in a cloud of dust, one behind the other.

I opened the breach of my M60 machine gun and snapped in a new belt of ammunition, scanning trees, bushes, and thickets, looking for anything suspicious to knock down. Having grown up outside of Cedaredge, Colorado where hunting was my hobby, I was good at this. I glanced around the cabin and read the guy's helmets, "Killing is my business and business is good." One had a peace sign, and another had, "It don't mean nothing" on his helmet cover.

I kept my mouth shut. These tough young men were tense, alert, and ready to spring into action. They had a crazy look and feel. *I ought to paint on my flight helmet, "What was I thinking?"*

The best part about going on a mission was we got temporary relief from the stinking air of Dong Tam. The nauseating smell was from fifty-five-gallon oil drums cut in half and used as toilets. When they were full, some sucker poured diesel or kerosene in and set it on fire. Then he had to stir the shit. The most disgusting odor imaginable got on the unfortunate guy's clothes and in his hair, and nobody sat next to him until he showered and had his clothes cleaned.

In one letter Dove said,

"The fight for freedom should always be alive in your heart regardless of corrupted political leaders and policies that harm people. When you fight for what is right, what is there to question? If you believe free choice is something everyone deserves, it's worth fighting for; it's all the reason you need."

I wanted to believe it, I really did.

The pilot turned up the radio. "I gave my heart and soul to a woman. She brought me along the road to woe and, In pain and agony, I called to God for company, white water running."

The machine gun stuck out from my lap like a monstrous phallus. I figured being a door gunner was better than being a ground-pounding grunt. The slicks transported these beat-up, tired warriors from one place of conflict to another. I felt sorry for them because they were always dirty and muddy, although my odds as a door gunner were worse than a grunt's – hence the chronic shortage of door gunners.

We flew over a huge defoliated area along a canal. All the plants and trees drooped, dripping poisonous toxins onto the underbrush and on any human who dared enter the dead jungle. It stunk of decayed animal meat and rotten vegetation and was the least desirable place to visit on the planet. Wide swaths of jungle, including border areas with Cambodia and Laos, were called "No Man's Land." Covering thousands upon thousands of acres, these dead zones were once lush, green environments. Now they were a putrid gray color.

Defoliants were sprayed by giant C-130 cargo planes, or by small single-engine crop-dusting planes like in the States. They also used Huey helicopters with 50-gallon drums of witch's brew. Vietnam was the armpit of the world and the defoliated areas were its cesspools. The dead jungle gripped and froze my thoughts.

We dropped straight into a hot landing zone. Bullets zinged past and instantly hyper-alert, I reacted from instinct. Time slowed, and I ignored the incoming bullets' slap. The sounds disappeared from my consciousness as shrapnel smacked into the helicopter. Feelings of dread turned to anger and became a creeping, subliminal sensation. I didn't understand it, but every time we came in hot, I got this sense of power and exhilaration as if I were king of the world, a rush of adrenaline, or insanity.

We swooped down to pluck grunts from the defoliated hellhole, mortars exploding, and gunfire whizzing by in streams of blinding frequency. There were no heroics. Everyone just did his job.

We took the men a few miles to another LZ to drop them off, and the slick crews kept pent-up, ambiguous feelings in check. We never knew the grunt's names and barely saw their faces through the grime, mud, and sweat. The crew chief said, "Get over it. Get used to the stupidity of war or you'll be slithering home."

At the LZ, in less than twenty seconds, we dropped these poor suckers to struggle through hip-deep mud and putrid water.

I had not been defoliated…

Yet.

29. The Old Stump

The morning was overcast, threatening monsoon rain. As we approached the PZ, seven helicopters shuffled into a single file, My ship at the end. We dropped to fifty feet and picked up speed as we entered the rice paddy. My aircraft dropped tail down, leveled, and hovered above the grass.

A gangly grunt and five companions rushed my chopper. Coming straight at me was a man I recognized. It was the way he ran. He took big strides with long spindly legs while running straight up. He pulled his knees to his chest, the right knee crossed over the left, and the left leg dragged.

It was Private Martin Moya, my old bunkmate from infantry school, a draftee born and bred on a farm in northern New Mexico. *Here he comes to save the day; Mighty Marty is on his way.*

Marty didn't smoke during basic, but a short cigarette was clenched between his teeth. Gunners or crew chiefs didn't help troops unless someone was wounded, instead, the first soldier in grabbed the litter pole and helped his mates. Most grunts wouldn't take my hand, not out of disrespect, but because they preferred to help each other.

Moya was written in black-on-green letters above the limping man's left breast pocket. I leaned against my monkey harness to reach out with my arm. Instinctively, Marty clasped my forearm. Dark glasses hid my eyes, and he didn't recognize me.

Wearing a beat-up green flak jacket with a single stripe, in his left hand Marty held his M-16 rifle by its suitcase handle; he was covered with mud splatters. Strapped to his thin, bony frame was a heavy, ragged backpack stuffed to the brim with grenades and ammo pouches laced to the webbing. His camo shirt was soiled with perspiration. Stuck in his camouflaged helmet were sticks, weeds, and a white stickpin with "Mom" on it. In the green elastic helmet band were three toothpicks, bug spray, and a book of matches.

A haggard look wrestled on Marty's face, a battle-worn gaze; he had aged years in the last four months. His six-foot frame was gaunt and his eyes vacant.

I gave a hard pull and Marty twisted to land with his butt on the aluminum-plated floor, his feet dangling over the edge. He took the cigarette from his lips and glanced up at me as he flipped the butt to the ground. He wiped the sweat from his eyebrows with the back of a grimy hand.

It was an unspoken rule to never remove your flight helmet because you must stay in constant radio contact with the pilot. We were so close, I thought about taking off my aviation glasses so Marty would recognize me. We had maybe thirty minutes to the next landing zone. Here we were, two teenagers eight thousand miles from home about to rock and roll into a battle together, perhaps for our last party forever.

I wondered if Marty was still homesick for his Ma and the farm life in New Mexico. There was no opportunity to speak because of the helicopter blades and the roar of rushing wind. It wasn't as if the mission could be put on hold so a couple of old pals could yuck it up.

I hesitated. Would talking to him create a distraction? Might it break his concentration as we landed? Could Marty get angry at me as a clean door gunner with a dry bed while he crawled in the stinking slime? I closed my eyes, imagining what might happen. Marty was always quiet, and a single phrase emerged, "I'd rather be home sitting on that stump my grandpa hammered the nails in."

I kept my dark glasses on.

I was a support personnel who backed up the grunts on the ground. Who were the others? There were cooks, clerks, doctors, and nurses. There were road engineers, construction workers, pilots, artillery gunners, truck drivers, paymasters, laundry techs, clerks, mechanics, chaplains, and more. The list went on and on. Thousands of bureaucrats, the local selective service boards, and flag-waving politicians – each had a hand in this mess. What about the weapons and ammo manufacturers? There were millions spent and made each day because of this war.

Do Marty and his pals take any comfort in knowing how many people they had behind them? I doubted it. This wasn't like his father's war where great armies marched across vast landscapes, fought, and held the ground captured. Marty and his fellow grunts probably conquered this defoliated section of Vietnam last week. The next LZ might be the exact spot they were delivered on a search and destroy mission a month ago and today, they'd do it again.

It was insanely stupid – sweep the area to make sure it was clear of enemy elements to the satisfaction of an intelligence geek in the Pentagon who was already drawing up the next confusing mission. New orders were conjured by a pencil-neck stiff hunkered down with statistics in an air-conditioned office thousands of miles away in Washington D.C. They looked for body counts. A war of attrition to kill so many VC they might give up. Genocide, like they killed the American Indians.

The problem was, you killed one, and it pissed off his relatives and friends. You'd have to kill the guy's friends and relatives. Those people had friends and relatives who'd want to kill Americans in revenge. You'd need to kill them too. General Westmoreland and General Ewing don't get it. To win, we'd have to kill everyone in the whole country, then kill most of the Cambodians, the Chinese, and the Russians – it would never end. So maybe we should just kill ourselves.

The pilot kicked on the radio and a song rang out, "We came to 'Nam to fight the commie devil."

I glanced down at Marty sitting with his feet on the skids. *That could be me.* The grunts don't get to keep the ground they captured. There was no booty, no loot, no maidens to ravish – nothing. If they were lucky, they might take an old, scrawny rice farmer as a prisoner. The VC soldiers disappeared into tunnels and down jungle trails. A piece of territory wasn't worth holding because it'd be bombed and scorched to smithereens by the U.S. Air Force.

The grunts were often pulled out as quickly as they were brought in. It was one reason they were so damned worn out. In the old days, when you took a piece of ground, you got to hold it for a while, and you got a breather to write a letter home to Mom. Not these men; once the area was secured, they were snatched from their hard-fought sector and flown sixty miles to another LZ to do it again.

I questioned whether we provided any real support. Would the ground troops rather walk the sixty miles as their fathers and grandfathers did through forests, swamps, and jungles to their next rendezvous with hell? It'd take them about three days since it's slow going in the mud and muck. By the time they arrived, would there be anything to do? Would they have pushed Charlie to the next area a few clicks over? Would this be followed by another 60-mile hike right back to where they started? These thoughts had no answers. My questions were as futile as putting these men in harm's way day after day. I tried to push it from my thoughts as I searched for something comprehensible. It was no use.

Far away, dark sheets of rain rose like black drapes. It swept across the horizon, drenching everything in its path. The captain radioed to indicate we were within minutes of the landing zone.

Our seven helicopters broke formation and shifted into a single file as we approached the LZ. My ship was in the middle. A smoke ship flew close to the ground to put down a trail of thick, white smoke against the edge of the trees to veil the transport slick's approach. It was rare to have a smoke ship and two

Snakes. Intelligence must believe a large NVA force was in there. Men will die.

Smoky was a quarter of a mile ahead with two Cobra gunships protecting its flank. The snakes packed the most lethal weaponry imaginable. A multi-barreled machine gun was mounted on each side of the ship. When the Cobras lit up their guns, it fooled a man's ear. It wasn't rat-tat-tat like a regular machine gun, but more of a burp, a continuous burst of lead stretching end to end – a fast, ragged sound like air blowing through tight, spitting lips - BrBrBrBrBrBrBr. There was a stream of white-yellow tracers, one of every fifth round. It was spectacular at night when the color changed to bright, wavy lines in ruby-red fluorescent liquid. They also had rocket pods mounted on each side. The rockets were so fast you couldn't hear or see them.

I suddenly thought of Devyn. He wanted to be a Cobra pilot. For a few seconds I wondered how he and Stormy where doing. It made me think of Dove. God, how I loved her. I thought about the last time we made love. I'd marry her the moment I got home, well, maybe we'd first stop in San Francisco for a night with the stripper. It was a fun fantasy.

Smoky had steel drums of assorted chemicals to create a mile-long stream of heavy fog against the tree line. It was a narrow stream that expanded to a height of thirty feet. It blocked visibility from the edge of a rice paddy to a tree line. It made a lane for helicopters to land behind. Smelled disgusting and burned your eyes.

The gunships worked back and forth on the flanks of Smokey. Cobras sprayed five-second bursts into trees and bushes. Rockets exploded in balls of blue and yellow flashes like bolts of lightning and camera flashes.

My ship came in parallel to the line of smoke. "Fire at will!" My index finger reflexively pulled back on the twin trigger rings of the machine gun; it jerked and vibrated, spitting brass casings as if it were loose popcorn. Open spots in the haze exposed muzzle flashes and I swung at them to fire. Time expanded in the center of a time warp.

Shooting bursts into the smoke, I was conscious of men stirring. Marty scooted closer to me, allowing one of his mates to sit on the aluminum edge of the doorway. They pulled back the bolts on their M-16s, pushing a round in the chamber. Locked and loaded, they tensed for action.

Behind the curtain of smoke, there was a tree line where hidden NVA waited. I wanted to be extra fierce – a maddened fiend, protecting my boot camp buddy. Fear subsided, replaced by exhilaration. Electricity flowed in my arms as if he's been shocked from sleep. Intuition took over. I wheeled the M-60 from left to right. My legs stiffened and stood up from the gunner's chair, jaw muscles in a tight grin and my eyes dilated, dark thoughts seeped into my consciousness.

Watching my crazy excitement, grunts shifted nervously. In my first combat, these sensations were frighteningly unreal, but now they were a welcome feeling of power. The machine gun transformed from a gun barrel into a pumping phallus. Firing, firing - killing, killing. A mind trip. The psyche slipped into madness, and I morphed into a crazed killer. I relished the punishment delivered to the enemy, unloading fears and frustrations in deadly bursts. It was a relief, draining haunts in lethal bursts of gunfire, pissing on the enemy, payback time, rising to a crescendo, an exploding orgasm.

The addiction grew stronger with each battle. Other gunners had told me about this fanatical sensation but this was the first time I felt it. For all the travails, fears, and pains, one phrase described it: "Getting your rocks off." The rush made it worthwhile. I laughed as my M60 roared.

The grunts looked up at me oddly.

The helicopter slowed as it dropped to the ground and we came to a stop with the tail down. We were eight feet from touching the earth. I did a quick inspection of the rice paddy underneath. "Clear left," followed by "Clear right" from the crew chief. The line of helicopters leveled and sat down in a single file.

Dust and debris flew up from the ground and a dew-like mist from the disturbed pools of water settled on my face. My nostrils filled with the odor of smoke, jet exhaust, and gunpowder. The blanket of smoke ripped open, whirling and blowing. Spinning funnel winds caused a vortex. The assault angered a nest of hidden specters, scampering above rice shoots. The little twisters melted away as I fired through the mist at dead, barren trees and dancing ghosts.

To my left, I sensed an ominous gesture as if to swat us down. I made out a faint helmet and shredded it and everything nearby.

Marty readied with his feet planted on the landing skids. The aircraft dipped and as it leveled, he plunged off in a quick, smooth movement but when he hit the ground, he favored a leg. He rolled forward.

Like clockwork, he was followed by fellow grunts; they ran with heads down because of the helicopter blades and that allowed my M-60 to lay cover fire. The ships quickly lifted and peeled away in different directions, gaining altitude at odd angles. My chopper banked to the left, twisting as it climbed higher directly over the LZ.

Sweat poured into my eyes as I squinted through the haze. Small parallel lines of dark forms lay next to each other, then men got up and ran at the smoke-filled tree line. Marty pulled his knees up too high, the right knee crossing over the left and one foot dragging. "Run Marty, Run," I shouted into the expanding gulf between us. "Damn it – Run Marty Run!"

He vanished, swallowed into another dimension. *Did he make it?* I wondered. *Did he get hit?* I imagined him charging into the defoliated trees, lifting his legs high, his right hand holding his helmet, and poof, he was gone, disappearing into the recesses of time. It was great to know Marty had made it this long. How about that!

I felt fortunate to speed away at sixty knots, a thousand feet above the ground, headed in the opposite direction for the next pickup zone. I thought of Marty and his platoon fighting communists in another search and destroy mission. What would he have said about his injury? Was it a booby trap, a toe popper, or a poisoned bamboo stake? Could it be jungle rot? A foot infection that ate away your flesh.

I remembered his sobbing spell in the snow during basic training when we saw him on his knees asking for Momma. Damn weird. The god of dumb luck had pulled him through.

I now understood why Marty avoided making friends, especially with a bunch of draftees bound for the meat grinder of Southeast Asia. The death of his father must have left him emotionally aloof. A good survival skill.

Dare we ask of the unseen scars, the ones no man can talk about? Is it necessary to wrap your emotions in a concrete cocoon? How does a guy get reconstructed without tripping over mania brought on by the insanity of combat? How do you get unwrapped? Abruptly, I was unfulfilled for reasons I couldn't explain. My curiosity about an old army bunkmate had uprooted another time and place. It was an intruding presence difficult to shake.

Marty ran, charging into the smoke veil and hopefully he came out the other side without mistrusting anyone who offered a hand.

For some odd reason, I found myself not thinking of Dove but of my elementary school friends. Guys like Vernon, Robert, Danny, and Ralph; girls such as Sandy, Sonya, Marlene, and Joann. We grew up together, played on the playground jungle gym and competed in spelling, and now they were all graduating from high school. Where will they end up?

I hoped none would end up here.

A quilt of mixed green patches of rice paddies spread underneath the ship. I closed my eyes and imagined what Marty might have said if we had talked. A faded image emerged of a once-frightened farm boy sitting in the snow with his back against a pine tree. "I wish I was back on the farm right now, sittin' on the stump my Grandpa left."

Good for you.

Run Marty.

Run for all you're worth.

30. Graveyard Attack

We picked up speed the closer we came to earth and a tree grove appeared larger and larger. The tree line was the drop site, and the pilot came on, "Prepare to lay cover fire on the thickets." In the center of the paddy was an island of dense trees and brush.

Fifty yards from the drop zone, I saw red and yellow gravestones. We dropped like a hawk on a mouse as the pilot called: "Commence firing."

I got a barbarous excitement from firing my machine gun until the barrel glowed red. A thirst to kill obsessively, devouring right and wrong. My machine gun sent a shattering burst, ripping through foliage, but the gun jammed. A spent shell held the bolt open. I saw figures in the field and cursed because I couldn't shoot them.

The other helicopters fired into the cemetery grove. As I fought to clear my weapon, I recognized a mother and child kneeling next to a grave marker. Dressed in a black robe, the woman was placing flowers near a headstone.

I had a headset and microphone inside my helmet. I pressed a button on a short cable and radioed the pilot, "Cease fire at the grave markers."

Terrified, the little girl ran at the landing choppers as if they had come to save her. I watched the mother scream as she desperately tried to chase her daughter down.

I cleared my M60 as bullets ripped into the child while the mother frantically threw herself over the little body. In a futile effort to save her girl, the top of the mom's head shattered open, splattering like a ripe pumpkin. They both went limp as blood coursed from their bodies.

I gagged.

I had shot deer, rabbits, birds, skunks, elk, coyotes, and other animals, but had never been so close to see a little girl and her mother die – right there, not more than twenty yards straight in front of me. As the chopper hit the ground, my stomach contents burbled up, and I fought to keep from puking.

Grunts scrambled out. I couldn't let the other guys see tenderness. They'd call me out on it… I'd endure harassment if they knew. I choked, heaved, and coughed as I pushed the microphone mouthpiece out of the way so I could spit. My nose dripped profusely. Embarrassed, I wiped my face and pulled my dark goggles down quickly.

"You okay back there?" The pilot called to me.

"Yeah, my gun jammed. I got it." I let go a short burst to prove it and since my gun was pointed there, a bullet shattered the dead girl's fragile wrist. Her bones stuck up as her partially cut-off hand flopped on her mother's shoulder.

"Shit! Damn it!"

No medic waved and no one ran at our ship so we lifted off into the blue sky. I saw no muzzle flashes in the trees – only two lifeless dots in a green field near the cemetery. The radio blared, "I got a line on you, babe, I got a line on you, babe."

In minutes, we were miles away, the rice paddies skimming by underneath. I stared out the open door, my eyes blank. The C & C radioed we were released for the day. We were to return to base for the night.

We flew at a safe altitude, two thousand feet high. Everything to our front is clear – empty rice paddies and a slow-setting red sun. You'd never guess there was a war below. Today made less sense than when I buried a truckload of black market materials. Strangely, I felt marvelous inside. Confused, I thought, *What the fuck? What the fuck?*

Late March 1969

31. Crushed

Devyn was working on the high jump at track practice when his older sister skidded into the high school parking lot. A pretty blue-eyed blonde, Gaylin ran to the track field with a frantic, wind-swept look. "You've got to come, Daddy's been run over by the tractor."

"What?" He jogged to her. "What are you talking about?"

"Daddy and my husband were pruning the apple orchards. He fell off the tractor, and it crushed him."

"Where is he now?"

"They took him to the Delta hospital but he's beyond their help, and the ambulance is on the way to the Veteran's hospital in Grand Junction. He may not make it."

"Where's Mom?"

"She rode in the ambulance with him. Come on, let's go, he may die before he gets to the hospital."

At the Veteran's Hospital in Grand Junction, the receptionist was cold. "He is in surgery. You need to wait over there."

Mr. McDowell's kids sat in the main area for hours. Mom came down. "Your father is in intensive care. You kids can't go in, they won't even let me." She explained that his dad did not sit down on the tractor seat to move to the next tree. Instead, he stood on the side of the tractor, stepped on the clutch, put it in low gear, and moved the tractor slowly to the next tree. Suddenly, the Massey-Ferguson had jumped into gear. It knocked him off. The big rear wheel had climbed up his right leg and crushed his pelvis. At the last minute, Dad threw his head back or it would have smashed it. It was a wonder he was alive.

Mom was devastated.

Devyn was surprised, *You'd think the way they fight all the time, she'd be relieved the crusty Marine might bite the dust.*

He wasn't allowed to see his father for several days and when he did, Dad wasn't the same. He was pale, weak, and humble. They said he may not make it.

Calum apologized, "I'm sorry son. I do love you. Because my dad died when I was nine, I wanted you to learn to be independent."

"It's okay. Mom needs you to get well."

"Call a reverend. Tell him to come to pray for me. I don't know if I'm going to live."

"Seriously?"

"Yes, call the one at the church where you play guitar."

Devyn called Reverend Wiseman who was happy to go. To everyone's surprise, after he and another pastor laid hands on Dad in the Veteran's Hospital, Calum McDowell started improving.

McDowell said, "Son, I'm not a religious man. I seen too much war to be, but when Reverend Wiseman and the other preacher prayed, the moment they put their hands on my head and my hip, I felt an energy and I knew I was gonna live."

Devyn was taking three days off a week from school to work on the farm. There was pruning, plowing, disking, and harrowing – otherwise, they'd be in deep shit come summer and the fruit wouldn't develop because of no water.

He was shocked when two dozen men showed up on a Friday at their hundred-acre farm. Their wives cooked and served the men breakfast and lunch. They helped Mom prepare her vegetable and flower gardens. The farmers and ranchers brought their tractors and went to work pruning, plowing, disking, harrowing, and marking the rows for water.

Mom cried because it was like the whole community came to help. That's Surface Creek Valley people. They would gossip and put you down, but when push came to shove, they were there for you.

The farmers worked three twelve-hour days. Devyn didn't know it was possible to live among such good people.

Dove dropped Stormy off at the farm after church on Sunday, and she helped prepare food. After a quick lunch, Devyn showed her the small house for migrants who picked the apples.

Naturally, they ended up kissing and fell onto one of the old mattresses.

A half hour later, "Where have you been?" his mother asked. "The men are asking for you because they need to know what you want to be done next."

It flattered Devyn. Here he was just seventeen and men his dad's age waited for his directions. "Just taking a break after lunch." He and Stormy had Cheshire cat grins.

Dove picked up Stormy soon afterwards.

Devyn got the men reorganized for the afternoon. There was still a lot of work to do, but those farmers put a huge dent in it.

One of the men who helped was involved in the Mularkey's water consortium. He told Mr. Falcon that Calum wasn't running the farm the right way to make money. Joe Falcon held a land contract against the McDowell place. Devyn also learned the Town of Cedaredge had filed a lawsuit to take possession of the spring that fed the Bonita Reservoir providing irrigation water to their farm.

Devyn's teachers were great. He went to school on Mondays and Fridays and the teachers waived his homework, saying, "We know you're smart and can pass the tests." He still competed in baseball and track and would graduate on time.

When he saw his father in the hospital, he asked Dad about the town's lawsuit.

Dad said, "They're probably going to get the Bonita spring because I can't afford to keep fighting them, especially now. The Mularkey's will make a fortune on their land development scheme to the southeast of Cedaredge. Political position and knowledge equal money and vice versa." Changing the subject,

Calum said, "You tell Rowdy and Big Owl, you got to fight through the pain. The gooks aren't your enemy, your fear of pain is. Once you overcome your fear, you'll survive." He took Devyn's hand for the first time since he was a kid. "Son, we'll survive. Ain't no point in being afraid.

32. BrBrBrBrBrBr

When an AK bullet hit my chest plate, I immediately thought of Dove. I was a pimple on the lips of eternity, but she'd have me sealed to her in the Mormon Temple if the commies nailed me.

I felt horrible about attacking the cemetery but the other guys didn't notice or care about the Vietnamese mother and her daughter.

The peasants resented the brutality from all sides, they asked, "How can the U.S. be fighting for our freedom if it indiscriminately bombs, burns, and imprison us, fearing we're the enemy?"

It got worse every day. Someone said, "We don't have ten years of experience in Vietnam. We have one year's experience ten times over." When the enemy was bent on taking your life, you didn't ask whether it was right or wrong. You pulled the trigger and wanted the enemy to fall. Broken boys bled on the chopper floor and it made me so mad I wanted to kill those who did it. That's when it changed inside.

Before, I never knew hate. A crumbling riverbank at flood stage, my moral aversion to killing died. Kill gooks. It was my job. Hated to admit it, but watching them fall before my hail of bullets was fun. My thoughts twisted: The enemy wasn't human – they were dinks, gooks, VC, yellow bellies. Body counts were what the superiors wanted and I gave counts to them. It was easy to kill from a distance. Nothing up close and personal like the grunts. Kill or be killed.

Devyn wrote about his dad getting run over by the tractor. I re-read what Mr. McDowell said, "Fear of pain is your only enemy. It's all in your head." There was too much in my head. I lost respect for the officers, clerks, and other pogues sleeping in air-conditioned bunkers deep inside the base. Officials had hooch maids and luxuries while we were being ambushed.

One evening as we straggled in from another mission, I noticed Darrel's stuff was gone. Was he transferred or killed? Did he desert? No one knew. No one had said goodbye to him. *Hope he made it out alive, not back to the world the hard way.*

Thinking it was the safest place, General Ewing ordered all ammo on Dong Tom stored in a central area surrounded by U.S. forces. On March 26, 1969, the Viet Cong put a rocket over the berm, scoring a direct hit. It blew up five hundred tons of ammunition. The explosions and aftershocks were so tremendous it felt like an earthquake.

I constantly thought of Dove – I was here because of her. She represented everything good and right with America. The pilot turned up the radio, "Say it loud, I'm black and I'm proud."

The helicopters formed a staggered line and dropped in a predefined order. I heated up the M60 barrel, firing short bursts. My ship was 2nd in and we went in low and deep. In combat, the worst thing was paralysis. *Stay alert - stay alive.* I faced the tree line and opened up as we lifted out, choppers peeling off at different angles to avoid hitting each other.

The squad of helicopters shifted a few clicks to pick up another platoon. Five squad members ran through tall Elephant grass, hauling a man on a poncho. They tossed him onto the chopper floor. I glanced down at him. The poor wanker's left leg was shattered. Punched up with morphine, he was silent with eyes rolled back in his head. The squad jumped in and we hauled ass into the sky.

The radio blasted, "There's just no place for a street fighting man, no."

I rocked the M60 to the music and the bitchy machine gun jammed again. "Motha-pucka!" I cussed and glanced from the tree line to my gun as I worked to clear it, a VC with his AK-47 pointed right at me. "He's gonna kill us!" I kept my eyes on the target as I worked to clear the jam without looking at the gun. I fired again and the gook folded headfirst. I couldn't believe it! I was alive and VC was dead. An incredible surge of happiness, an elation better than the afterglow of great sex hit. I yelled, "I'm alive!"

The grunts looked up, confused.

I looked down at the grey-faced man on the floor and felt guilty for my grandiose, wonderful emotions. Here I was celebrating being alive, and this poor grunt on the floor was bleeding out. Adrenalin mixed with sweat and gunnite – the smell was addicting.

We took the wounded man to the 3rd Surgical Hospital. The radio blasted into my headphones, "I met a gin-soaked bar room queen in Memphis."

One of the grunts asked, "You get hit?"

I looked down and my pant leg was soaked red. Suddenly, it hurt like a muther-fucker. "Shit!" I said over the headphones. "I took a hit in the leg."

They made me report to the hospital while the chopper immediately took off. Fortunately, it was a minor flesh wound, and they patched my calf. "Be careful to keep this clean and use the antibiotics on it because infections are bad over here."

I got the afternoon off. One of the guys in the bunkhouse said, "Hey, you can get a purple heart for that wound."

I laughed. Who gave a shit about purple hearts?

I heard about Thursday, May 20. 1969 when Governor Ronald Reagan called in the National Guard to spray tear gas and skin-stinging powder on thousands of protestors at People's Park in Berkeley, California. Police killed a man, and they hospitalized 123 for protesting the Vietnam War. It didn't stop the war.

The next sunrise, I was back on a chopper. The Huey carried a max of eight troops plus the four-man crew. I knew the next one would be a hot LZ because two cobras and three Huey gunships escorted our flight group. The gunships had grenade launchers mounted in their nose and two miniguns above the rocket pods. They spun so fast it went BrBrBrBrBrBr.

We must be hitting a raging hot LZ in enemy territory because we also had a smoke ship (smoky) with two miniguns and chemical drums to create a heavy greyish-white smoke. The gunners on smoky came back from their day greasy, black, and coughing. The smoke spread thirty feet wide and thirty feet high behind the chopper. They lay down a mile of smoke. A few minutes behind, the gunships threw rockets, hoping to kill anyone who could shoot back.

The Army used this strategy one in ten hot LZs because there weren't enough smoke and gunships available. They were sent when intelligence believed an NVA company or battalion were there. Even with this protection, it was easy to knock a slick helicopter out of the sky.

In the headphones, I heard, "I see the bad moon arising. I see trouble on the way."

My ship came in at 1200 feet. We geesed into a V wedge with their blades so near it looked as if they'd slap each other. Our ten-ship group landed to let the troops off.

No enemy contact as the grunts dismounted, but as the helicopters raised broadside to the tree line, a machine gun stitched our right side. The crew chief took a slug in his arm as rounds ricocheted around the cabin. One lodged in the side of the copilot's helmet, jamming his head down. I couldn't do anything since there were empty rice fields on my side.

The crew chief was enraged. He screamed and with one hand, blasted away with his M60, ignoring the blood soaking his uniform. As we gained elevation, I lashed down my machine gun to helped my crew chief. His face was white from blood loss. I pulled him to the main floor area and wrapped bandages in a tourniquet.

I turned to check the copilot's pulse. He was alive. I pulled off his helmet. The round didn't penetrate but had enough force to knock him out. At that moment, more bullets smacked the aircraft and the pilot ordered, "Get back to your gun position, we're taking rounds."

I jumped back to my place and scanned the fields. We were in a free-fire zone, kill anything that moved. I fired a few random bursts for effect. Whoever shot at us must have popped up, fired, and dropped. The rice paddies had a uniform somberness. *How do you control a place covered with water?* It was akin to shooting into a lake to catch a few fish. I scanned the beautiful green and fertile countryside.

The co-pilot regained consciousness by the time we landed at the base, but the crew chief shivered with shock.

Medics ran with stretchers to pull the wounded men off. The aircraft had taken too many hits to go back out, so me and the pilot were shifted to another helicopter with duct tape patched bullet holes, but it was airworthy. We shook hands with the new crew chief and copilot and were off again.

I caught a shiny flicker from the corner of my eye. KABOOM! A huge explosion rocked the ship like it was hit by an RPG (rocket-propelled grenade). A second later, I was sailing out on my own – sky, rice paddy, sky. Humph, my breath was knocked out and my head rang with the spots that danced before my eyes. Another helicopter flew just over the top of me.

Catching my breath, I discovered that my retaining strap was still on, but the bolt and plate that held it to the ship had broken. I was fifty feet from the smoking helicopter with crumpled blades. Dust hung in the air and soldiers were flung all around.

Rising, I took fire in my chest plate. Knocked me down. I was surprised I still held my machine gun. Rolling, I put bursts into the dismal tree line. I crawled up a slight rise; *I gotta kill these dinks before they kill me.* Men and materials were scattered from hell to breakfast.

"Medic!" Someone yelled.

The situation made me think of Big Owl. *Glad he's not here.* Owl was probably drunk and stoned and he'd kill himself by running off the road since he drove trucks – enemy not needed.

They say there ain't no such thing as an atheist in a foxhole, but I disproved it. Terror made me more cynical.

A couple of slicks came in and I climbed aboard one, exhausted. Lifeless bodies had been tossed onto the aluminum floor while others lay in a morphine-induced stupor. Men grinned as we do when you cheated death. The crew chief radioed the AC, "Loaded and clear."

At fifteen hundred feet, the crew chief gave us cigarettes.

I lit up, inhaling as if I broke the surface of a deep pond of stale, stinking water.

Back at the base, I was immediately assigned another chopper despite being dazed and confused. The radio came on as Hanoi Hannah announced the 162nd Assault Helicopter Company was being blown away in a contact half-hour northwest of Dong Tam. "And GI, this song is for you, this is what your girl is doing back home." The radio played, "It's not the way you smile that touches my heart. Cheat, Cheat."

I pressed my mic button. "Hey, can we get another song?"

"These eyes watched you bring my world to an end."

I hollered into my mic, "Geez man! How 'bout a combat tune?"

He fiddled with the dial. "Paint it black, black as coal. I want it painted, painted, painted black!"

"Thanks!"

33. Gunnite

I sent a poem to Devyn. "The Last Night…sleep, restless Sweat, cricket, breeze, screen door, grass, naked, Tremble, leaves, moon, silver, BOOM-BOOM-BOOM. Nova - Nova where nightmares never end."

Devyn wrote back quickly, 'Hey guy, what's up? Bang any of those little Vietnamese honeys? I know you – even if you had the chance you wouldn't since you're devoted to Dove. She has straight A's at Western.

Two weeks ago, Ms. Knutson let me take Stormy to see *Waterhole Number 3* at the Egyptian theater in Delta. I used to the restroom and ran into Steve's little brother, Donny. Although he's only a freshman in high school, Donny is a virtuoso on the piano. The last time I did anything with him, we went hunting. I hit this mallard way up in the sky and it came crashing down. I picked it up and couldn't find where I had shot it. On close examination, there was a bit of blood on one side of its neck. Just one BB to take a life.

Anyway, Donny and I talked. He asked, "You remember Wayne Flayhand?"

"Yeah, Wayne used to live down the road from us and he beat me up every chance. He's nineteen now."

"Don't tell anyone, but Wayne made me give him a blow job last month. He forced me down on my knees. He's twice my size."

That pissed me off. I told Donny, "I'll help you kick his fagtard face if you want. It's not right to force someone."

"You might think it's weird but I liked it." He went on. "I could do it for you if you want." He nodded at one of the toilet stalls.

My mouth fell open.

Donny said, "Don't tell my brother, he'd kill Wayne if he knew."

I backed out of the restroom. "No worries, you can be queer if you want – just don't force it on someone like crud-faced Flayhand did you."

The Knutsons received the painting of Dove you had made. Wow! It's amazing the way her blue eyes follow you around. They hung it on the middle wall of their living room.

Stormy sends her love. You can keep sending me your strange thoughts in the middle of the night. Man, I miss you.

I re-read the sentence about the duck. One BB in the neck was all it took.

I had the portrait of Dove painted by a local Vietnamese artist. The artist had her high school photo and captured her intelligence and compassionate spirit with a gaze looking straight at the viewer. It cost ten dollars to have it made and the Army shipped it free to her home in Delta, Colorado.

Dove wrote to say thank you for the painting. As usual, she included Bible verses. "Isaiah 41:10 So do not fear, for I am with you; do not be dismayed, for I am your God."

In contrast to the strange, troubled nights I described in the poem I sent to Devyn, I loved flying. It was tranquil with the green earth pictured below framed by the open doorway. I had incredible views from a small corner of the helicopter. Facing out and strapped in with the ceramic plate covering my chest, I felt safer than in a bunker because tracers worked both ways and here, and I could shoot back. A thousand feet below, flowed the sparkling snake of the Mekong River on its way to the South China Sea.

The sea, a dirty green, was dotted with black toy boats. I caught glimpses of rolling mountains that peeked from behind a curtain of grey clouds.

For some reason, I stopped getting letters from Dove after her thank you for the painting. It was odd. She had written every day from the moment I went to boot camp. Sure, they weren't newsy and mostly just religious drivel, but at least she wrote. I began worrying.

We flew in the daylight and missions were usually short zooms across rice paddies to pick up men and drop them back down. Land and do it again. There were hundreds of helicopters in the air. Usually, we were in groups of four to six ships, and the missions were thirty minutes to two hours.

Some days were boring like flying a chaplain around for services, or taking the mail to firebases. The guys in remote bases were grateful to see us. They watched jealously as we lifted off back to Dong Tam. Those were the toughest days because there was nothing to keep my mind off Dove. A cold, shallow loneliness rose from my bowels every evening I didn't get a letter from her.

A platoon might radio and give their grid coordinates, pop yellow smoke, and wait for pickup. While in flight, the pilot learned about the landing conditions, whether the PZ was hostile, and after we got them out, where to take them next. A high-powered taxi service.

It wasn't like Dove didn't know my address. I hadn't been moved anywhere.

Some of the guys kidded me because she used to write every day. "Jody's got your girl and gone."

"No way," I said. "She promised she'd wait. We're engaged. I gave her my grandmother's engagement ring."

"A ring never plugged a hole."

"Fuck you!" I went to my bunk and stared at the ceiling, wondering what the hell was going on back home. I thought of Devyn's comment – 'My luck, if I was on a mission or in the Army, Stormy would run off with a Mexican, and there I'd be, stuck with no way to talk her out of it.' It was hard to sleep.

The rough stuff was when we loaded dead bodies onto the ship, especially those already decaying. It's hard to describe. Nothing like a dead animal rotting on the side of the road back in the semi-arid climate of Colorado. This was a jungle – it was wet and squishy with weird creepy things that crawled inside and sucked on decaying corpses. No body bags like in the movies. We covered the men's faces with rain ponchos, green shirts, or a towel because it's hard to look at a dead guy's face.

I thought about calling home. Maybe I could talk to Dove and find out what happened – why did she quit writing? If I couldn't get her on the phone, I might be able to talk to Devyn or even Stormy, but it was very expensive and cumbersome to call home. I decided to wait.

The worst was when a man got ripped open from kidney to kidney and the contents of his bowels spilled. The grunts hauling dead bodies to the helicopter wore the essence of sweat, defoliant, and adrenalin. I wondered if they bottled it, would women like "Scent of War" cologne?

The stench of a burned body was rough. Start with singed hair and combine it with burnt sugar beet pulp. Add the stink of overcooked and burning animal fat. The longer the body was dead, the stronger the bouquet. Made you want to puke.

The best fragrance was gunnite. It was the whiff of gunpowder after pulling the trigger – lovely.

34. Heart Cut Out

The first task at the end of the day was to clean the helicopter of blood, mud, and debris. The crew chief and I checked the mechanics. The last thing was to cleaned our weapons. When we were done, we hit the showers and ate, then went to the enlisted men's club or headed for the barracks.

The St. George's medallion Dove gave me had disappeared, probably ripped off when I had crashed three days back. Because my calf wound continued to bleed and due to the danger of infection, I went to the 3rd Surgical Hospital.

They X-rayed my leg. Whistling, the tech said, "Man, *that* was clo-ose!" He called a doctor to examine the picture.

"That wasn't a graze, it scraped the bone. I'm surprised you're doing okay."

I shrugged. "This isn't bad compared to some of the guys. I didn't know I was hurt until someone said, 'Hey, are you hit?'"

Dr. Valk was a new surgeon straight from medical school. She smiled. "You must have high pain tolerance." She cleaned the wound and gave me oral antibiotics.

We were face to face as I sat on the ER table. I realized she was quite attractive with long reddish-blond hair and blue-green eyes. Because she had a doctorate in medicine, she must be at least ten years older than me but she didn't look it. The thought bubbled up: *Sex is not the answer. Sex is the question and yes is the answer.* I kept it to myself, but she was major fantasy material not only for me, but most guys who saw her at the 3rd Surgical Hospital. She reminded me of Dove and that empty pang in my heart rang like a bell.

Today was my nineteenth birthday. Hoping for a letter from Dove, I went to the barracks. I hadn't heard from her in two weeks. It was strange because she had been writing every day and suddenly – nothing. I figured the Army would eventually bring a bundle of her letters. Dove used a light turquoise blue-green stationary; I could spot it from way across the barracks. I loved to sniff its soft perfume before opening her missive. Letters were the only contact with the outside and helped you feel you still belonged to the real world.

Mom sent airmail letters – the ones with an imprinted flag and stripes around them. Everybody else used plain white envelopes, except Devyn who sent window envelopes intended to mail bills since he didn't have money. He snagged them from his dad's office desk and stole the stamps from a drawer. Devyn wrote my address to the side of the little window and folded the letter so you couldn't see anything but paper.

He said, "Not bragging, but Stormy and I made love. Incredible to touch her and be touched. I've been floating down the school halls. Now I understand why you are so deeply in love with Dove. Somehow, making love changes you. Before I thought you were nuts to go to Vietnam, but I'm now so committed to her that if she wanted me to join the army or go on a church mission, I would."

I wrote him, "Take my advice since I'm not using it. Whatever you do, don't enlist. Go on a mission for the Mormons if you have to but don't come here – it's a totally fucked-up war."

Mama wrote that my younger sister, Hetty, was pregnant by a guy out of high school. They planned to get married when she graduated at the end of May. His family was religious and they went to the Assembly of God church that Cherry's parents had joined. Momma didn't sound too thrilled with Hetty's choice.

A day later, relief at last! Excited to get one from Dove, I sniffed her letter, but there was no perfume. Perhaps it lost the fragrance on the long trip to the Mekong Delta. It was cryptic:

Rowdy,

I'm going to help Alayna in Africa on her mission. I'm sorry. I won't write anymore.

Best of luck,

Dove

Stunned and confused, I stood there, staring at the letter. Once I felt the ground again, I rushed to the company clerk's office. Luckily, Bill was still working.

As I walked in, Bill jumped up, coming around the desk with his hand out. "Hey, fish sticks! Great to see you! Man, you're alive and kicking!" Bill slapped me on the back and started to give me a he-man hug, but stopped when he saw the look on my face. "Que Pasa, what's up?"

My lips twisted with anxiety and pain. "Good to see you too, but I have a family emergency. Is there any way I can place a call home?" A call to the States was expensive and cumbersome – after each exchange, a guy had to say, "Over."

Bill had a memory like an elephant, remembering damn near everything about everyone he'd ever worked with. He checked the time. "You think there's anyone awake at four-thirty in the morning on a Saturday in Delta, Colorado?"

My face fell. "No. Dang! Oh, man…."

Bill wanted to know what was going on so I handed him the letter.

"This ain't good. This is a Dear John letter without the dear in it." Bill put his hand on my shoulder.

Speechless, I stared at the letter. I hadn't put it together it was a Dear John letter. My heart started pounding. I was under heavy fire with a napalm bombardment blasting my hot face.

Bill patted me on the back. "Listen, come back in four hours after chow and a rest. You're barely back from a mission, and you're exhausted. I'll meet you here and put through a call." He walked around his desk and fumbled around. "Who you going to call?"

"I'll try Dove's home and dorm room and if she's not there, I'll call my best friend, Devyn – he'll tell me what's going on."

Bill handed me some little white pills, "Take one of these. It'll calm your nerves."

I staggered back to the barracks and lay on my bunk. I read and re-read Dove's letter, trying to imagine what happened. *Why did she break it off with me? What is going on?* My brain ran in circles.

I found one of the little white pills Bill gave me. It had a tiny heart cut out from its center – Valium. I swallowed one.

My imagination ran wild. *Did Dove hook up with some guy? Is she quitting college? Is she seeing Gabe Falcon for his money? Why would she be going to Africa? Jeez, weird shit.* My thoughts were jumbled but the little pill started to help, making me less jittery. No appetite, and couldn't keep it down if I tried. I debated taking another of Bill's little pills with the tiny heart cut out from the middle.

Fit my feelings to the T.

Late May 1969

35. Over

Back at Bill's office hours later, I had no luck connecting with Dove's home or her dorm room. It rang and rang without an answer. I called Devyn and his mother answered.

She was excited. "We miss you! Oh, so much has happened around here. Let Devyn tell you." I heard Mrs. McDowell calling my best friend.

"Wow! It's great to hear your voice!" It was the first time we had talked since I went to Vietnam. I explained the structure of saying "Over" each time he finished speaking. I let Devyn settle down by answering a few questions.

"Yeah, I've been killing lots of gooks. They're everywhere. When I get back, I'll tell you about it. Over."

Devyn asked, "You heard from Big Owl? I haven't heard a thing. Over."

"No, last I heard he was driving a transport truck from DaNang. Over." I cut him off, "Listen, Devyn, you have to tell me what is going on with Dove. Over."

The line went silent. "You there? Over."

"Yeah, where to start? Over."

He gathered his thoughts. Devyn said he didn't think Dove was headed for Africa, rather something was going on between her and Gabe, maybe something to do with the mortgage on the sawmill. His theory was that Mr. Falcon had offered her a small fortune, maybe inheritance rights if she took care of Gabe. "Hell if I know, but that family has problems. Over."

I was too shocked to speak. If we had the time to discuss, it would have taken hours to comprehend, but the overseas line was limited to fifteen minutes, max. I asked, "Why would she need to take care of Gabe?"

Bill waved at me to get off and the line went dead.

Laying the phone on the desk, bubbles came from my gut to float around my brain as if I had drank a pint of Everclear grain alcohol when we were at Hart's Basin dancing around the fire in the rain when me and Big Owl had decided to join the Army, and now here I was in Vietnam and stuck while the love of my life was with this slimy slug of a guy. *Now if that ain't a total pickle?* It was all too damn crazy.

I asked Bill, "How can I get a leave home?"

Surprised, Bill shook his head, no. "When your tour is done, you get a leave home before your next assignment, that's it."

"You don't understand, Bill. I got a crisis. I need to get home."

"Army won't see it that way. Nobody gets a leave until their tour is complete. I've seen guys not get a leave even when one of their parents or a wife was dying or dead. They've cut 'em off completely because those anti-war protestors are marching on Washington and servicemen are being harassed – they spit on us and call us baby killers. Too many guys don't come back – they run to Canada – so now there ain't no way to get a leave. Not gonna happen."

Several nights later, the Viet Cong rocketed the barracks next to mine. It penetrated the roof, exploding before it hit the floor. Four men were instantly killed. The next morning, me and other gunners walked around its Swiss cheese remains. The bodies had been removed but not the bloody fluids and parts they left behind.

Made me want to throw up.

I helped move shattered timbers and clean up body parts. Everyone hated this gory detail and wondered why these guys instead of our bunker? My former dreams of being a heroic warrior felt like a comic book superhero – it ain't real.

At lights out, after smoking grass and taking one of Bill's little pills with the heart cut out of the middle, I fell into an exhausted sleep. I came slightly awake when the U.S. artillery started up and I listened in a state of fading consciousness. The big guns were a few hundred feet from my barracks. They fired incessantly. No one was sure what they shot at, maybe an enemy position, saving some platoon's asses. They got a call on the radio from a higher-up who gave coordinates on a map, then blasted away, one round after another, hour after hour, day and night.

In this semi-aware state, I flashed on Dove being with Gabe. It hit me – going to church didn't make you a Christian any more than standing in a garage made you a car.

I wondered if maybe I should join the other guys doing the cute Vietnamese whores who asked, "You want Boom-Boom? Me fuck and suck you good, GI." Up to the time of her Dear John letter, I could not imagine sampling one. But now, it would sure feel good to hold a woman in my arms even if I had to pay for it.

My mind drifted to more immediate concerns. I could tell how close an incoming rocket or mortar was by how quickly debris hit roofs. If it was close, you heard dirt and gravel on the tin roof – it made a sound like a typewriter. An outgoing round made a loud, crisp bang, like the sharp crack of a rifle shot but a whole lot louder.

I wondered about the men of the artillery battery who loaded and fired, loaded and fired; worker ants feeding great, explosive machines. They must be deaf. Blast after blast created invisible shock waves penetrating every niche and cranny – piercing walls and pillows smashed to your ears. Compression waves rippled in a shallow stream, tumbling over stones, wearing me down until my surface was smooth.

The sound from an incoming rocket or mortar shell was like no other. Some nights I heard the high-pitched whistle of a rocket as it flew overhead, but in-coming mortars made little or no sound during flight. Whether from a mortar shell or a rocket, the closer it fell, the louder the detonation. Each type caused a distinct sound – mortars created a dull blast as if coming from deep inside a pit of mud. When it hit closer, it left an impressionable crushing thud. The first man awake shouted, "Incoming! Incoming!" Then sirens wailed and thousands scampered to the safety of the nearest bunker.

A dim light from the company light pole flickered through screened windows and on the guys sacked out. I tried to sleep but had an ear exposed like a watchdog with one eye open. I imagined the VC lighting fuses. They were three or four of them, jumping up and down and chuckling with excitement in the dark night.

Suddenly wide awake, I couldn't move. It was an odd paralysis. I was conscious but unable to speak. I heard a quiet, but urgent voice, "Incoming."

I tried to sit up, but could only lift my head.

This dark, shadowy figure stood at the foot of my bed. We woke a guy by pulling on his toe because men were allowed to sleep with a weapon. You didn't want to shake someone's shoulder because he could startle and shoot or cut you. This strange figure grabbed my toe, saying with a soft intensity, "Incoming, incoming."

I didn't get it – why was the guy so quiet? Normally, if there was enemy fire, a man hollered, "INCOMING!"

The figure pulled on my big toe again. It was a hard pull and the voice whispered forcefully, "Incoming."

My rigid body was still frozen, but I tilted my head in the voice's direction. I heard again, "Incoming." I moved my neck to scan the barracks, but there was no one there. In the half-darkness, I saw from one end of the open hall to the other. All was clear, no one in sight.

There was a thud as clear and distinct as a dinner bell. It was the muffled sound of a mortar hitting dirt. I got my body to move and shot up in bed, "Incoming!" I shouted louder, "Incoming!"

Men stirred and rose from their bunks, shuffling. Someone swore, "God damn it, not another attack!" They got up and grabbed lawn chairs and cigarettes. I snagged a lounger because a guy might have to sleep in the bunker; otherwise, you were on the pallet-covered floor. Rats and mice lived between the pallet boards and they attracted snakes. Vietnam has many poisonous ones that made you shudder. I looked for the shadowy figure but there was nothing.

Men got outside into the warm humid air. Two dozen all-but-naked troops walked toward our bunker. Oddly, the artillery guns next door momentarily stopped firing. There were no explosions. "Hell, there's no incoming!" Someone shouted in frustration. It was a false alarm.

"Who called it anyway?" They grumbled and started back to the barracks.

I kept my embarrassed mouth shut. Those who had waited on the stairs were already hitting their bunks. I felt like a fool. It must have been a dream, but it was so damn real.

BOOM... BOOM... BOOM! It was 80mm mortars walking straight at us. Mortars walked in like the crushing feet of marching giants. Seldom were the first rounds on target. Usually, they were too short, landing on the outer grounds.

Not tonight.

A siren wailed, and thud, the mortars hit closer, almost on us. Usually, we counted 1001, 1002, 1003, and 1004 to figure out how near incoming rounds were by how long it took the falling debris to come down. There was no time to count because shrapnel and debris immediately rained down on our tin roof and our heads. Wood splintered as a mortar hit the far end of our barracks.

Everyone quickly sprinted to the bunker. Inside, my eyes hurt from the naked bulb's bright light. Men scrambled to find places to sit or sleep, either on a bench or in a lawn chair.

We heard shrapnel puncturing barracks and vehicles. Rocks fell and dirt clods banged or bounced off the bunker roof. More mortars shredded things. Shattered earth broke apart and pieces hurled up into the air at various heights. Chunks of rubble rained down in thumps and plops. We heard the sound of splintering wood and ripping tin.

I stretched out on the lounger in an empty corner. Taking a deep breath, I wondered what had happened. Who pulled my toe? Who whispered incoming? Was it a dream or paranoia?

Under the single light bulb overhead, I saw dirt falling between the planks of the hard-packed bunker ceiling. One of my hooch mates said, "Close call, huh, Rowdy?" It was Garett. He was short, meaning he had twenty days before he shipped out. May he live so long.

"Yeah, it was."

"You called it – wasn't it you? I recognized your voice." He lit a cigarette.

"Yeah, I heard something. Didn't you?"

"No. I didn't hear a damn thing and I was wide awake."

"Garett, did you see anybody? Did you notice someone walking around?"

"I didn't see a thing and I didn't hear a ffin' thing either. It was quiet for a change."

"You didn't see a dark tall guy walking around? He grabbed my toe and shook it hard. He's the one called it, not me."

"There was nobody, Rowdy. I heard your voice, nothing else."

Someone butted in, "Hey, you saying you saw a ghost?"

Everybody laughed.

"I'm telling ya, I saw this dark fellow but I couldn't tell for sure – could have been a woman with long hair – had a hood. He stood at the foot of my bunk. Whoever it was, called it, not me. I heard it plain as day."

Another voice from across the bunker chimed in. I couldn't make out who it was since he wore sunglasses. "Sounds like you saw The Man."

"What do you mean?"

"Not everyone sees him but maybe you did. Only drowning men can see him!"

"Drowning men? Doesn't make any sense. I wasn't drowning." I stared at Mr. Sunglasses. The guy rolled on his side, turning away.

"It means what it's supposed to, The Man up in the sky paid you a visit. Or it don't mean nothing. What do I know? I heard it in a song called *Suzanne*, only drowning men can see him."

"Did you see someone at the foot of my bunk tonight?"

"Not sure who or what you saw, Bud," said Sunglasses.

"A tall dark man in a hood woke me up, pulling on my toe and said, 'Incoming.'"

"Yeah, well, it's clear nobody else saw your phantom. Let's give it a rest, huh? I wanna get some sleep, Pal."

"Okay, forget it." My fellow bunkmates were settling down for what little remained of the night.

The next morning, we were allowed out of the bunker. We were stunned. Our barracks was gone – totally destroyed. A piece of shrapnel the size of a walnut had shattered a two-by-four where my bunk once sat. What would that do to a guy's skull?

I was freaked. *Who was at the foot of my bunk?* So weird. I kept my mouth shut. *I have no reason to be alive but The Man woke me and saved us all.*

Up in the sky on a new mission, I wondered how it would feel to unhook my monkey strap and step off the chopper into the sky. But me and Devyn had promised each other at Hart's Basin that we would never kill ourselves over a woman. I flipped between hating Dove as much as I loved her. She had pushed me into signing up. I could have gone Air Force or Navy, but she insisted on the Army. I did it so she would love me.

My beliefs about her had been phantoms.

36. Pickle Farts

I paced the grounds of the Dong Tam Base after the latest mission. I was up all night. Good thing Bill gave me those pills; otherwise, I might have used the jungle gun on myself. I had snagged it when working in the supply depot.

It was a monster shotgun. The Army called it the M79 grenade launcher. It fired a newly minted shell designed for jungle warfare. The round was the size of a coffee mug and was filled with steel shot. You loaded it like a break-open shotgun. The shotgun was two feet long and kicked like a pissed-off mule. You had to stand a certain way with your legs spread wide from front to back to keep from being knocked down. You leaned into it and fired from the crotch of your elbow and not from the shoulder. Firing it from the shoulder could snap your collarbone or jerk your shoulder from its socket. I considered shooting the whole nasty base up and offing myself. It wouldn't be fair because the grunts don't want to be there any more than me.

The next days were a blur. I couldn't sleep and didn't rest although I was exhausted. Because I couldn't sleep, I walked around at night with the M79, hoping some Vietnamese sapper would break through the wire. I was about as useful as anal taste buds.

The Viet Cong secretely packed mortars to the outskirts of the base and set up mortar tubes. Waiting until after ten PM when lights were off, they landed two or three before the siren went off. The guards and MPs ran around waking everyone to go to a bunker.

I begged Bill for more of the white pills with the cut-out heart. When mortars came in, I didn't bother going to the bunkers, instead, I headed to the tarmac where somebody always smoking weed. Helicopters were the Viet Cong's favorite target. Watching the fireworks, I figured if I was hit, so what? Dove was gone. My reason for being in Vietnam had vaporized and I was stuck in this mad war.

The sweet-smelling herb was better than cigarettes – at least it relaxed me a little – almost like those white pills with the heart cut from the middle.

Like my own heart.

Empty.

The Viet Cong targeted the flight line along with the rows of barracks and other military buildings, airplane hangars, and supply sheds. A single mortar shell hit nearby the one I was in, taking out several helicopters although each one has a four-foot-high sandbag wall on three sides. Me and the other door gunner just laughed. "Look at those fireworks." We lit another joint.

Because I couldn't sleep, I volunteered to guard the base at one of the towers. Other times, I squatted inside a big pipe on the ground. I watched with red blurry eyes, my heart cracking and tearing a little with each passing hour.

I kept trying to call Dove and again asked Bill about a leave home. "Isn't there some way? You've got to help me?"

Bill shook his head. "I wish I could. Nixon is turning the war over to the ARVN. The 9th Infantry Division is pulling out next month. We've lost more than a dozen men from our company because of the anti-war protests back home. Too many deserters. There's this former Navy man, John Kerry, who started an organization called The Vietnam Veterans Against the War. As soon as a serviceman gets home on leave, they're on him. They work him until the moment he's back on a plane, trying to get him to desert." Bill ruefully shook his head. "Only three ways you can get a ticket home."

"What?"

Snorting, Bill said, "Well hell, the obvious one is in a black rubber bag, or two, if you're wounded badly enough that they can't patch you up here or in Japan, and they have to send you to the States. But the reality is our 3rd Surgical Hospital has a hundred beds and is a world-class facility. Guys can stay there for up to forty-five days because it's quicker to get you back into action. No point in shooting yourself in the foot because you'd be limping back into the field. It means a guy has got to be so badly wounded they have no choice but to ship you home."

"Similar to the book, *Johnny Got Your Gun*?"

Bill nodded.

"You said three, what's the last one?"

"Pickle farts, man, that's not for you. I don't even want to tell you about it."

"Come on Bill, I'm desperate."

"Don't ask me to help you, but if you extend for another tour in 'Nam, they'll give you a thirty-day leave home. They figure if you want to stay here and kill communists, you ain't gonna desert."

"Is it on top of the one-year combat obligation or ten months from now that I'd get released?"

"On top of it. Let's see," Bill thought, "You arrived here at the end of January this year, so it would be next year late in January 1970 plus another ten months, so you'd be done with your Vietnam combat obligation around the first of October 1970."

"After that, what happens?"

"You still have to finish your contractual obligation. You enlisted for three years. Who knows, you might get stateside, you might get Germany, South Korea, or Japan. They might change the rules and you could end up back here."

"But for sure, I'd be in Vietnam until the October of 1970?"

"Yep, and you won't get any more leaves, except a three to five-day pass for R&R. I don't recommend you extend, not unless you love this shit."

If I extended, I'd be in combat for an additional ten months beyond this tour. Through the foggy haze of exhaustion, I couldn't figure it out. Should I extend so I could get home to talk with Dove, or fight here until next January? Damn Vets Against the War. They're the ones screwing me.

Phoning the Knutson home time after time, I finally caught Stormy. Initially, she said Dove was going to Africa to help Alayna, but when I probed, she admitted Dove was helping Gabe because he had been badly injured while working at their sawmill, in fact he had been paralyzed from the waist down. "She doesn't love him, but they have a lot of money. Over."

Oh, shit. Images ran through my ragged brain. I was deeply disappointed that Dove didn't keep her promise to me. Losing respect for her, something clicked inside, and I stopped caring; I didn't care she dumped my ass, I didn't care about nothing. Couldn't.

As Bill said, "Pickle farts."

37. You Pay?

A few days later, I went back to talk with Bill. After telling him about the strange experience with the phantom pulling my toe, I was adamant, "I need to go home. Bill, I need to get things straightened out."

"Believe, me if there was any way, I'd send you, me, and the rest of the 162nd Helicopter Assault Company to Hawaii with the 9th Infantry Division." He snorted. "Can you imagine – beaches and Polynesian girls?"

I didn't see the humor.

"Anyway, the 3rd Surgical Hospital is also pulling out soon. But nobody is going home from *any* helicopter company in Vietnam unless your tour is done or you're in a black plastic bag. The helicopter companies will be flying the ARVN until the war is over no matter how many years and how many American lives are lost."

"Of all the luck! I'd have been better off as a grunt."

"Yep – you'd be heading to Hawaii in August. The door gunners and pilots are getting screwed."

Bill reached into his desk drawer. "I've been saving this for you." He wrote on the form. "The eagle shits today – so take this three-day pass and catch a chopper to Saigon. Get drunk, get a great massage, and bury your sorrows between a girl's legs."

He handed the pass to me. "Trust me, put Willy into wonderland and it'll make you feel a whole lot better. The best way to get over a girl is to get on top of a new one." Bill grinned. "So you heard about this soldier whose girlfriend wrote him a Dear John and she asked for her photograph back?"

I shook my head no.

"The guy asked all his buddies for any unwanted photos of women. He sent a half dozen to his ex with a note, 'I regret that I don't remember which one you are. Please keep yours and return the others.'"

"Ha, Ha." I mentally wrestled with taking the three-day pass. I had never paid for sex and had vowed fidelity to Dove. But she had dumped me, no doubt about it. Dove wrote it, Devyn confirmed it, and Stormy corroborated it. I owed her nothing but a heartache. Maybe she didn't fake orgasms but she had faked our relationship.

Bill said, "You should send her a card, 'I'm so miserable without you it's almost like you're here.'"

Hard not to laugh. I decided to take the pass and look around Saigon. This was my first opportunity in five months to see any part of Vietnam other than Dong Tam and the fields of war. Before I left, Bill said, "What is the difference between a Vietnamese Ho and a Vietnamese mosquito?"

I shrugged.

Bill said, "The mosquito will stop sucking after you slap it."

I laughed. "Guy, I sure miss working with you. In more ways than you can imagine."

Surprise, surprise, there was a steam and cream place near the Saigon heliport. It was a series of tin, mud, and straw hooches strung along the road. Despite strong encouragement from a Vietnamese hawker, I had trouble going in.

"G.I. need a good massage? My girls take good care of you, you come out very happy, only ten dolla."

Continuing down the road, I kept an eye on the fellow. The pimp ran and stepped in front to stop me. "Please friend; tell you what, I got new, young girl today. Virgin – you first one. I make you deal. You see her and you not happy at end, you no pay. I take risk. You not happy, it free."

The idea of being with a virgin grabbed my imagination. If true, I wouldn't worry about catching anything. The Army had all kinds of inventive ways of not giving the soldiers the truth. They claimed the Vietnamese sex workers had black syphilis so incurable, unlucky men were shipped to an island where they spent the rest of their short lives with horrible sores all over their bodies. Like the idea we're winning the war, black syphilis was made up. They also claimed the hos were Viet Cong with razor blades inside their fur tacos so when a GI slipped inside her sleeve, it ripped a guy's cave dweller to shreds.

I remembered a joke Bill told, "When I was turned sixteen, my uncle said, 'Bill, someday you're gonna meet a girl who is so right and perfect you're not even going to haggle over the price.'" I decided that I may as well have some fun.

She was a darling peasant girl with little nipples capping a palm full of cams. It was hard to tell how old she was. I hesitated, then thought, *Would I accomplish anything by passing her by? The pimp outside would offer her to the next serviceman who'd be more than happy to take her virginity. Why not treat her to a real date with gentle and erotic seduction?*

Trembling, she showed her anxiety as I slid her blouse from her shoulders. Gently smiling, I knelt and carefully pulled her jeans and panties down her ankles. She kicked her peasant sandals off and stood with bare feet on the dirty floor.

I stepped back to admire her. She was petite and developing a cup's worth of creamers. As the guys said, "More than a mouthful is wasted." There was a wisp of pubic hair. She was afraid and sad about what she was about to do and started weeping.

Tears are poison to a man's logic. I felt guilty. *Is she just a child?* Asian girls are late to mature. One of the gunners told me about hooking up with a twenty-year-old with only a tuff of coochie hair who was flat as an ironing board.

Certainly, if tears were an indicator, she was a virgin. I suspected she was too young by Western standards. But there was only one standard in Vietnam – survival. Selling a daughter to pay off the Viet Cong or the South Vietnamese police was common.

I'd be ever so gentle and kind. If she was a virgin as advertised, I'd show her how to make love within the limits of my experience. I pulled her to the bed and invited her to lie down beside me.

Drying her tears with a finger, I tried to talk with her, but she didn't know English. Having learned a little Vietnamese from the guys in prep for my Saigon leave, I said, "Bạn đang đẹp, you are beautiful." And she truly was. Slender, perfect heart-shaped face, brown innocent eyes, and black hair down to her butt.

Hearing her native tongue, she brightened and snuggled to me. "Tôi thích bạn, G.I.;" Meaning, 'I like you, G.I.'

I took her long black mane and wrapped her hair around my neck, enveloping us inside its silk.

Hesitantly, she kissed me softly on the lips.

Tears of sadness, thankfulness, and guilt rolled down my cheeks. My thoughts needed soothing.

She touched my face with a slender hand. It was so fragile a fairy could dance on the tips of her fingers. Everything about her was delicate and delightful.

She pressed warm breasts to my chest. No longer were we American or Vietnamese, rather, we were one in the silent hands of a loving energy field. There was no war raging outside this space. The world disappeared as we melted in a soft embrace. She didn't know what to do and I happily taught her. She was scared to put her mouth around my member, but after licking her until she orgasmed, I gently encouraged her.

Gradually, she got into it. "Tanks."

"My pleasure."

When it was over, she said, "Me good fuck, G.I.? You pay?"

Snapping back to the world, I shook my head and tipped her three bucks, making her smile. I paid the pimp his ten-dollar fee and marched down the street to the center of Saigon. The young girl's fidelity would run off to the next soldier and she'd forget me, but I would never forget her. She'd live in my memory as the second girl I had made love with. Bill was right – it was healing; I had been imagining Dove and pounding the pud far too long. And I needed healing in a bad way.

Another GI was walking from the heliport to Saigon, and we hooked up for protection and company. He said, "Let's go to Sin City. It's near the central area. They have hookers and the MPs control who goes in. American docs check them for VD and it's the safest place to have sex."

I walked with him. "I just got laid and it was great. She was a virgin."

"Ha, Ha, Ha!" The grunt said, "Yeah, right. The young ones all claim they're virgins. I banged this little sister three different times. Every time I did her, they sold her as a virgin and she played the part convincingly. Had the crying act down tight like she was ashamed to be doing this." He caught my eyes. "Didn't bother me none. They think we all look alike and she didn't recognize me. I kept going back because she was tight and had the innocent virgin act down. She acted as if it hurt each time. Pretty funny if you think about it. We're a paycheck. Ain't nothing to it."

My disappointment was palatable. "I need to get something to drink and eat. I want a big steak and potatoes, or maybe a lobster. Anything to get the taste of greasy Army food out of my mouth."

We parted ways near a hotel sporting a batch of women in tight pants or short skirts who called out, "Boom, boom G.I.? I fuck you good. Me the best. I make you come many times."

Finding a decent-looking French restaurant, I sat down to my first real meal since leaving the States. Pulling a stack of letters from my back pocket, I re-read the last weeks of Dove's letters. I didn't see it coming. They were sweet and loving. Each cited Bible verses and romantic poetry or song lyrics, and were signed, Love. A gap, a two-week gap. The abrupt letter saying she was going to Africa. Good luck, that was it.

God, it hurt. My dream of eternal love and marriage was lost – a vision she had created. Now there was emptiness.

I wondered at my experience with the young sex worker who made such wonderful love with me. Why did I respond so passionately? Is love nothing but hormonal gibberish? The result of endorphins and enkephalins released into my bloodstream? What the hell is love? How to tell it from lust? How to tell fact from fiction, reality from fantasy? Will I be man enough to face the darkness of truth? Once I had imagined myself an emissary of light, but I was an imposter, a pretender. The oppressive humidity drowned out clear thinking.

Outside the café window, I watched crowds of rural Vietnamese who came to the city to escape the war. They hocked all kinds of things, including drugs and sex. But what could one man do? Could I rescue all the peasant girls sold into prostitution? Would it make any difference if I refused to partake of their lovely young bodies? Even more important, could I refuse to fire my M60? I knew the answer. "No, I must protect the men and the ship."

Given Dove's abdication to become my wife, I was only in Vietnam because it was impossible to escape.

I was in prison.

I read about a chemical war agent supplied by the Soviets called yellow rain. The North Vietnamese dropped the poison on the Hmong hill tribes of Laos because they were anti-communist. Refugees described attacks by low-flying aircraft in which a yellow, oily liquid was dropped on them. It caused seizures, blindness, and strange bleeding.

It pissed me off – this is such an unnecessary war. Atrocities on both sides resulted from the strategy of attrition. American papers were filled with the Mai Lai massacre trials – as if Mai Lai was the only one. If the media knew how many peasants the Viet Cong, NVA, and ARVN had wiped out…

After three days, two more girls, and some great meals, I returned to Dong Tam. Bewilderment and rage danced among my tears. Innocence lost, I drifted past the edge of logic and like the military commanders, I decided that killing – killing them all was the only way to bring peace.

38. Slicker Than Shit

Because our bunkhouse had been destroyed, the gunners were moved to a barracks even closer to the artillery and few of us slept. I thought about the shadowy figure who woke me the night our barracks were destroyed. What did the guy with sunglasses mean about drowning and seeing The Man? It was too damn weird.

I received a letter from Devyn, talking about the Falcon's offer to the woman I wanted. "You might have a slim chance with Dove, but hell, could you ever trust her again? I imagine she's giving Gabe a show even though he can't get it up since he was paralyzed up at their mill about three months back. I understand Mr. Falcon initially offered her just a job and then he turned it into inheritance rights if she would marry his boy. That's when she wrote you the letter."

The image sickened me. She was worse than a prostitute because she pretended to be a good Mormon.

Our company patch was a square with a flying vulture holding a helicopter. The motto on the Vulture patch was "STS" for "Set the Standard." Most say STS meant "Slicker Than Shit" because we quickly picked up and deliver troops – whoosh, we were gone!

Going into a hot LZ, I got so excited I couldn't remember what happened. It was a blur. Occasionally, I experienced combat in slow motion as if I was underwater and I remembered every detail with crystal clarity.

Approaching another pickup zone, we dropped to a thousand feet in elevation and I didn't know where we were. Huey transport helicopters were everywhere like great flocks of Canadian geese. We were the number one target for enemy fire.

Taking out a bird costs the U.S. a million dollars and kills men. We were easy targets while landing because we slowed to a stop and hovered. It was during these moments we took the most hits.

Suddenly, a bullet punched through the left side and mushroomed a grunt's head. It pissed off the crew chief and he unloaded a thousand rounds into the tree lines. All the way back to Dong Tam whenever he saw anyone working in the rice paddies below, he tried to kill him. I mentally cringed in the recesses of my thoughts.

We were out ten to twelve hours a day six or seven days a week and flew five to twelve missions a day. It took two-hundred-fifty hours to get flight wings. I had earned mine in a little over a month. We flew sixty miles an hour in the monsoon rain and, at the next LZ hit the ground so hard that the M60 ammo can slammed into me, cutting my leg in the same place the shrapnel had hit. Hurt like hell but I was alive. It started bleeding and throbbing. I'd have to find a medic or go to the hospital once I got back.

An infantry squad ran at my open door while a rain of gunfire followed them from the tree line. I fired back. Unfortunately, the last guy lost the side of his face to an AK round. The body twitched on the ground as his squad members froze in horror.

I jumped off, dragged the body to the chopper and tossed it onto the floor. We were supposed to drop these guys off at another LZ, but due to this grunt's death, we flew back to base. His squad members stared blank-eyed, saying nothing. A pool of blood formed around my feet.

The crew chief said, "Ain't no discharge from this shit until your tour is done."

I was happy my leg was bleeding because I got a couple of hours off to get patched up. But as soon as I left the hospital, they put me back onto another helicopter.

We picked up a load of South Vietnamese. As we slowed to land at the next LZ, all the ARVN bailed off my side. The resulting imbalance caused the ship to rock and tilt back and forth. I was thrown out and rolled up in time to see the blades slam into the ground, pounding until the engine died. My head smacked the ground and I went black.

I saw my grandmother. She asked if I was okay and offered me a cup of hot chocolate but for some reason, I couldn't get ahold of the cup. I really wanted that hot chocolate.

When I regained consciousness, I grabbed my M60 and set up to defend the helicopter but there was no incoming fire. I felt guilty because I had been told to shoot ARVNs in the back if they tried to jump off one side before we touched down.

Rescue ships came in using a left formation as a huge red sun climbed the eastern horizon. It was a hot and muggy day. When the slicks touched down, mud-covered, torn-up grunts and my bloody helicopter crew slung the dead and wounded into the ships. Boarding the ships, men patted each other on the back. Some men smelled like hell, having accidently shit or pissed their pants in terror during the holocaust. It was the body's way of preparing to run for its life.

The last to load up, me and my crew chief, Jon, climbed aboard, exhausted. Lifeless bodies lay splattered on the aluminum floor while others lay in a morphine-induced stupor. Guys grinned as humans do when we cheat death. The crew chief radioed the AC, "Loaded and clear." Surprisingly, the crew chief and gunner handed us oranges and water.

Jesus, how do you describe the taste of an orange after surviving a crash? It was magic, a gift of life. Ten minutes of combat was more life than most people live.

We lifted off. At fifteen hundred feet, they gave us cigarettes.

I lit up, inhaling as if I came up from a deep pond of stale, stinking water. Behind my dark sunglasses, tears formed and ran down my cheeks...it was too much of a relief. Catching Jon's eyes, I saw fluid rolling down his face. We pretended it was the smoke. I didn't bother to wipe it off. It meant I was alive.

I was taken back to the base hospital because my calf had started bleeding again due to the crash. I was dizzy and had a hell of a headache.

Dr. Valk checked me and said I had a mild concussion. "I don't want to keep seeing you here, you understand, even with a minor flesh wound."

I tried to laugh. "I'd rather see you rather than the inside of a black plastic bag."

She didn't laugh.

I was released to the bunkhouse since the day was winding down. One of the guys said, "Hey, you can apply for a purple heart for both your calf and the concussion. Every injury counts."

I shrugged. What was the point of receiving a Purple Heart?

I kept thinking of Dove. *Why? Why? Why?* I couldn't believe that she had hooked up with Gabe. I knew the answer but was dumbfounded. Her logic was as wacked as someone hit by a helicopter blade. How could she go from an intelligent, wise, and compassionate woman to an unstable female who lied to herself and me? Jody had her on his lap – using fear and greed to trick her. *If I could only get home and talk some sense into her. We don't need a lot of money to be happy if we loved one another.*

June 1969

39. The Bodhi Tree

After the destruction of our bunker in Dong Tam, things really heated up. Knowing of President Nixon's plan to pull our troops out, the VC wanted to give the American infantry a send-off party with the most causalities possible. We started searching a section of the delta based on intelligence that the North Vietnamese Army and the Viet Cong were planning a huge offensive.

On the edge of the canal there was a giant Bodhi tree with dozens of branches reaching to the ground where they became stabilizing roots. Villagers said this sacred fig tree was a thousand years old; it was a hundred feet high and its canopy spread three hundred feet across. There were clusters of wild orchids scattered among its many branches.

It was said that Siddhartha Gautama meditated under such a Bodhi fig tree. The tree symbolizes death, awakening, and suffering with dignity. It was liberation from materialism to choose the right way of living. The Bodhi tree's leaves wiggle even when the air is still and the villagers attribute this movement to devas or tiny fairies jumping and playing on the leaves.

An old papasan's hutch was under the ancient fig tree. He had mats, pottery, kitchen tools, and other stuff in a cave he had dug among the roots of the Bodhi tree. Its trunk was a series of twisted and gnarled roots at least twelve feet in diameter. He slept under a thatched straw porch that kept rain out. A footpath ran along the canal under the huge fig tree's canopy to the village.

Out of respect, the flight group always landed on the other side of the canal away from the sacred Bodhi tree and we never went into the village. But one day, after eating lunch, curiosity got the better of me. I had been in country for six months but my interaction with Vietnamese, other than trying to kill them, had been with Dong Tam base workers who smiled as they lied and cast hateful looks as they walked away – viewing all Americans with suspicion.

Army policy was never to go into a village unarmed, but I thought if I didn't have a weapon they wouldn't be scared. The higher-ups didn't want us going into villages except on a mission. If they must, grunts were to be wary and armed to the teeth because of the VC who had killed many unsuspecting soldiers. How to win the hearts and minds of the people 101.

My crew chief said, "Man, don't go over there. You never know what might happen."

I waved him off, leaving my .38 semi-auto on the aircraft. I casually walked across a narrow footbridge to visit the little old guy.

He was the perfect stereotype of an Asian wise man – a long thin white beard and scraggly white hair. Looking as if he were a hundred years old, his skin was thin with blue-veined arms. He was pale, wrinkled, and skinny. Using a stick for a cane, the old Papasan got up slowly, and smiling, bowed to me.

I dipped my head politely. We gestured, laughed, and tried to communicate. Papasan had white rice wine he offered in trade for cigarettes. I handed him a smoke and tried a sip of the wine. It was stronger than Japanese Sake, and I choked it down. "Wow!"

We laughed.

I learned the old man was called Khôn Ngoan, which means wisdom.

Seeing us make motions with our hands and laugh, the village children watched from a distance. I hadn't expected to be feared by them but couldn't blame them since there was so much corruption and brutality on both sides. If the peasants supported the U.S., the Viet Cong or NVA came after them. If they supported the communists, the ARVN, Vietnamese police, Army, or Marines burned their village. It was a no-win situation.

On another afternoon, I walked over to visit the old fellow, and children tiptoed from the village to the giant Bodhi tree. Previously, when helicopters landed on the canal berm, they closed their doors. This was a primitive place – there was no electricity, telephone lines, or radios. The paths were hard-packed mud and the shacks had dry grass-thatched roofs. They'd go up in a bonfire if someone lit a match. A narrow dirt road ran past a small mud-brick school into the jungle. Chickens clucked and walked around and there were penned hogs. Farmers went about their business of growing things. If there was a war going on, these people weren't in its way and wanted no part of it.

The kids were more curious or foolish than the adults. They were the first sign of life from the village. Because of me and Khôn Ngoan's ongoing laughter, they sensed we meant no harm. As soon as the kids got a nod from grandfather, they ran and surrounded the Americans at their helicopters. Begging for handouts, there was much joy.

It took the guys from the war for a few precious minutes.

40. Raucous

Door gunners got positive feedback the wilder we were. There was a door gunner everyone called Wildman Dan. He was on his fourth tour and had been shot down a dozen times but couldn't get enough of it. He said, "Ain't nothing the same at home after this. It's boring, but war is exciting."

The 162nd airborne would remain behind after the 9th Infantry pulled out. We'd fly the ARVN wherever they wanted. We called them "Ruff Puffs". We'd drop a platoon, let them wander around for a while, and after no contact, pick them back up, then drop them in another LZ.

One day we moved a platoon six times with no enemy contact. Seemed odd. Our guys always immediately got nailed out in the bush. We figured the Ruff Puffs avoided the Viet Cong or paid them off. South Vietnam didn't draft eighteen-year-olds; twenty-one was the minimum age for military service. I thought Vietnamization was a sure-fire formula for failure. The only thing that counted for Americans was getting back safe. Wild Dan said, "Stress is when you wake up screaming and you realize you haven't fallen asleep yet."

History shows that nations behave wisely once they exhausted all other alternatives. General Ewing obsessed about killing as many Viet Cong and NVA as possible before the 9th pulled out. We were sent on killing sprees, not because there was a military objective. Everyone knew America wouldn't win the war. We were pulling out and there was no point – the generals, not the grunts, should have been tried for war crimes.

I didn't follow U.S. or Vietnamese politics but my Dutch homeland had been occupied by the Nazi Germans. Here I felt more like a Nazi than an American soldier.

Bill Gordy said, "Politicians and baby diapers should be changed regularly for the same reason." The peasants were resigned to becoming communists because it was better to live under any one system instead of being attacked by both sides, and everyone knew Nixon was pulling the infantry back. It was a matter of time that the Americans would all be dead or gone.

Flying into another PZ, I wondered about death; it would be simple to unhook my strap and step off the aircraft into the sky. It didn't matter if I lived or died now that Dove had abandoned me. I felt almost as much distaste for her as I once felt love for her. She was the one who had pushed me to sign up. Who knows – I might not have been drafted. I did it to ensure she would love me, for the love of a woman. A song kept running through my head, "Blue, blue, my world is blue."

Every day we were in firefights. Pissed at Gabe, Mr. Falcon, and Mrs. Knutson, I imagined them as the dinks I mowed down. Why can't Dove see how foolish she's being? I had to get home to see for myself.

I tried not to dwell on her – bite down and shoot to kill. Shooting helped because while I fired, I went into another zone.

The Twilight Zone.

There was always a crew chief right there with me, shooting to kill. Being on a crew took the edge off my sense of isolation. Wild Dan grinned, gestured, shook a fist or acted like he was jacking off. We were twin robot door gunners programmed to go rat-tat-tat.

In between missions while fueling and loading more ammo, Dan cracked one joke after another. "If people from Poland are called Poles, why aren't people from Holland called Holes? If you take an Oriental person and spin him around, does he become disoriented? Don't tell my wife I'm a door gunner, she thinks I play the drums in a blues band."

Assault helicopter companies suffered one mental health casualty for every four physical ones. It came from knowing you had no control and there was nothing you could do to get control. As a result, door gunners had more psychological problems than pilots. Phantoms came to me again at night – strange illusions brought on from lack of sleep and seeing too much gore.

Devyn wrote,

Stormy says Dove is trying to escape from the Falcons. She can't stand Gabe, yet believes being with him is security for the family, and that it is God's will. I'm not so sure it's over for you and her, but it might be better if you let her go. Dove cloaks herself in religiosity and traps herself with it. If she's this moralistic, rigid, and illogical, who knows what she might do next? When you get to mourning, remember what she probably does to keep Gabe happy.

Stormy doesn't want to believe Gabe is her half brother. She hates him and Mr. Falcon. She also hates her mom and says she's nothing but a slut. Wants us to run away to California. She's fifteen, and they'd toss me in the slammer quicker than shit.

Gotta go. Tell me what's happening. Maybe I'll join the Army after a year at Colorado State. Wish we were going to college together. When will you get a leave home? Maybe you can come to Fort Collins and stay with me.

Dev

Pilots looked at me oddly because I came alive and laughed hysterically when I lit up the M60. I was accurate and fearless. They started calling me and Wild Dan the raucous brothers. The ACs talked about putting each of us in for a Bronze Star.

Although I was treated at the 3rd Hospital and they put it in my medical record, I didn't get a purple heart for my calf wounds, the head wound or for several concussions. We heard that most medals went to officers floating high above safely directing the helicopters below into the kill zone where they were shot up.

We dropped the ARVN into a hot PZ. Two men stumbled and went down spurting blood. Hearing their screams, I jumped off the helicopter and ran where they fell. I picked up the smallest man and tossed him across my left shoulder and heaved the other ARVN over my right shoulder, then hauled ass back. The Vietnamese were surprised. Americans seldom risked their lives for one of them.

Leaping into my gunner seat, I yelled, "GO-GO-GO. GET OUTTA HERE!" One of the wounded ARVN rangers screamed, thrashed, and died.

Wildman Dan shrugged as the AC pushed to get the bird into the sky; he put an index finger into his open mouth like he wanted to puke, then grinned and lit up his machine gun.

I laid suppressive fire into the trees as flashes popped. I felt slugs hitting the aircraft, hundreds of them, Thunk-Thunk-Thunk.

An ARVN ranger stood in the open chopper door with his gun on full automatic and unloaded thirty-round clips one after the other. Whoever said these scrawny guys wouldn't fight was wrong.

The floor was slick with blood. The dead man had emptied his bladder and bowel. Stunk to high heaven, similar to a slaughterhouse with screaming horses and raging adrenaline. The dead guy rolled around on the aluminum floor while his comrades hunched away. The Vietnamese were superstitious about the dead. Cleaning the bay would be a nightmare when we shut down. The weather was so hot and humid that burning shit woulda have been a better detail.

Bouncing down on the Dong Tam tarmac, we dropped the ARVNs off and medics got the dead man. Dan said, "There are three simple rules for making a smooth landing. Unfortunately, nobody knows what they are."

On inspection, it was a wonder we made it in because the main rotor blades took so many rounds. Momentum had kept us flying.   Dan said, "The rotor is just a big fan on top of the helicopter to keep us cool. When it stops, everyone sweats."

We were assigned another bird, and Dan yelled for me to join him. "We ain't cleaning this one. It ain't ours now."

Yes! A gift.

41. Precious Orchid

The sacred Bodhi tree became our regular stopover for breaks. As soon as the helicopters shut down, a small group of children appeared under the tree's ancient limbs. Running to the aircraft, they begged for treats and C rations. Old women with stained black teeth chewing betel nuts joined the kids, bringing fresh fruits and handmade items. We traded them C rations, trinkets, and cigarettes.

It was several days before I saw a young lady they called Cây Lan, which means orchid. Named after the beautiful flowers clustering among the ancient Bodhi tree's branches, Cây Lan was taller than the others by several inches. Her hair and skin were light and her eyes were a beautiful hazel-green color. A velvet blush touched her cheeks when she came in from the paddy. She held a fruit basket and lifted it to me. Her delicate features mesmerized me.

There was something familiar about her. A face I had seen before. Was it the virgin girl in the boom-boom shack? Or was I just a homesick boy who saw the eyes of my youngest sister in this Vietnamese girl? She had high cheekbones, a small chin, and lovely pink lips. I noticed pert nipples pressing against the coarse material of her dress.

As she leaned to set her basket down, the front of her top fell open and my heart leaped at seeing her sweet plums bounce, right there, within reach. I had to restrain myself; she had cantaloupes – larger and rounder than most Vietnamese women who lacked in that department.

Cây Lan looked up and caught my stare.

My face grew warm.

With a soft smile, she held out a fresh banana.

I could have eaten her fruit right then and there, no questions asked. My fiancé had just sent me a Dear John letter, and I was hurting.

Our eyes connected and the war stopped. I saw in her eyes curiosity, wonder, hope, and yet, anxiety. I realized she was French-Vietnamese and astonishingly gorgeous – the best of both worlds. She was slender and shapely with big round eyes and delicate features that included an elegant nose and exquisite ears.

She said, "Hal-lo, Xin chào. How yu?" She giggled lightly.

We stared at each other like two lonely puppies in a thunderstorm. Cây Lan became aware the other women watched and she stiffened.

I opened my hands, smiling warmly. "Xin chào, hello."

I bought all the fruit in her straw basket, giving her everything I had, including a cigarette lighter inscribed with, *When the power of love overcomes the love of power, there will be peace.*

The babysan (children) begged for C rations, especially canned cookies, crackers, and peanut butter. They wanted cigarettes to trade with other villages for more valuable things.

Each day afterwards, Cây Lan sold bananas and pineapples from a straw basket, but she always came to me first. If I couldn't buy all she had, she reluctantly moved on to the other guys. She often came back and gave me a little homemade item.

My crew chief gave me a hard time. "Gonna try to put your stinger in the little honeysuckle, are you?"

I waved him off.

Cây Lan kept an eye on one small boy, calling him Quy, which means precious. He played with other boys who threw rocks in the canal or tossed sticks for a skinny dog to chase.

I learned her family was the five-year-old boy who was her sister's child, and a skinny old lady who was her aunt. She had lost everyone else to the Viet Cong. She showed me a

Catholic cross around her neck. "Mẹ," meaning it was her mother's.

Cây Lan was a young fawn and I wanted to take her home to protect her. I had lovely fantasies at night and it helped the pain in my chest. Truly, she was precious.

During the next weeks, we landed nearly every day across from the ancient fig tree. We had lunch and waited for the next pickup. Realizing we meant no harm, villagers traded us pineapples, cooked rice, bananas, and figs.

The commanders strongly discouraged us from eating any native-prepared food because of poisoning danger, but what General Ewing didn't know wouldn't hurt him.

One of the gunner's jobs was to make sure we had a week's worth of C rations in the helicopter. One C ration was the size of a six-pack of soda. In those packs were a variety of canned foods. Now and then, I accidentally grabbed an old case of C rations from the Korean War or occasionally, even from World War Two. The new stuff was often traded on the black market and old C rations were sent in place. Even some the newer C rations were scary looking and smelled like a dog wouldn't touch – the canned eggs were green, black, and horrid smelling. Everyone hated getting ham and beans because of the smell.

The villagers and helicopter crews developed a brisk trade. We received fresh fruits, fried or steamed rice – sometimes with a bit of chicken or pork, and villagers got chocolate, cigarettes, C rations, and trinkets from the PX. The villagers started making special souvenirs for us and crew members picked up things at the PX to trade.

As everyone relaxed, the children climbed on the men's backs, played with our hats, and treated us like visiting dignitaries. Young gunners with dozens of confirmed kills laughed and played with the Vietnamese children, handing out candy like it was Christmas.

A glow began to replace the thousand-yard stare in our eyes. It was a feeling most hadn't experienced since leaving the States. I was enthralled by Cây Lan and listened to Quy read a Vietnamese myth in a lute-sounding voice. If the helicopter crews could adopt a village, we would have taken them home.

One day near the Bodhi tree, a pack of cigarettes went missing from a helicopter where the babysans played. A burly gunner shouted, "God damn it where's my ciggies?" He stormed into the frightened children. They scattered like a flock of chickens and most escaped, except for Quy, Cây Lan's five-year-old brother. The G.I. grabbed him by the shirt collar and picked him up, shaking him.

Instantly, Cây Lan ran to him, yelling in Vietnamese, Dừng lại! Dừng lại! (Stop, Stop).

I walked briskly behind her.

The GI shook the boy, demanding, "Give me those cigarettes!"

I stepped up. "Relax guy – let me check his pockets." Feeling the cigarette pack, I pulled my hand out empty. "Wrong one – sorry."

The gunner let him go. "Damn-it These little shits will steal you blind."

Saying, "Cảm ơn bạn," (thanks) to me, Cây Lan quickly herded her little brother away, boxing him gently on the side of the head, "Xấu con trai" (bad boy).

The next day, she approached and gently pushed her lovely twins into the crook of my arm. Looking up at me with her jeweled eyes, she said in broken English, "Tanks help." Her brother handed me a bunch of tiny delicious bananas and the pack of cigarettes.

I grinned at the boy whose head was bent down. I'd give the cigarettes back to the gunner who lost them. Pointing my finger at the child. "No steal!"

Cây Lan shooed Quy away and we went for a short walk away from everyone. When we were out of sight, she faced me, taking my right hand with both of hers. Looking up into my eyes, she slipped my hand under her shirt onto her lovely breasts, saying, "Dưa tôi," she pointed to the helicopters. "Sợ hãi Viet Cong." She pointed at the village and then at herself with a heavy accent saying, "Công giáo Pháp." Seeing my confusion, she said "Cat lic" and held the cross around her neck to my face.

I was so entranced with the feel of her bare breasts, I didn't comprehend her words. Instantly erect, I wanted to slide my hands all over her sweet young body to massage, suckle, and make love to her as no man had ever loved a woman.

Pulling my hands from her breasts, she pointed desperately at the village people. She made a slashing motion against her throat, "Họ không thích tôi! Kill me!" There was real fear in her eyes. "Công giáo - Cat lic."

I got the picture. She was half French and a Catholic in Viet Cong territory. She was afraid they'd kill her. *Jesus. What could I do?* Having practiced with some of the other airmen, I said, "Tôi yêu bạn." I love you.

She looked surprised and smiled happily. Spontaneously, she offered her lips.

I could not resist, no, I could not. There wasn't the slightest hesitation. Within moments, we became invisible to the world; this kiss, this pressing of the lips, slightly touching tongues; she felt my strong lean body towering above her, offering a strength she had never known; I felt her tender, yet firm body with magnificent peaches pressed to my sternum. My one-eyed willy went bananas and she knew I wanted her. Positively, without question, our lovemaking would reach the stars, the divine, and beyond.

Quy ran up yelling, "Chopper, Chopper!"

I jerked away and in a daze, walked back to the aircraft.

"Đưa tôi với bạn….Tac me!" Cây Lan closely followed, running to keep up as I jogged past the giant Bodhi *tree and* across the canal bridge. "Tak me. Pease Tak me." The birds were winding up, rotors turning. "Xin, pease, tak me!" She hung onto my arm until I stepped onto the helicopter skids.

I pushed her away, saying, "Tôi xin lỗi… I'm sorry. I'll be back tomorrow.

Cây Lan looked crushed and frightened.

The crew chief, AC, and copilot gave me shit-eating grins. "Yer da man! Seducing a young village girl. Bet your hotrod is fired up and ready to race!"

The pilot's voice came over the headset, "Nice set of howitzers, bet you were squeezing those a minute ago."

Embarrassed, I didn't want the guys thinking of her like that. "She ain't no ho, guys. She's Catholic and she's very scared the Viet Cong will kill her if we don't get her out."

The mood shifted as we thought of the Viet Cong coming into this village, our village. No doubt what they'd do to a girl like Cây Lan. A deep sense of anger and determination filled the space as we headed for the next PZ. It'd be a hot one. Over the radio came, "We gotta get out of this place if it's the last thing we ever do."

I thought of our last party at Hart's Basin with Devyn. Owl and I had sang this song and laughed in his face when he said, "Don't be fools. We're losing the war."

42. Orchid Love

Hey Rowdy,

Well, we finally graduated. You should have walked with us. Your sister Hetty walked even though she was showing – the administration pretended they didn't know. Hope things work out with her and her new husband.

Have you heard the news? Nixon and Kissinger are trying to negotiate a "peace with honor" with the North Vietnamese. Anti-war protests are going on all around the country. Some are for the war and others are against it. Everyone's embarrassed about losing.

Right after graduation, Dad said he'd sign the enlistment papers. It started a big fight because Mom doesn't want me to go to war. She yelled, "Devyn belongs in college, not the military!"

Regardless, Smith and I went to Grand Junction where we took the ASVB test. The Army recruiter said my scores qualified me for officer candidate school and I could be a Cobra pilot. He gave us plane tickets from Grand Junction to Denver where we were to get physicals. I was excited. It was a beautiful day, but at two in the afternoon at the Walker Field airport, out of nowhere, this monster thunderstorm blew in and the plane couldn't land. The recruiter told us to go home and catch the plane tomorrow.

Remember my grandma who reads palms? She said it was a sign, an omen, so I got to thinking: Why would this storm suddenly blow in and the plane couldn't land? They divert planes from Salt Lake and Denver to Grand Junction due to weather, not the other way around.

Grandma said I should let fate be my guide. It freaked me, so I called Smitty to say I wasn't going. He called Kenna, you remember him? I gave my ticket to him, and he took the Army physical in my place. Smith flunked the physical so he doesn't have to worry about the draft, but Kenna is now in boot camp.

Instead of Army Basic, I'm driving out to California with Art. Stormy wants to run away with me because her mom is crazy. They would arrest me for taking her across the state lines. She's mad at me now.

I'm totally worried about you. You haven't written anyone. Hope you're okay.

Dev

The ugliness of the war roared into my brain when I heard of the Mai Li prosecutions. Together with Nixon's announcement that the U.S. was pulling out, there was a noticeable shift in attitudes – servicemen in every branch were confused. No longer were we gung-ho. No one said, 'We're going to win this war.' Morale deteriorated into drug use, racial tensions, and lapses of leadership. We were pissed at the officers. Even the colonel who fought in the field with his grunts out of Dong Tom, David Hackworth, was said to have a bounty on his head, and he was a total stud who didn't sit in an air-conditioned office.

Knowing our Division was pulling out for Hawaii, men didn't want to get limbs blown off by a mine or booby trap. Who wanted to be the last American to die in Vietnam?

The fighting got more intense. Reconnaissance by fire meant we wasted anyone in the free fire zones. I was in a paradox, a Catch-22. There was a license to kill but if I did, I might be arrested and charged with war crimes. There was no real objective, and the enemy wasn't identifiable. A dozen Mai Lai's happened every week. Any goals for this war were gone.

About three weeks later, I got another letter from Devyn.

Rowdy, life is strange. One night after work at this pancake house, I went for a walk on Pacific Beach. I didn't know there was a curfew if you were under eighteen, and I was arrested as a runaway. I told the police that my parents knew where I was but they didn't care. They threw me into San Diego Juvenile hall where I spent the night and a day. I prayed and promised to join the Mormon Church. To my shock, the next evening, they released me on condition I went back to Colorado.

Stormy was cold when I arrived. She acted as if I had abandoned her. I heard she already stated seeing some returned missionary. Guess I won't have to join the Mormon Church, ha, ha. (It hurts like hell).

Anyway, I went back to work for Tongue Creek Orchards. They put me on a new cherry-shaking machine that eliminates at least two dozen pickers. Got our pictures into the paper with it. I'm camping at the cherry orchard.

I'm not so sure things are over between you and Dove. Heard she's moping around the Falcon's big house. If you were here, you might be able to patch things up, but could you ever trust her again?

When you get home, remind me to tell you about the offer the Falcons made me if I married Stormy. (Like that's gonna happen now). Man, I'm in confusion land.

Maybe things aren't over with Dove? I thought, *What the hell is Devyn talking about?* If I wasn't conflicted before, I was now.

It was a typical rainy day in South Vietnam when we were ordered to haul an ARVN platoon out of an area. The tropical heat exploded when the sun came out. It was so blistering hot, it sucked my sanity.

The pilot gave the command, "Lock and load, fire at will." RPGs and mortars exploded around the chopper. I hosed down the area to the front and below the helicopter.

Settling to the ground, we were shocked that villagers rushed the aircraft to get away from their burning hutches. I tried to block late arrivals because we couldn't lift off with too many people on board. The pilot put all power to the rotor and red warning lights flashed across the dash. He yelled through the radio, "Get those people off now or we're going to crash!'

The crew chief couldn't get across the cargo bay to help me fend off the villagers. He started tossing them off the other side to lighten the load.

I stepped on the hands of those hanging on the skids. The helicopter whined loudly, vacillating between becoming airborne and dropping like a rock. The crew chief tossed a couple more off and the ship floated up, struggling to climb. I thought, *You can't save them all.*

I was unsure who to spray with my machine gun. The crowd was mixed ARVN grunts and villagers. Who set fire to the hutches? Where are the Viet Cong? Who is the enemy?

The pilot wound the helicopter up an invisible spiral staircase into clouds. The mist was dangerous because even the best pilots could get disorientated and think he was headed up when he was flying into a hill. The smell of burnt hair and skin filled the cargo bay. These people were torched inside their homes. They whimpered and cried.

My heart broke for them.

Fortunately, we came out of the clouds at about two thousand feet. For every thousand feet in elevation, it cooled two degrees. The sun was a beautiful sight for the people on board. They were packed in the cargo bay like sardines – more than double a standard load of six to ten men. Good thing the Vietnamese people were skinny. These poor traumatized people would live to see another terror-filled day.

Out of small arms fire range, my fear and anger dissipated. People cried and my ears rang from shooting the M60. Their horror swept out the open doors as we flew above rice paddies far off into the horizon. The reflection of sunlight on the water was beautiful.

I hadn't received mail for days. My mother was in Holland and Dove never wrote. I thought about how to rescue Orchid from the Viet Cong, maybe by sending her to Saigon where it was safer. I asked Bill for help.

Bill said the only way I might get the Vietnamese girl out would be to find some ARVN officer or a Vietnamese Policeman to take her to Saigon for a big fee, or I could marry her. No clue how to could get in touch with the right ARVN officer or policeman. That wasn't feasible.

I wanted to believe the impossible. "So what would I need to do to marry her?"

"Are *you* serious?" Bill grinned with a wide, mocking smile. "You ever wonder what it'd be like if you had gotten enough oxygen at birth?" He waited a minute and seeing the worried expression on my face, said, "Do I have this straight? You get a Dear John letter and within a few weeks you're trying to marry a Vietnamese girl?"

"She is precious – we could make it work. Cây Lan deserves to live a long life."

Rolling his eyes, he said, "It's too bad stupidity isn't painful." Bill explained, "To marry a Vietnamese girl, the Army requires you to extend your tour for a minimum of six months and up to a year. Anything to keep servicemen in country – especially door gunners. You have to fill out a bunch of papers and identify how long you've known her, where you met her, and other pertinent information. You *have to* extend and wait."

I shrugged. "Feel free to use me as a bad example. That way, I won't be totally useless."

Bill shook his head. "I won't miss working with you."

I figured I'd need approval from Khôn Ngoan, the old village chief who lived under the Bodhi fig tree so I'd start there. If it went well, I'd apply to marry Cây Lan and extend for another six months. I could move her to the base and also get a thirty-day leave home to find out if Dove could look me in the eye and say she didn't love me anymore. If she didn't, I'd be free to marry Cây Lan. Either way, I couldn't lose.

The supply officers still owed me for helping them pass the GI Inspection audit. I went to the depot where I had worked for two weeks at the beginning of my Vietnam tour.

Rummaging through piles of new black market stuff, Ernie found a gas-powered irrigation pump. "Hey, how about this? Could they use a pump?"

I looked it over. Fire engine red, it had a five-horse motor, a gas tank, and a two-inch hose. "This might work. Can I get a five-gallon gas can too?"

"Sure, no problem. Small payment for how you helped us out."

We packed it in a wooden grenade box along with hoses, and I hauled it and a full gas can to the tarmac. My crew chief asked, "What the hell are you doing?"

I grinned as if I had a big secret. In my imagination, marrying Cây Lan was worth a six-month extension. After all, I had enlisted for three years to be with Dove. But in the back of my mind, I worried – six months in a war zone could change everything. One or both of us might be dead or crippled. I'd have to take her little brother and aunt. The five-year-old brother was cute if impish, but how would I handle the aunt? It was a complex conundrum that distracted me from the painful rejection suffered at the hands of Dove. I imagined her reaction if I showed up in Delta with a Vietnamese family in tow.

It made me smile.

43. The Red Irrigation Pump

We were temporarily grounded due to heavy fog but by afternoon, it cleared. In between hauling the ARVN around, our squad of six helicopters took a break near the Bodhi tree village.

I lugged the grenade box with the gas-powered irrigation pump and my crew chief carried the five-gallon gas tank to the orchid-enriched Bodhi tree. The old man was curious to see what I brought.

Pulling it from the box, I motioned for the small group of curious watchers to follow me to the canal bank. I dropped a hose in the water, filled the gas tank, and got the pump running. The villagers were astounded, murmuring among themselves. The people were excited and wanted me to take the pump to the village well to see if it would work there. But old man Ngoan stopped me, "Đúng!" No! Waving hands, he put the palm of his hand in my face. He turned to the people, talking rapidly in Vietnamese.

The villagers' happy smiles turn into frightened frowns. They started leaving.

I was confused, "What's wrong?" I asked Cây Lan, turning my palms up.

She tried to explain in a broken mixture of English and Vietnamese. "Viet Cong họ đến outil. Kill us."

After several repetitions and pantomiming the actions of soldiers shooting and cutting throats, Cây Lan pointed at the irrigation pump.

I realized my error – the Viet Cong would kill them for accepting American aid.

I pointed at the helicopter, making a lifting motion with my hands. "You come with me to Dong Tam. We marry." I struggled to say my proposal in Vietnamese, my pronunciation way off, "Bạn đến kết hôn?" (Will you marry me?)

Processing my words, Cây Lan was confused. Something connected as I showed with my arms and hands that I gathered her up and we flew in the helicopter.

Her face burst with excitement. "Oui, vâng," she found the English word, "YES," and to the astonishment of everyone watching, she hugged me firmly full on the lips. Very odd for a native village girl where the public display of affection was strongly frowned upon.

I resisted wrapping my arms around her, instead, I held her lightly and as gently as a hummingbird.

Hearing my fellow squad members jeer, whistle, and yell catcalls, my face turned hot and I stepped away.

She turned to the villagers, explaining something in Vietnamese. Their mouths dropped open. A few applauded while others looked away with concern. She pulled Quy to her side. "Prendre, lấy, Quy?" Replicating my flying motions, she made it clear her brother must go.

I shook my head to mean, *I don't know.*

Cây Lan took it as no. She burst into tears.

I motioned with my hands to calm her and nodded my head to mean, "I'll figure it out."

The old village leader hobbled to us. Having picked a bouquet of orchids from the Bodhi tree, he held it in both hands to the front of my chest. Khôn Ngoan bowed.

Surprised, I bowed with hands steepled and accepted the fragile, red, and white flowers. They had tiny blue dots patterning the petals. I tried to place it in Cây Lan's long black tresses. It kept falling out.

Her skinny little aunt came over and worked with the orchid until it was established in her lovely hair.

I held Cây Lan's hands. When her aunt got the orchid to stay, we turned to Khôn Ngoan who presented us to the villagers.

They clapped and cheered.

The old man presented us to the watching Americans.

After a moment's hesitation, they clapped and whistled.

I didn't understand what just happened but knew I'd been accepted by the village.

Cây Lan snuggled up to me, tucking herself under the arm of her man.

The airmen and gunners laughed and applauded, throwing catcalls, "Way to go lover boy. Got you a sweet young one." One pilot understood Vietnamese culture. "Now you're married and you can lick her honey pot."

"Load 'em up!" The squadron leader yelled. The men lost their smiles as they turned back to their jobs.

I picked up the irrigation pump, put it back in the grenade box, and carried it to the ship. Cây Lan and Quy walked with me to the helicopter. In a bind, I asked the pilot, "Lieutenant Bean, may I please have permission to take my wife back to base?"

The AC shook his head. "You know better; we're going into a hot PZ next. You'd need to get permission from our company commander or someone higher up."

I argued briefly, "If they were wounded, couldn't we take them?"

"Sorry gunner, no cigar. Let's go!"

Cây Lan was surprised when I shook my head, putting my palm up to stop her. "Đúng!" No, not now. We're going into a hot PZ, I'll be back." I sat the pump near my gunner's perch.

She had no idea what I said and her disappointment was obvious.

I bowed to her and got onto the ship. Picking up my weapon, I pointed it in the air and made shooting sounds, "Pow-Pow-Pow!"

She understood.

Embarrassed, she and the boy turned back to their village where her people stood in surprise. Some sniggered as if happy she was rejected. Khôn Ngoan had a serious, concerned expression on his face. He shook his head and opened skinny arms to Cây Lan and Quy.

Over the radio, my crew chief teased as we lifted off, "Didn't have to buy her love, did you?"

I pressed my button, "I wasn't expecting that. I wanted to give them the irrigation pump and ask permission to take her to Dong Tam."

The copilot cracked up. "You're a married man now! Better keep your head down."

Flying on to the next PZ, I was pissed to the max. I was angry at the Army, at the Viet Cong, and the whole god-forsaken situation. In a fit of frustration, I kicked the grenade box with the irrigation pump off near the edge of a big rice paddy. The radio played, "What do you get when you fall in love?"

That evening, I talked with Bill about getting her out of the village. I told him about the ceremony. "I'm a married man now. It's my right to have my wife with me."

Bill choked back a guffaw. "You have the right to do whatever the Army orders you to do." He slapped me on the shoulder, "Man, we ain't got no rights. You got to get permission to do anything, to make the smallest choice. Crikey, you might get an Article 15 for getting married without the commander's permission. You better not tell him."

"Well, shit! What can I do?" I paced the office. "What would you do in my situation?"

Bill thought about it. He was a smart guy, smarter than ninety-five percent of the men in Vietnam. That's not saying much, given that General Westmoreland came up with the American strategy of attrition with a zero percent chance of winning the war.

"Your best choice is to extend. If you extend for six months, you'll get a thirty-day leave home. You can check things out with your former fiancé and get clear on whether you can work it out with her, or whether you want the sweet little orchid. Eventually, you will have the approval to marry her. You'll need to claim the boy is your child because they won't let you bring a relative into a secure area." Bill looked at me, his lips pursed with certainty. Nodding, he said, "Yep that is exactly what I'd do. Kill two birds with one stone."

"Exactly what I came up with. Let's fill out the forms. I'll extend." I clenched my jaw. "I also want to fill out the forms to get approval to marry Cây Lan."

"If you want to get home in a hurry, you can re-enlist for another three years, and I can get you home in under a week. You're a friend and I ain't gonna do anything until you've thought on it a few days."

Re-up for three more years?

Everyone tried to talk me out of it. "Ain't no woman in the world worth three more years of this shit. No way. You'd have a year and a half of combat!"

I wavered and talked to Bill again.

Bill wanted to slap me up the side of my thick Dutch head or tear one of my big ears off the side of my face. "If you enlist for three additional years, you won't get Dove anyway; she couldn't wait three months before she was off with some dude – you think she'd wait five and a half years? Get a clue – she's a bird that flew the coop the first chance."

"But if it doesn't work out with Dove, I'll marry Cây Lan. She could go with me wherever the Army sends me."

"What happened to your brains? That bullet that scrapped your skull do you in? In your dreams, you can have your wife with you. Look, do you see my wife and kid with me?" He pranced around me, swinging his arms as if he wanted to box. "Come on, I'll knock some sense into you."

"Hell, man, I'm in a bind."

There was a lot of travel time between missions, watching the rice paddles flow past. Up in the air and again at night, I stewed on it for several days, then went back to talk to Bill.

He said, "If you extend for six months, I can get you a promotion to Specialist 5 plus a pay raise. Better do it immediately because the idiots upstairs keep changing the rules."

I signed the documents to extend my Vietnam combat tour so I automatically received a 30-day leave home. I also filled out all the forms to marry Cây Lan. I was Saint George and the Dragon, saving a lovely damsel in distress.

Bill said it sometimes takes a month to get it through the chain of command but once approved, I would be on a plane back to the world.

44. Die Trying

It was another search-and-destroy operation across sparsely treed rice paddies. Gunships flew tree top level to engage the enemy as the slicks dropped off ARVN platoons. We airmen felt strange working only with the South Vietnamese Army instead of our own troops. "Why can't we go home too?"

Secretary of State Henry Kissinger negotiated with the North Vietnamese, hoping for peace with honor. Who cared? We've lost the war. Lets punt and go home.

Drop off ARVN; pick them up – one firefight after the other. It was an intense adrenalin rush every time. Taking a break, we dropped in near the ancient Bodhi tree alongside the twelve-foot-wide canal. People were digging into the berm. I jumped off to find her.

Cây Lan and I hugged, quickly kissed and then went for a private walk. Something was wrong. I read fear in her face, pressure in her voice, a nervous shudder of her shoulders under my arm. In broken English and Vietnamese, she got across the Vietcong were there last night, and it was very dangerous for the helicopters to keep landing nearby. The VC had brought the irrigation pump in the grenade box. It was proof Americans were in the area, and the villagers supported them.

I was stunned. I was sure we were miles away when I kicked the pump out the helicopter door. How could they find and connect it to Cây Lan's village so quickly? "Không. I'm sorry." I didn't know what else to say.

The VC had searched for a woman who had recently married an American but the old man hid Cây Lan in his dugout underneath the ancient tree's roots. Everyone knew they would rape and torture her if they found her.

The VC took revenge for the CIA-sponsored Phoenix Program. The Company, as the CIA is called, believed a morally corrupt South Vietnam government could not be maintained without a secret military force to suppress opposition. The CIA killed or captured suspected civilians believed to have information on Viet Cong activities. Villagers were afraid to say anything about the Viet Cong so the Phoenix team grabbed any villager as a possible informant. Putting a bag over his head with holes for his eyes, they put wire around his neck like a leash and walked him through the village saying, 'When we go by the VC's house, scratch your head.' Phoenix agents came back later, knocked on the person's door, and whoever had the misfortune to answer was wasted as a communist sympathizer.

In reaction, the Viet Cong also policed the peasantry using the same torture and threat tactics as the Phoenix program. Last night, the VC had grabbed a friend of Cây Lan's aunt and walked her through the village using the tactic. Her face itched from the dirty bag and she accidentally scratched her nose as they walked past the village school.

The VC ordered the villagers to close their school, and threatened to cut the fingers off any child who defied their order. To drive the point home, and believing they had caught the girl who married the American, the female teacher was kidnapped. The people were sure she was tortured and died in the nearby jungle.

I ran back to the squadron of helicopters, telling everyone about the Vietcong's actions last night. The flight commander radioed headquarters and received permission to make a perimeter search of the area. One gunner stayed with each Huey slick while gunners and copilots spread to cautiously search for the teacher. The helicopters floated above the area, making slow figure eights, watching for Viet Cong movement.

The teacher's body was found in the undergrowth not far from the village. Violently raped, her vagina and anus were torn as if an entire platoon took their rage out on her. Finishing their buggery, the VC made thousands of deep flesh cuts everywhere on her body, leaving each muscle in bleeding strips. *Lingchi* – the Chinese death by a thousand cuts reserved for the most dishonorable crimes; it was extremely painful. We hoped she died quickly.

The Viet Cong were nowhere to be found. But being masters of camouflage, they may have heard the helicopters and hidden. They could be grinning at us right now.

I begged my AC to take Cây Lan and her brother with us. "I've completed all the papers to marry her. I've put in to extend my tour for another six months so they'll approve it. Please, we got to get her out of here!" Desperation filled my voice.

Even though the AC was sympathetic, Captain Badwin in the Command and Control helicopter loafed above at two thousand feet. He said it was a no-go. We'd be in firefights all afternoon, and Badwin said they couldn't risk having a civilian abroad.

My head nearly exploded. Sure, it was risky to haul her in and out of hot PZs and LZs but at least she'd have a chance. We could drop her at Dong Tam when we refueled. Leaving her in this village was a death sentence.

She was with the old village leader under the Bodhi Tree. Cây Lan presented me with a silver chain and a Catholic crucifix similar to the one she wore. She placed it over my head, hanging it around my neck, and said, "Christ được với bạn." (Christ be with you). The crucifix represented the faith of Christian Vietnamese the U.S. would win against communist aggressors.

She kissed my crucifix and I kissed hers; desperately we hugged and kissed. I must be off. "Xin lỗi. Goodbye." Sensing a great loss, we let each other go. I tried to act hopeful to avoid alarming her as I said goodbye.

The crew chief tried to reassure me, "Hey man, we'll come back and get her. If we have to, we'll steal a bird tonight, and you and me will come out to pick her up. I can fly this thing."

A smidgen of hope – I remembered how my parents worked in the Dutch underground. Poppa was an active resistance fighter and my mother was a nurse. He was wounded and Momma cared for him in an underground facility deep beneath the streets of Rotterdam.

I thought the villagers were like my parents – ordinary people who wanted to get rid of conquerors and their collaborators. Cây Lan's village was among the last friendlies; they had been tolerant and congenial until last night. Someone jealous of Cây Lan's marriage to an American told somebody in another village and so on. Such an unusual event would be big news, capturing the interest of the Viet Cong. And miles away, someone found the red irrigation pump in an American grenade box. Two and two equals a harsh lesson to those who resisted the communists.

I realized, *If she dies, it's because of me.* It struck me between the eyes: *Had I never met her, she may have survived the war.* Instead of being the hero who rescued the damsel in distress, I was her executioner. *I've got to get her out of there tonight!*

I watched the war-torn land unfold beneath us. Miles to our left, smoke from a burning village rose to the clouds, and kilometers to the right, artillery and bombs ripped away a jungle forest. I felt like an invader as we swooped in. Most of the guys didn't care – they just did their jobs, doing time until we got a ride home, not a far cry from prison, but here a guy was more likely to die.

Something had changed inside me. I was a shy kid from Cedaredge who didn't know what was going on when I enlisted. I never knew hate and wasn't mad at anybody. After Dove sent the Dear John letter, I stopped caring, but now I cared about Cây Lan. And lick a duck, by landing at her village; we had brought the VC in on them. *We have to get out of this country to let them have peace, communist government or not.*

I was going off the deep end. Ain't a pretty sight to watch a teenage boy with a machine gun lose it.

A .50 caliber round blew through the aircraft right where my head was moments before I bent down to fire under the skids at a running dink. My brain fogged up like a car windshield on a cold January morning in the Colorado Rockies.

Son of a gun!

Trying to nail the .50 cal machine gunners, I spewed thousands of rounds until I ran out of ammo. Looping around, we hurtled past enemy bodies scattered in strange positions.

I pulled out my semi-auto .38 and shot clip after clip at anyone resembling a Viet Cong until I ran out of bullets. I was killing for peace – the philosophy of this war. Fight and kill for peace. When everyone is dead, there will be peace. Tell Secretary of State Kissinger and President Nixon to suicide out.

Landing at Dong Tam, I counted the bullet holes in the helicopter. There were twenty-one from AK 47s and ten from the .51 caliber. There was no reason we were still able to fly.

My crew chief said, "These Hueys are amazing!"

I had no time to run into the company commander's office to beg permission to bring Cây Lan back to the base. We immediately took off with another platoon of ARVN grunts. A sinking feeling hit me, *I may not get her out dead or alive.*

Heavy winds and rain rattled the helicopters as we formed into a "V" coming into the landing zone. A skinny Viet Cong soldier froze and yelled something from the trees. Fire in his eyes, he faced the incoming aircraft and his muzzle flashed.

One of the gunners sprayed the VC and bullets tore his shirt open. The body was right under our aircraft skids as we landed. The crew chief gestured and making cups with hands over his chest, he pointed down – the soldier had breasts. This VC was a female.

Sweat ran down my neck as I squeezed off bursts as we climbed out of the LZ. A loud thud, KA-BOOM!

An RPG round exploded on my side of the aircraft, shaking the snot out of everything. The pilot was a pro and managed to stabilize the helicopter. I felt a sting in my calf and glancing around the cargo hold, I saw sizzling pieces of shrapnel scattered about. The smell of gunnite hung in the air. Red tracers bent downward from my M-60. Green ones sprung back up at us.

The medical tech at the hospital said, "Hey, didn't I patch this same leg up a couple weeks back?"

I shrugged. It didn't matter. The only thing that did was getting Cây Lan to safety.

In the morning, gloomy clouds brooded over Dong Tam as the cloud ceiling dropped to three hundred feet. Our squadron of helicopters lifted off in drizzling rain and scattered ground fog. Such weather didn't give much room to maneuver. It was dangerous because helicopters could slam into each other in these conditions.

We had five slicks, a command and control chopper, and two Cobras for the insertion. My ship was third in line. We slid up through the soup to two thousand feet, getting above the cloud bank. Cruising at over one hundred knots, we flew in a left stagger formation.

The pilot kicked on the radio. "Some folks are born, made to wave the flag."

Dropping down through the clouds, the cloud ceiling was a little better than at Dong Tam at three hundred feet, but thick patches of fog caused the pilots to intermittently lose ground contact and sight of each other. Mist enshrouded us in a white haze that played with your senses. At less than two hundred feet in elevation, the ground was still challenging to see. Everything was wet and soggy from the rain.

I spotted peasants working in the rice paddies. They didn't look up or wave. That could be good if they were unconcerned because there was no danger around, or it could be a very bad sign if they didn't dare look up because the Viet Cong had the area surrounded.

I heard the voice of Captain Badwin far above in the C&C helicopter speaking to the pilots. "Intel is the VC are nearby."

My heart jumped into my throat. Where was Cây Lan hiding? Is she still alive? We flew inches above a large stand of trees and made a quick U-turn, going back the direction we came.

In a few minutes, I heard the AC again, "Approaching target, stand by. Could be a hot LZ. Prepare to fire on command." If there was VC hidden in the trees and bushes, something bad was about to happen. Although the C&C helicopter couldn't see shit because of the monsoon weather, Captain Badwin micromanaged the mission. He couldn't pass up an opportunity for a combat medal. He ordered us to fly straight through the next village.

What? Usually, we came into a clearing or rice paddy and dropped the grunts off because helicopters were extraordinarily vulnerable and troops were much safer on the ground. Didn't Captain Badwin know? He was going after a Silver Star for himself.

Flying at forty knots over a rice paddy in single file we were ten to twenty feet above the ground. The cloud ceiling had risen to eight hundred feet but there were still wispy patches of fog. I saw small haystacks and wooden pens with pigs. This meant a village was nearby. Villages weren't military targets unless VC were confirmed. *Why not first drop the ARVN grunts off and let them search?* The situation was out of control.

The other rule was to never fly between two hooches because it was too easy to get caught in crossfire. The enemy seldom was fast enough to shoot at the first helicopter, but they always got the next ships – the second, third, fourth, and fifth aircraft. *What the hell is Captain Badwin doing to us?*

The AC gave the order: "Commence firing, fire at will." A rain of gunfire exploded from all the helicopters as door gunners opened up. Cobras hovered above. I felt a moment of panic but pulled the trigger. I couldn't help smiling with excitement as my M60 machine gun rattled off bullets. We were coming in very low, three feet off the ground. Tracers set grass roofs on fire. Someone in black ran into view, and I mowed him down.

An AK-47 opened up with bright green tracers. *My side!* All the gunners opened up on the enemy. ARVN shot their M16s from open doorways. The scene unfolded in surreal gunfire. The Cobras were awe-inspiring with guns, cannons, and rockets bristling. One opened up its mini-guns spraying bullets at 4000 rounds per minute. Rockets hit a little school building, blowing out windows as the roof came apart in splinters.

I recognized the school. This is Cây Lan's village! I quit firing. I saw no fleeing civilians and tried to justify their absence – maybe they heard the helicopters and ran for cover. A pig had escaped its pen and ran around confused. It took a round, flipped over, and blood squirted from its front shoulder, spewing against the wall of a grass hut. Chickens scattered, trying to flutter out of harm's way. One exploded in a puff of feathers. The roofs of grass huts burned from tracers. Big water pots outside huts were blown to smithereens. The Viet Cong ran zigzag and fell when hit by machine gun bullets. Everyone blasted into hut doorways and through windows. A large ceramic water jar blew up on the front porch of a hooch directly in front of me causing its bamboo awning to snap and fall over. Small clouds of dust puffed up in front of the next hooch as it was peppered with gunfire.

Where are they? Where are the people? I hoped the villagers had cleared out and Cây Lan was far away. From the corner of my eye, I noticed tiny flashes of light, as if someone had struck a match and put it out.

Muzzle flashes.

Aiming into the tree shadows and thick shrubbery behind the huts, I directed machine gun fire at the striking matches. Holding my barrel at those points as the ship rose in elevation, I released the trigger ring once we were out of range. The barrel pulsated red-orange.

In the C&C ship safely high above the clouds, Captain Badwin ordered us to put the ARVN troops on the ground. We banked over the trees on the other side of the village and came down to hover two feet above the rice paddy near the Bodhi tree. No one had to tell the ARVN grunts to bail out; they'd much rather be on the ground than in the air. At least they could dig a hole and hide.

Plop, splash, they hit the flooded rice paddy, some sinking, and some splatting like a bad dive into a swimming pool. Everyone carried at least sixty pounds of gear. Back and knee injuries were rampant.

There was no incoming fire. Relieved, the ARVN troops cautiously stood and walked toward the village.

Laying deathly still and camouflaged like a brood of poisonous vipers, the enemy force had waited until the ARVN stood and moved forward. Suddenly, the ancient fig tree lit up with bright flashes like a long string of cameras shooting off. The Viet Cong were everywhere – in, under, and around the Bodhi Tree, having taken positions among its massive branches.

The helicopter in front of us was hit by a B-40 rocket. Exploding in a ball of fire, the crew got toasted in a violent death of flaming debris. Many ARVN grunts weren't making it to the canal berm; they dropped like wheat under the reaper's scythe.

The rain increased intensity, coming down in sheets – it was difficult to see. My heart raced, my head pounded, and beads of sweat were trapped under my aviation glasses, making them fog.

Our ship rose, flying straight at the ancient Bodhi tree. A torrent of VC fire targeted us. In the heat of the firefight, the power of my M60 bouncing in my hands gave me a heady, exalted clarity. Everything slowed down and in a weird time warp, and I knew exactly where to shoot. Skinny men in black PJs fell from the giant old tree, plop, plop, plop like plums falling in a windstorm. A U.S. Army five-gallon gas can leaning against the tree trunk exploded, throwing fuel. The ancient Bodhi caught fire – whhooosh!

The Cobras worked in pairs: one fired rockets and then the other let loose. Rockets exploded into the ancient Bodhi tree, tearing limbs and shattering the main trunk, bursting support trunks and branches. *No, no!* I yelled in my mind.

I quit firing. I caught glimpses of black-clothed bodies flying through the air framed by red and orange high explosives.

Another slick started smoking from being hit and headed for home. Our Huey climbed out of the target zone. Banking to the left, we circled back over the rice paddy. We stayed close to the ground between the trees and headed west to loop into the village. *WTF? Are the Viet Cong now in the village?* I saw ARVN soldiers kicking in doors and setting hutches on fire. I couldn't see any Viet Cong but the VC saw the helicopters. The air was full of their tracers and muzzles flashed from around the base of the ancient Bodhi Tree. Resilient little pukes.

The Cobras and gunships attacked with everything they had; rockets tore into its massive trunk. Already on fire, the main tree trunk exploded outward in a starburst of huge splinters that went in all directions.

Fog and smoke from fires and rockets mixed and swirled in the chaos. As our slick came at the remainder of the ancient fig tree, the AC yelled, "Full suppression!"

I didn't fire because my side faced away from the tree, but my crew chief blazed away, yelling obscenities while firing. "Take that you commie &*()%$*)!.

The return fire stopped. Looping back around above the village, I had no idea how many people we had killed.

My AC yelled out, "Cease Fire! Cease fire!"

I went numb as we pulled up. Over the radio, I heard Captain Badwin say, "Cease fire."

Returning to base, my brain was rattled, *She's dead, she's dead. Cây Lan is dead because of me.* I looked down. My pant leg was bloody again. More shrapnel. It was same damned spot on the same damned leg. It suddenly hurt like a mother. Fuck!

The radio played, "If I had my way, she'd be back today."

45. Three Purple Hearts

A week later, limping in with a cane, I reported to the Company Clerk's office. Bill popped up and rushed around his desk. "Hey! You're alive and well! Dang, I've been worried about you. Heard you took a piece of shrapnel in the same leg for the second or third time. Great to see you." He grabbed my hand and pumped it. "Sit down, sit down. You got your medical release?"

I handed it to him and Bill shuffled through several files. "You're going home for thirty days. Congratulations!"

"What about when I come back?"

Reluctant to say, Bill twisted his face. Glancing from me to the paper, he said, "You'll still be a door gunner." He shook his head and shrugged. "Big shortage."

I felt my face crinkle as I gritted my teeth. "Sounds as exciting as having hemorrhoids cut off my butt."

Bill gave him a quick hug around my shoulders. "I'm so sorry about Cây Lan and her village. I don't know what to say." He shrugged. "Maybe she survived."

Stoically, I pursed my lips, but my guts clenched with guilt and emptiness.

Captain Badwin came out and patted me on the back. "You did a great job for us. You set those Viet Cong up at the village, you got us the right Intel, and we blasted the holy bejesus out of 'em. Made our body count for July shine."

I felt nauseous as Badbutt continued, "I'm getting you purple hearts for wounds sustained in combat. Three for prior injuries and one for this last action."

I felt like putting a V finger sign astraddle the Captain's nose – he was blind so it wouldn't hurt him.

"I'm also putting you in for a Bronze Star. You deserve it; you're a real war hero." Badwin grabbed my hand to shake it.

Feelings stormed around my chest as I shook the captain's hand, thinking, *I'm no hero, I'm a war criminal. If they give it to me, I'll throw it.*

Captain Badwack returned to shuffling papers in his office.

To lighten the mood, Bill said, "What do you call a Marine with an open head wound?"

"You joker… What?"

"Ajar Head."

Bill patted my shoulder. "Listen, pal, I'll see what I can do about your assignment." He whispered, "And if the Captain actually puts you in for three or four purple hearts, you got nothing to worry about. There's this policy if you're wounded three times, they can't send you back into combat."

A glimmer of hope. "For real?"

"Yep. Three purple hearts and you can request a non-combat assignment."

"What needs to happen?"

"The captain has to put in the paperwork, then they verify your wounds through the 3rd Hospital Group. Shouldn't be a problem." Bill said the 9th Infantry Division and the 3rd Surgical Hospital were pulling out before the end of August.

"Seriously – we're pulling out?"

"The 9th Division is going to Hawaii and the 3rd Hospital will move to Binh Thuy. They'll be attached to the 29th Evacuation Hospital. The 162nd Assault Helicopter Company stays in Dong Tam to transport the ARVN around until Nixon negotiates his 'Peace with Honor' with the North Vietnamese." Bill held up two fingers on each hand to emphasize "Peace with Honor" in quotes.

I shook my head. "President Nixon doesn't need to bang his wife because he's screwing us."

Door gunners were extremely hard to find. Nobody volunteered because they knew the infantry was being pulled out and the helicopter crews would stay in Vietnam for who knows how long. I was surprised they didn't just forcefully start assigning infantrymen to the job.

Bill tried to be positive. "Assuming you get at least three purple hearts, maybe you can take my job because I'm going home at the end of August." He handed me a paper. "You got a promotion and a pay raise for extending your tour – you're to report August 26th as a Spec 5."

"How likely is it that I'll actually get three purple hearts? My calf was injured three times and I never got a purple heart for those, not counting a couple of concussions."

Bill shook his head. "Ain't it the pits man? Seems the officers get all the awards and few Purple Hearts."

The day of my departure opened with low clouds and patches of fog. I climbed into a helicopter bound for Saigon.

Bill ran out to the tarmac with a sealed envelope. "I don't know if you want this for a memory, but do both of us a favor and don't open it until you're about to return to 'Nam. Please? If you wait, it will help you make a major decision. Promise?"

I chuckled. "Anything for you, Bill. See you on the back side."

"Look me up in the States when you have a chance. I'll be home before you come back."

"Will do." My head bent beneath the clear morning. I was as emotionally dead as a defoliated strip of Vietnam. I felt a hollowness as if a stake was driven through my groin.

One last time, I looked out the open helicopter door at the ugly, muddy, and rocket pockmarked base of Dong Tam. No living trees, bushes, or grass. War material was everywhere. No happiness here.

Devyn said if you didn't want to return to a place, you had to kiss the ground goodbye. I jumped out and to the surprise of the guys waiting on the aircraft, I kissed the sandy oily ground three times.

Tasted like shit.

From two thousand feet, I saw miles of rice paddies and dikes. Everything was flat with hundreds of tiny suns reflected in the pools across the fields. Vietnam was as beautiful as its women. Though riddled with shell craters the lush green environment emitted a fertile ambiance.

Today was humid and extremely hot at Togn Nuewts Airbase in Saigon. When I first came in country it was dry, dirty, and dusty. Now it was muddy. I walked with other veterans, our faces brown and eyes narrowed with a wary coldness.

New recruits walked past in a daze. I didn't speak to them. What was there to say?

To my surprise, I ran into Rayferd in the terminal. We went through basic training together and had helped Marty pass. His eyes lit up. Rayferd pressed his neck stoma and a robotic voice came out. "Yer alive!" He had been hit in the throat by a chunk of shrapnel when the Viet Cong mortared the base where he worked on helicopters. It had destroyed his vocal cords.

I was shocked and felt sorry for him, but Rayferd shrugged and wrote a note, "They'll never send me to 'Nam again, and I'll get disability."

It was strange to hang out with him, strange to hear his robotic voice, and strange because this talkative guy couldn't crack jokes. He had to write them down.

We went through a line of clerks typing in forms. The Army returned my civilian clothes and shoes. Once I was on the Flight manifest, I could exchange my military script, MPCs (Military Payment Certificates) for American dollars. The ticket was for San Francisco. "Hey, I'm from Colorado. Don't I get a ticket home?"

The bored clerk didn't bother to look up. "You enlisted near San Francisco; you get a plane ride back there."

"But I need to get to western Colorado where I live. How can I?"

"What do you think? You buy a ticket when you get to San Francisco." The clerk looked at the guy behind me. "Next."

Damn, I'll have to pay for my ticket to Denver then Montrose or Grand Junction. The Army dropped a billion dollars a week in Vietnam but couldn't spend a hundred bucks to get me home.

Once I processed through, me and Rayferd got seriously drunk. Lurching up the stairs to board the Continental Airlines flight, we staggered down the aisle and quickly fell asleep.

Awakened by cheering voices as the plane lifted off out of Vietnam, we high-fived each other. "We're going back to the world!"

The flight was quiet because the men slept. It was the first time since being shipped to Vietnam that we felt safe. Everyone was bone-weary.

Midflight, I retched and grabbed the barf bag. I made it down the aisle to the toilet and threw up until I stopped dry heaving.

"You alright?" A stewardess tapped on the door.

"Yeah, too much beer."

There was a line of troopers waiting outside the door holding barf bags. For most, it was too late.

I sat back down next to Rayferd who snored loudly, his trach made a whistling noise. I thought of his wife sleeping next to him and grinned. She wouldn't mind – her man was home at last. It was still, the whoosh of air rushed past. There were no rockets, mortars, or bombs, no helicopters, artillery, or machine guns. A large yellow moon rose in the sky. There was nothing to fear and it felt strangely unreal.

I pulled the bundle of unopened letters I had lacked the energy to read. My mother, Hetty, and Devyn had written. Some were from a month back. I saw one from Big Owl and opened it first. It is very short; scribbles ran in different directions:

Hey my frend,

Wear you at man? Drivin this son of a mother trucker ain't bad. I ken drink and drive and do drugs all I wat. Got ta wach for mines. How you got infantre? Nothin' make no sense no how. Mines r bad. My buddy took a bullet in his side. He died. You alive?

I couldn't help but chuckle. He even made a rhyme.

Dear Favorite Brother,

I wish you could be at my wedding on June 1st. I realize you never liked him but I'm getting married to Mick Woolhead. I'm going to be a mother in a few months. We plan to move to Arkansas where he's from.

I always thought you would marry Vernie and I'd marry Devyn, but you never know how things will turn out, do you? I'm so sorry about Dove. It's too bad. See what I mean? You can't see what the future brings. Are you OK? You haven't written Momma in a long time. Everyone is worried about you. Please come back safe and whole.

Love, Hetty

The sun was rising in America for a new day. Coming awake, I looked out and saw rice paddies passing underneath us. The fear and resolution of going into battle ran through me. I realized I was seeing the San Francisco Bay. I shook my head to make the rice paddies go away. I wondered if I could look people in the eye knowing I had committed atrocities nearly as bad as My Lai. I was alive and dead. As Hetty said, you never know how it's going to turn out.

Never.

Landing in San Francisco, anti-war protestors paraded through the airport. A young lady toting a "Stop the War" sign slapped me with it on the shoulder as I limped across the terminal.

I stopped and stared at her. "Why did you hit me for serving your country?"

"You don't understand, do you? The Paris Peace talks are stalled. The war is wrong."

"Unfortunately, I understand more than I ever wanted to. Why do you think I escaped from Vietnam?"

"Good for you!" She turned away to harass another serviceman.

America was an odd and chaotic space, far different from the one I left behind. Rayferd wrote a note, "Too many freaks, not enough circuses."

We went into the men's room, peeled off our uniforms, and changed to civies. Rayferd gleefully dumped his in the trash bin where several other uniforms rested in peace. Reluctantly, I stuffed mine in my duffle bag.

We gave each other a hug goodbye – his long black arms wrapped around a tall skinny white guy. Odd in a time of racial tension, it drew stares. Rayferd pressed his stoma, "I started out with nothing and still have most of it left."

It was odd to hear Rayferd's chuckle because it was a kind of loud breathing as if he couldn't catch his breath. I retorted, "See no evil, hear no evil, date no evil." We laughed like brothers because we were. Our brotherhood went deeper than skin color. It was love and loyalty to the depth of one's heart where there was no race, religion, or politics.

We banged knuckles and slapped hands, promising to look each other up, knowing it may or may not happen. I headed to the ticket counter as Rayferd softly whistled through his stoma on the way to freedom and a new life.

No one noticed me once I put on civilian clothes. Nobody knew what I had been through in Vietnam and nobody cared. No one saw the horrid experiences carved into my soul. I mourned – not in self-pity – but for my lost innocence.

Somewhere deep inside there was a growing determination, a sense of integrity, to act on what I knew was true, right, and correct instead of letting Jody run my life. *I must protect, not kill people.* I had become a Buddhist without realizing it.

Late July 1969

46. When You Get Home

On the plane to Denver, an older couple next to me stole looks. I had short hair and my big ears stuck out. Everyone else had long scraggly hair.

The man said, "You're in the military aren't you?"

"Yeah, I just got back from Vietnam." It was good to talk to civilians. Everything in the war was far away and a long time ago – death, fire, blood, mud, smoke and rain, rot, and stench. Now I was talking to nice people who were interested in how I was doing.

It felt incredibly good, but unreal to fly above the Rocky Mountains of Colorado. It was beautiful. The sun was bright and the sky pure blue. I was coming home. Devyn was right – The Ute Indian Curse rubbed off on you.

It was a dream to wind around the mountains as the sun threw a golden glow on everything. Felt like I was floating in Ouray's hot springs.

Meeting at the Montrose airport, Devyn grabbed and squeezed me. "Man, I've missed you!" He looked at me. "Leaping lizards, you've gotten bigger and stronger. Look at you."

"They work us pretty hard." I was thinking of my family who we were meeting in Delta. I wondered what to tell them about Dove and how I managed to get a leave.

Devyn got gas because it was only twenty cents a gallon in Montrose. I called my mom to let her know I had landed and was headed for Delta where we planned to meet for lunch. Once we were on the highway, he said, "So tell me about it. What's it like? Did you kill a lot of gooks?"

I shook my head. "Not now. I need to get my feet on the ground." I sensed jealousy from not being in the war or a part of this men's fraternity. I wanted to shake some sense into him.

"Is it pretty rough coming back?"

"No, it's wonderful to be out of the war zone, but I'm in shock. I'm a different man now. I've changed, the U.S. has changed, and I'm not sure what's going on here. Hell, I'm not sure what is going on with me."

Devyn had lost the car to Mr. Falcon to help pay his parents mortgage. He got the Cadillac back by teaching Gabe to play the guitar. "It's not going great. Gabe has no sense of rhythm and he's tone-deaf. He doesn't know that he sings off-key."

"Thanks. Maybe it takes some pressure off Dove."

He was going to the Mormon church so her mom was letting them date. "Stormy broke up with her returned missionary and we're seeing each other again. I sure love her."

We met my family at the Highway Café in Delta. To my surprise, Dove pulled up in her Rambler right behind my parent's station wagon. When I had called home, she was at my parent's house telling them that we had broken up and she was going on a mission to Biafra, Africa. Since I was home, everyone insisted that she see me in Delta. She was tight-faced with embarrassment.

Everybody was happy to see me, but I felt strange. I was on a mission to see what was going on with Dove, and she was just telling my parents we broke up. I couldn't imagine more peculiar timing. I wasn't prepared to talk to her.

Dove looked at my cane. "Rowdy, you were injured; what happened, Sweetheart?"

"Took some shrapnel in my calf."

"Oh, you should have called me." She sat next to me. I wanted to tell her that I tried and tried to call her but she had ducked me. Man, talk about a barrel of mixed emotions charging around inside my body.

Everyone kept asking questions about my wound. I told them I was eligible for at least three or four purple hearts, but I refused to talk about the battles. I was in some strange place. Nothing felt real and my feelings went flat.

By the end of the meal, Dove cuddled under my arm. Her very own wounded war hero.

Before taking off for home, Devyn offered, "If you need to use the Caddy, it's all yours – I'll come up to Cedaredge and pick you up, then you can drop me back at my house on the way to Delta."

"Thanks, man."

"You need money?"

"No, I got plenty. Never spent much while I was over there." I pulled out my billfold, showing a couple of dozen crisp new bills lined up.

Dove leaned over with a thirsty expression.

"Wow, those are hundreds. I've never seen so much cash at one time."

"It don't mean nothing."

During the next few days, I got ill from the farmer spraying his apple orchard around the house. "This stuff smells like the defoliant they use in Vietnam. Makes me sick."

Our Dutch relatives were visiting from Holland and they probed me, "Why are *you* in Vietnam? You should come back to Holland with us. You're a Dutch citizen and we don't believe in that war."

I was surprised to learn that my parents had never surrendered us kid's Dutch citizenship and I wasn't officially naturalized. "You mean all of us guys didn't have to register for the draft?"

Papa got mad and yelled, "This is our country now and you should do your duty."

The Dutch relatives argued and it got hot. Should the Jaeger boys serve with the American military in an immoral and unnecessary war?

I couldn't deal with it and went up to the shared bedroom.

Devyn called, "So how has it gone with Dove?"

"Things are different. I'm not sure if I can trust her after what she did. She sounds committed to this mission to Africa."

He didn't say anything, but I sensed he wanted to tell me something important about Dove. We didn't talk long.

The world looked frivolous and dull because there was nothing at stake. In combat, everything is important and nothing can be taken for granted. Your relations in a battle were based on whether you could trust your life to the other men. It was a life of adrenaline, meaning, and purpose that amped you to the max, and left you feeling wonderful when it was over – even better than sex. Everything you did was essential to the other men. I suddenly understood why Wild Dan was on his fourth tour.

I read in the Grand Junction Daily Sentinel about the last action I was involved with – the Bodhi Tree Village. The paper said that only two dozen civilians were killed while 327 Viet Cong had bit the dust. My squadron had reported ninety-two enemy dead. However, at each level, the commanders manipulated the body count. "Hogwash," I said aloud.

Momma asked, "What's wrong?"

"This makes me mad. I was there – I was in this action. The Army claims we killed over three hundred Viet Cong but there were less than a hundred. This war is crooked from the top down."

Late at night, a panther tiptoed in, seeking its evening meal. A soaking rain fell in the waiting jungle. The VC lured an ARVN platoon into their killing zone and sprung an ambush. Landing next to a pile of dead South Vietnamese troops, I helped pile rotting bodies on the slick, their arms and legs twisted or missing. The smell was indescribable. The helicopter downdraft covered me with fluids from the dead men. Rayferd was on the pile with a huge bullet hole through his neck. The first trace of a yell came as Rayferd's reflection vanished. I was lost in the darkness. I screamed and jumped from bed.

My younger brother woke from across the room. "What's wrong? You okay?"

"Yeah, just a bad dream."

I was wacked out and wandered around the house at night, sweating and shaky. There was no glory in what I had done. I was a pawn in a monstrous political game. The storyline was that we were there to protect American interests. Whose interests were those? Which ones? Huge businesses owned by wealthy people all named Jody? And what was in it for me? Not the American Dream, apple pie, and a Chevrolet, or a hero's welcome. I was from Holland and this was not a Dutch war. Dove was the prize and she was sullied. She no longer told me the truth, and claimed she was headed to Africa. Devyn said she had hooked up with Gabe, but she wouldn't admit it.

47. Moral Duty

I borrowed the Cadillac from Devyn. Wearing my Army uniform impressed Dove. "You're so handsome! I'm proud to be seen with you."

I took her to Teryal's restaurant in Delta. Hardcore patriotic, Western Colorado was not a place to find anti-war protests. People stopped and shook my hand when they saw the uniform. "Thanks for doing the job." They asked about my cane. "How were you wounded?" I tired of telling the story. "I'm healing, it's no big deal."

We made small talk throughout the meal. Dove shared her family's financial problems and how Mr. Falcon had threatened to repossess their sawmill.

"Why didn't you tell me the truth? Why write and say you're going on a mission to Africa?"

A guilty expression. "I didn't know what to say. It's so complicated."

I stared into her eyes. "Tell me the truth."

"I was trapped into being with Gabe. At first, I was a nurse to him. He was in a wheelchair since he was paralyzed from a tree falling on him up at the sawmill and they blamed my father." She looked up at me, trying for sympathy.

I had none.

"Mr. Falcon and his mother talked to me. They want an heir to their family fortune." She glanced around the restaurant and smiled casually. "I could be worth millions."

Fuck a duck. She's a gold digger. I tried several times to get her to confess what she'd been doing with Gabe, but she was as slippery as a U.S. President in the making. I doubted that since Gabe was paralyzed from the waist down that he could get it up, but Devyn had mentioned that Stormy said her sister was likely doing oral with him because she loved it. I knew that was true. I damned near urped at the image.

I wasn't sure why her sexual behavior mattered. There was nothing wrong with being a sex worker since they were upfront about it, but Dove was a prostitute without acknowledging it.

Why this jealousy? I couldn't explain it. But she was so damned beautiful, I kept sitting there, fighting the impulse to jump up and leave her.

"Please understand. It's my moral and ethical duty."

Moral and ethical duty – my ass. "For life?"

Slowly shaking her head no, Dove said, "It's a terrible burden. Gabe is very demanding of my attention and time. He yells and throws things over stupid things. I talked with his grandmother, Tempest, and she understands." Her blue eyes begged for understanding. "She's the one who suggested I go to Africa so Gabe would have time to adjust to me not being around."

The thought of Dove being yelled at made me angry, but there was nothing I could do. "Why Africa? Why not Vietnam? You could enlist in the Army nursing corps, and we may be able to see each other."

"I thought about Vietnam, but Alayna is in Biafra. It's very difficult for her and she needs my help." She took a breath and looked me in the eyes. "Rowdy, terrible things are happening there, similar to Vietnam. The Igbo people are Christian. They are democratic and Westernized. They seceded from Nigeria two years ago. The Hausas in the north are Muslims with an autocratic sultan." She flipped her long blonde hair. "We have a chance to do a lot of good there. Many are starving. My mother had a dream that I went to work there."

I held my tongue about Mrs. Knutson; she wasn't exactly a paragon of virtue since she got pregnant with Stormy through the affair with Mr. Falcon. I decided not to share my desire to never return to the Vietnam War, or for that matter, war of any kind.

If I played my cards right, I may be able to seduce her again so I drove up to Grand Mesa, parking in our favorite spot. Given the uniform, I was right. What a contradiction she was – rigidly moralistic and religious, but horny. She was ripe to the point of bursting. The front seat of the cherry red Caddy was the perfect vehicle for us to re-consummate our relationship.

Dove ripped off her clothes and pulled at my pants, saying, "I haven't had sex since you."

"Wait a minute, be careful. I still have stitches and they hurt."

Her expression was like one of those bitchy models, prancing down a fashion walkway with an expression, 'serve me or die.'

I tried to bury the death of Cây Lan inside her. By the time we, or more accurately, *she*, was done, my stitches were on fire.

I felt an odd detachment as we drove back to town. In the wee hours of dawn, we walked to the door of the Knutson home and kissed, but there was coolness without passion.

Tonight we had sex.

48. Little Big Man

We used to play music in Devyn's apple shed with Art and Big Owl. I'd been in the army for nearly a year and couldn't play my harmonica well, so Art and Devyn skateboarded around the apple shed and snuck cigarettes as if old man McDowell wasn't smart enough to know they were smoking.

Art always cracked jokes. "Hey, is today trash day? I can't believe they'd dedicate one day of the week to me." He went on, "The only time I'm funny is when I insult myself."

You had to laugh.

He pulled his shirt up and wiggled his fat belly around. "Look at this," he grinned, "It's a girl doing the hurdles."

I could only shake my head. They were still kids.

I didn't ride the skateboards. I didn't care because nothing was a thrill after swooping down on a hot LZ firing your machine gun with the Viet Cong trying to kill you.

Devyn kept talking about Stormy. He was head over heels in love with her. "I'll join the Mormon Church and go on a mission to marry her in the Temple."

I wanted say he was a fool like me, but kept quiet, letting him enjoy the passion of his dream. I knew what it felt like. It was hell when it popped like bubblegum and splattered over your face, then you couldn't get it off your mustache. Who knows? Maybe it would work out for them. Stormy was different from Dove.

They talked about Steve, an older friend of Dev's, going to Woodstock in two weeks. I couldn't enjoy the surface conversations. Sneaking smokes was silly. The carnage of war was beyond the comprehension of my friends. We lived on different planets.

A few days later, Devyn picked me up. He laughed. "Worrying works! More than 90 percent of the things I worry about never happen." He had been worried Stormy was pregnant.

I knew the feeling, but I hoped Dove *was* pregnant. Maybe she'd fall back in love with me. I couldn't think. My brain was in a stew, all mixed up with carrots, potatoes, and chunks of fat.

We went through the speed trap town of Eckert, twenty-five miles an hour on a major highway. Devyn insisted we stop at his grandfather's house. "He was a .50 caliber machine gunner in the First World War, and he wants to talk with you."

When we walked in, the old man grasped my hand firmly. "Glad you made it back, come in, come in, please. How did you manage to get a leave home?"

I explained I had extended my Vietnam tour to get a thirty day leave home. We sat down.

Offering a cup of coffee, he said, "My division was the first to land in France and the last to go home." He showed us his citations and medals for bravery during World War 1. He was a cook and .50-caliber machine gunner in the great battles near Argonne, France. Mustard gas drifted across the torn-up, barbed wire fields and the gas masks weren't snug. As a result, he suffered from debilitating emphysema. He wore an oxygen tube up his nose and wheezed.

We talked about war. He told about the Germans coming across gas-covered fields looking like evil zombies as gas sirens wailed and huge fans blew the deadly mist back at the enemy. He cut enemy soldiers in half with his .50 caliber machine gun.

I said, "It sounds strange but I liked killing gooks – it's a rush. Sitting behind a machine gun is a drug better than sex or alcohol. It's power. But… I have nightmares every night. I kill everyone with my machine gun. But it's gory and scares the shit out of me."

"Yes, same for my generation, for every generation that went to war. I'm 72, and I still kill Germans at night when they come swarming over the trenches into no man's land."

He gathered my brown eyes into his own. "You need to quit. You love it and I understand. But you got to get away from it or it will take your whole mind and soul, and you'll be a killer, wanting to hunt and kill your whole life."

I shared my nightmares about Cây Lan, the girl I had fallen in love with over there. The village elder had married us to my surprise, then the VC infiltrated their hamlet, and the Army had blown it to pieces. I didn't know if she survived.

Grandpa said, "You'll never get over her." He told about his French girlfriend and the heartbreak of her death. "She was hit by a Kraut artillery shell. She and some other girls were washing our clothes in a creek. We were engaged to be married." He shook his head. "It's fate – you never know what will happen."

Our eyes teared slightly, remembering the girl we had lost.

"I joined because of a girl," I said, "True love is the willingness to step up and take a bullet for someone you love."

Grandpa said, "Fiddle Sticks! Who told you that rubbish? We go to war because the government tells us to go. We don't pick our enemies, and we don't make policy! Once you're on the battlefield, you fight for your survival. Take love and idealism from it and the truth of combat comes out."

Devyn interjected, "If you took a bullet for Dove, all you did was save her for Jody, not you. It's self-deception, a lie."

Grandpa looked at his grandson proudly. "I'm glad to see you're using your head instead of your wiener schnitzel."

I held my palms out. "Dove wants me back in Vietnam. She's religious and extremely political. She writes letters to the newspaper about the communists in Vietnam, and how we should stop them. I'm her warrior for God."

Grandpa said with anger in his tone, "You need to decide what you believe instead of listening to some horseshit because you got your trouser snake wet! There are plenty of girls who won't make you do things that aren't right for you. Go back to Holland – that is who you are, not some warrior for her god."

I felt like he had slapped the side of my head. "The officers tell us we're winning but there's nothing to win. It's wishful thinking because all we do is kill, kill, kill."

The old man said, "You're wavering. You're wavering because you're listening to other people, to a Jodie – spelled i.e. – a female who has you by the short hairs. Listen to me – your gut is telling you one thing, but your yippee rod is saying something different, and your head has another story. You got to get everything in alignment, all your parts got to agree. It's simple: Are you a born killer or not?" He was out of breath and he had to lay down.

On the way to Delta, Devyn told me about Mrs. Knutson. "Stormy said her mom is up and down all the time. She's been this way ever since her little baby died in a car accident."

"Tell me."

He chuckled. "She doesn't suffer from mental illness. She gets excitement from every second of it."

I didn't laugh so he went on, "There was a baby boy between Dove and Stormy. The kids are stair-steps every two or three years. The mom had the baby in the car when she ran off the road at the Cory Store. It rolled and put Mrs. Knutson in the hospital. The wreck killed the baby. Fortunately, the other kids were with their grandmother.

Mr. Knutson was most attached to the baby compared to the other children. He was supposed to be the last child, and he went for a vasectomy. After the baby died, they were in financial trouble because of hospital bills so he sold his Delta sawmill to Joe Falcon and bought the field one up above Glade Park with a loan from Falcon. He started spending all his time up there, avoiding Mrs. Knutson because she went nuts." Devyn laughed without humor. "She thinks angels command her." A breath.

"When Cheri ran away to find Big Owl, she dug holes in their back yard, thinking I had killed and buried her there." He laughed again, but his face was red and his expression was serious. He said quietly. "She filed a restraining order on me, saying I was a murderer and she feared for Stormy's life."

"Go on."

"Mrs. Knutson has more conversations with the voices in her head than with actual people." He took a deep breath. "Mrs. Knutson became extremely religious. She was at the Delta Ward all the time where Jose Falcon was the Bishop. He counseled her several times a week. They got too close and Stormy resulted."

"Why didn't their dad divorce her?"

"They were married in the temple for time and all eternity. Similar to Catholics, you don't divorce. The church authorities dis-fellowshipped Mrs. Knutson and they ex-communicated Joe Falcon because he was the bishop and priesthood holder. They said it was his fault."

"Sounds like a progressive and tolerant religion."

We laughed.

"Dove told me some of that story last Christmas, but I didn't have the details.

As we approached the city limits of Delta, Devyn said, "Rowdy, you're distant and detached. What's going on?"

"I don't know. I can't get a handle on anything." I shrugged. "I'm different, Dove is different, and I've got to decide between her and the Army." I explained that now it was just sex, not lovemaking with her. "Devyn, the Vietnam War is like getting banged in the butt with a razor dildo. The infantry's pulling out to Hawaii, but because I'm assigned to helicopters, I have to stay." I shook my head. "Mr. Knutson said I can work at their sawmill in Glade Park anytime I'm ready. Felt like he was trying to tell me something."

"Are you thinking about deserting?"

"I can't be a door gunner anymore. Like your grandfather said, I started loving the killing." I choked back a sob. "I have to get out."

Devyn was shocked at my tears. Men don't cry. You don't cry if your momma died, you don't cry if your girlfriend used your buddy for a revenge bang. You don't cry if you're whipped with a cat-o-nine tail. A man doesn't cry. He looked up at the headliner. "Now I get why the big thunderstorm blew up in Grand Junction. I wasn't supposed to enlist. I let fate be the guide." He looked at me. "It's that bad, huh?"

"Worse. I can't tell you. I'm tied up in a bundle of knots. I have nightmares about Vietnam every night. I wake the whole house up screaming and yelling. I'm angry and depressed. I don't want to kill anymore." I stared at the floorboards.

"What does Dove think?"

"I haven't told her. I'm sure she'll think I'm anti-American, a communist, and a puke SOB." I was silent for a few minutes, then said, "I've got to tell her that I'm not going back. Maybe she'll understand."

"Dove is more complex than Stormy. Stormy thinks their mom is a slut, but Dove's got it wired her mom did the correct thing with Mr. Falcon because it saved their house from repossession and produced Stormy."

Devyn cleared his throat. "Mrs. Knutson convinced Dove it was her duty to see Gabe. It was a business deal, but they've turned it into this odd religious obligation because Gabe is also Mormon and Dove thinks she can get him to the temple." He went on, "The two of them are twisted, and their beliefs are as flexible as a rock. I've had debates with them and once their minds are made up, the Lord Jesus himself could strike 'em with lightning, and they'd still hang onto what they decided, no matter how illogical."

I lit a cigarette and offered one to him. "You're on the money. I have to find out how Dove will react."

Devyn insisted we see *Little Big Man* at the drive-in theater. I enjoyed it until the cavalry attacked the Indians. Bullets rang out and zinged. Suddenly, I was back in a helicopter in the middle of a firefight. I slid to the floorboards and covered my ears. "Get me outta here!"

"What? It's a good movie and it just started."

I pointed my index finger at him as if it was a pistol. "I said, Get me the fuck outta here – Now!"

Devyn put the speaker back on the post and peeled out.

On the highway, I crawled back onto the seat. "Fuck, I'm sorry. Suddenly, I was back in 'Nam in the middle of a horrible firefight."

Devyn patted my shoulder. "It's okay, man." He shook his head. "If I was you, *no way* I'd go back over there."

August 22, 1969

49. Tell The Truth

I could delay the inevitable discussion with Dove only so long because I had to report to OAT by August 26.

One night after having sex at our favorite place on Grand Mesa, we were watching a falling star and I said, "I'm thinking about not going back." I explained the carnage, the foolishness of the battles, Hamburger Hill, My Lai, the corruption, and how the peasants were being brutalized by five groups – the ARVN, Viet Cong, Americans, the North Vietnamese Army, and their own police.

She said nothing as tears ran down her face.

"Dove, if only you knew what is going on in Vietnam – this is hard for both of us. I'm not doing this to hurt you – my tears should tell you."

She stared silently out the windshield, her ivory cheeks wet and streaked. Her long blonde hair was still perfectly straight after our wild sex. It shined luxuriously in the moonlight.

"I can see this hurts you, but I can't go back. Not only is the war strategy completely wrong, but the government has admitted we've lost the war. The US is pulling out all personnel but the helicopter crews. I'm sorry now that I volunteered." I tried to catch her eyes unsuccessfully. "There are atrocities on both sides. I've committed war crimes myself by shooting in the free fire zones at innocent civilians who are just trying to survive." I took a breath. "There are a dozen My Lai massacres every week. I cannot participate anymore. I can't go back." I tried to take her hand, but she pulled it away and scrunched up against the passenger door.

Brushing tears from her cheeks, Dove gritted her teeth and flipped her hair over a shoulder. She pouted with unfocused eyes, staring out the windshield.

Sensing I may never again be able to make her laugh or smile again, I wished I could turn back time. I longed for winter and snow angels, for orchards in spring, for when we first dated.

Sometimes it's the unspoken words that say the most. No, not necessarily what those silent voices mean, but what we should have said and did not. It's the hush, a lingering silence that dashes understanding. What more could I say? Love was lost now, and the meaning was gone.

She was quiet and pale, sitting with a stunned, incredulous expression. Blue eyes without sparkles stared out the windshield at the twinkling lights of the valley – The Valley Of The Ute Curse.

Shuddering, I asked, "Can't you say anything?"

Slowly, she shook her head. "Take me home."

Total silence during the twenty miles to Delta. I wanted to apologize, to say I'd go back to Vietnam for her.

I could not.

Inside the car was a hush, a lingering, limping silence that dashed hope.

I walked her to the door.

Turning her back to me, she opened it. There was no kiss, not even a polite handshake. She whispered something under her breath without looking at me.

I wondered what she had whispered but only stared at the door.

50. Four Bad Choices

The next week, I tried to act as if everything was fine, but Devyn knew it wasn't, especially when I told him, "My luck, I'll probably be reincarnated as me."

He tried to make a joke of it. "I don't know, I'm just a potato." He saw my face and said, "I have a good heart, but I really should fix this mouth of mine."

His silly expression made me laugh.

Stormy reported Dove was bestowing everyone with the silent treatment. I thought about giving her a gun so she could simply kill me. Maybe that was the way to go.

They say money talks. But all mine said was goodbye. I began giving it away: to my brothers and sisters, and a chunk to my parents.

I insisted Devyn take my .22 rifle, a .38 pistol, and my 12 gauge shotgun.

He shook his head. "Why are you giving everything away?"

"I don't see myself coming back." I was going back to Vietnam and would be killed. "I don't need it."

Everyone in the family was confused and wondered what came over me.

"This isn't good. You should put the money in the bank to give you a start later."

I shrugged.

Two days before I was due to get on the plane for Oakland Army Terminal, Devyn brought the .22 rifles to the house and tried to get me to shoot cans. I refused. "No, I'm not into guns anymore."

"Huh? When you and Owl came back from boot camp, all you guys wanted to do was shoot guns."

I shook my head. "Yeah, they had us brainwashed. I don't want to shoot anything, not even cans."

Dove showed up.

My younger brothers and sisters were thrilled to see her, and they surrounded her like little Vietnamese children. My mother loved her too. She made Dove instant coffee, and we sat to visit.

I looked at her. "I wouldn't settle for me, so why would you?"

She stared at me. Tears ran from her blue eyes. "Please, will you go back?"

I nodded. I felt like the human equivalent of a typo.

Devyn said nervously, "I've got to go. See you." He jumped into the Cadillac and quickly backed up. CRUNCH, his right front wheel buried itself into the left front of Dove's little grey Rambler. She had parked in an odd position where he couldn't see her car.

Everyone came from the house to see the damage.

Devyn apologized up and down. "I'm sorry. I'm so sorry. I didn't see your car. It's so small." His hands shook.

I said to Dove, "I got the money. I'll pay for the cost." Opening my billfold, I handed her five hundred dollars – three hundred more than it might take to fix it.

Devyn kept apologizing, trying to make a joke. "Well, look what we have here – if this isn't the consequence of my bad decision to back up without looking."

I stopped him. "It's okay, I'm paying for it."

She happily took my money.

Two days later, Dove drove me to the Montrose airport. We had made up and had sex a couple of times because I was going back to Vietnam, and it would work out according to the Lord's will. A song by Oliver came on the radio, "Jean, Jean, you're young and alive."

At the gate, I touched Dove's cheek with the back of my index finger. "Tell me the truth. What happened? Why did you stop writing?"

Her deep blue eyes pled. "Rowdy, I had to stop caring about you. I loved you so deeply that I hated myself for pushing you to join the Army. How stupid and selfish of me." Her voice faded. "I wanted to commit suicide."

I pulled her to my chest and gently kissed her. "Dove, don't hate yourself. You're too precious. If I die, then I die, and you'll have us sealed together for eternity in the LDS temple anyway. Who knows?"

Settling on the plane to Denver, I imagined things were patched up. I came home and fixed it with Dove. I was honorable but was she? Maybe I was lying to myself – again. *Damn, am I my own Jody?*

It was a beautiful sunny flight over the Rocky Mountains from Montrose to Stapleton International Airport in Denver. We boarded the plane to San Francisco, but it just sat at the gate in Denver. They announced there would be a short delay. Half an hour later, the pilot said we may need to transfer to a different jet because it was taking too long to make needed repairs.

I thought that the last thirty days may be the last peaceful stretch of river I'd ever see. My life was a school exam that I didn't study for and was a cautionary tale for others.

I thought and thought. Nothing could cool the fire of dishonor. If I returned to Vietnam, I must accept the will of the military and be a door gunner. Killing, killing, killing.

When I got back to Dong Tam most people I knew would be gone. They wouldn't be able to verify the treatment of my wounds because the 3rd Surgical Hospital will have moved, and it was unlikely I'd be able to track down Dr. Valk so I wouldn't get the Purple Hearts. I'd be forced to kill to protect the helicopter and the South Vietnamese squads we ferried around. How could I cherish life and freedom while working in the most anti-life and anti-freedom environment mankind could devise?

The pilot announced there were no other planes available and we had to wait for repairs.

Sitting on the tarmac, I thought through my choices. I came up with four:

1. Go back to Vietnam as a door gunner for another thirteen months and kill or be killed. If Captain Badwin was honorable, which I strongly doubted, I'd receive at least three promised purple hearts and get a safer job in the rear, but I knew he would conveniently forget because there was a tremendous shortage of door gunners.

2. Wound myself – it had to be a terrible wound to get shipped home. If I wounded myself it was chicken shit, but worse, it could have a crippling effect on my life and may not work. Hell, I could paralyze myself.

3. Try for a mental disability, but it was a Catch-22 as described in the novel. In that story, the only way out of flying extraordinarily dangerous bombing missions over Germany was to be crazy. If you asked to be grounded, it proved you were not crazy because asking to be taken off the missions was the only sane choice.

4. Desertion – I would be on the run for life at the risk of twenty years in prison if caught. It would be impossible to get back to Holland because I needed a passport, and they checked for deserters at airports. There was Canada, Mexico, or hiding in some isolated place in America.

If I went back to Vietnam, I'd kill many others before either I was killed, or I killed myself. If I deserted, for sure, I'd lose Dove and worse, the FBI would be after me for years. Four extremely bad choices.

Mr. McDowell told me just before I left, "Rowdy, if I had come home in the middle of the Korean War, I don't know if I would've had the balls to return to combat. Who lives and who dies is random. I don't envy your position."

Confused, my thoughts flitted between two lovely young women. Memories of Cây Lan shadowed me. I felt her innocent presence, heard her voice, and occasionally caught a whiff of her delicate flower scent. Like a horror movie, we had attacked her village. I wondered if somehow, some way, she had survived.

In the next image, I was having sex with Dove. Beautiful, compassionate, horny, and morally rigid, Dove. A woman I could not resist nor trust – who insisted that I go 8,000 miles away to kill more of Cây Lan's people. In the meantime, because I wasn't home to keep her satisfied, she could not be faithful and had sold her soul for money.

There was Devyn's grandfather. "You'll dream of these horrid things your whole life. Try not to think about it during the day. You need to get out."

Dove's father had offered me a job in the sawmill anytime I wanted it. It was an isolated place where I could hide from the FBI. Was Tom Knutson trying to tell me something?

I decided to use Devyn's mystical approach.

If we transferred planes, I'd walk out of the Denver terminal and decide what to do from there. If we took off on this jet, I'd go back to Vietnam.

At last, the pilot announced, "Ladies and Gentleman, I'm pleased to announce they have verified all conditions are safe and sound to fly. We will be departing soon. Please fasten your seat belts."

"Today is not my day." I had muttered this to myself every single day since I arrived in Vietnam. I resigned myself. I didn't feel anything for the Vietnamese – it was their war and none of my business. I didn't hate them, the Viet Cong or the NVA, and not even the Army.

It was a tough decision: What to do when ordered to act immorally and unethically? The villagers were victims. Was I also a victim? Like Joe Bonham in *Johnny Got a Gun,* I had the choice to face the consequences of refusing to go back. Therefore, I was a willing participant and not a victim. I had the power to exercise choice.

I remembered the sealed envelope Bill gave me when I loaded onto the helicopter for Saigon. That is one promise I could keep. I'd open it just before I get onto the plane for Vietnam.

Flying into San Francisco's grey clouds, I was aware my emptiness was a reflection of shame and guilt. It was more than the pain of Dove's infidelity, and the probable death of my lovely, innocent Cây Lan. No matter what I did, my moral compass was destroyed and without it, I was lost.

51. Too Poor To Party

Devyn's mother dropped him off at Ingersoll Hall at Colorado State University in Fort Collins the fall of 1969. He panicked. It was six hours and 350 miles away from his girlfriend and he couldn't sneak over to see her. He was afraid that like Dove, Stormy would end up with someone else while he was gone. "Take me home, I don't wanna go here. Take me to Mesa College. Please, Mom, I can't go here."

"You have to stay. You have a scholarship here and we can't pay your tuition at Mesa. If you don't go to college, you'll end up in Vietnam and for sure, you won't see Stormy."

This muscled-up black dude walked in, tossed a big duffle bag on the empty single bed in Dev's room, and put his hand out. "Hi, I'm your roommate. Name's Harley. What's yours?"

From North High in Denver, Harley had walked onto the CSU football team. The guy did pushups on his fingertips; his body was chiseled out of black marble. He transferred to Ingersoll Hall because it was across from the practice fields. He was also on an equal opportunity grant. He said, "A football ride would make all the difference."

Devyn was a poor white farm boy and Harley was a poor black ghetto kid. No movies, rock concerts, or taking girls out – neither had money or a car. But Harley was a stud athlete and the girls were all over him.

Cultural shock. Braless girls sat next to him in class and he had trouble concentrating on the lectures. A guy on his floor teased him, "Where's your accent from? Why do you wear cowboy boots? Are you a country hick?" The other freshmen had hot cars and designer clothes with smartly placed ragged holes. He walked across campus in cowboy boots and new JC-Penny blue jeans.

Other guys hit the bars but he didn't have enough money to buy a beer. They went to shows, concerts, and parties. Devyn was poor to the point of shabby. "Yep, I'm just a country hick."

This dude across the hall asked if he was gay since everybody was having sex while he studied in his room. Had to. Cedaredge High hadn't prepared him for this. The professors graded on a strict bell curve. His smile faded. Extremely lonely, he sent Stormy a song, "I'd wait a million years. Walk a million miles, cry a million tears for you." She didn't write back. Scared him.

His classes were in huge lecture halls with four hundred plus students – the professors a tiny dot at the podium. Thinking of getting done in three instead of four years, he signed up for eighteen hours. His underwear, socks, and T-shirts came out pink in the laundry because he didn't know you should sort. The guys in gym class saw it and called him a gay wad. His papers came back, "Good ideas, style poor C-." His rural high school education sucked compared to other students and he had to work his ass off. Part of his financial aid was work-study, so he showed films twenty hours a week for different professors.

One night Devyn asked Harley, "So, as a nigger, do you experience prejudice?"

Harley looked like he'd smack him. "Don't use that word, man – it's offensive."

"That's a bad word? Sorry man, where I grew up, there are only Mexicans and whites. Everyone calls blacks niggers. You're my first nigger friend."

"There you go again, say black. Nigger is an expression of hatred and bigotry and is the worst racial slur you could call me."

His face hot, Devyn stuttered, "I…I thought it was short for Negro, I apologize from the depth of my heart and I'll never say that word again."

Harley's expression softened. "You're going to get a real education over here, aren't you?"

Harley was cool and introduced him to his cousin, Bianca, who lived on the girl's wing of Ingersoll Hall. She was gorgeous with muscular legs that coalesced in a bubble butt that looked like two cats wrestling in a gunny sack as she walked. Every guy in the cafeteria stared when she left. Funny and bright, she planned to be a veterinarian.

They started eating together in the dorm cafeteria. He told Bianca about growing up on a farm and about his girlfriend whom he hoped would wait. Her mother was a strict Mormon who demanded that he attend their church to see Stormy. Girls were expected to marry a returned missionary and he worried she might start dating one.

Bianca said, "You need to move on. You're too young to get married. This is the time to explore and figure yourself out."

"I know." He thought for a moment. "Guess that's why I'm interested in getting to know you."

She saw him staring at her arm. "Are you looking at my skin color?"

His face felt hot. "Yes, it's interesting. I was thinking you're not black, you're brown."

"Haven't you been around blacks before?"

"No." He shrugged and shyly asked, "Can I hold your hand? I think the contrast would look beautiful."

Bianca smiled and took his hand.

They sat looking at their fingers locked together.

She said, "They are beautiful wrapped as one. I hadn't thought of it that way."

He nodded. "Looks like a sensitive black and white photograph." He resisted the impulse to kiss her hand.

Other students stared at them. Some smiled while others looked disgusted or angry.

She said, "Actually, there is no such thing as race. We're not separate species that can't interbreed. Race is a construct to justify enslaving black Africans and is a means to scapegoat us."

"We ought to try and change it." He caught her brown eyes.

She grinned. "We should walk around campus holding hands with you in black and me in white."

"That would be fun."

As he left, two big black athletes came up to him. "Hey, what you doing with one of our girls?" Bianca was likely the most beautiful black girl on campus and they wanted to date her.

"Just getting to know her. My roommate, Harley, introduced us. She's his cousin."

"You're a friend of Harley's?"

"Yeah, like I said, he's my roommate. We're getting to be good friends."

They looked confused, then shrugged and left.

Despite the attention she got from the black athletes, Bianca was interested in helping Devyn lose all vestiges of his prejudices. If he hadn't given his heart to Stormy, no doubt, they would have become an item. They talked about the Vietnam War, inequality, and racism. She pointed out, "James Baldwin said, 'Not everything that is faced can be changed, but nothing can be changed until it is faced.'"

Devyn said, "I'm committed to ending the war and stopping racism if you'll help me."

In a burst of emotion, they hugged. Some students stared. It was uncomfortable but they were emboldened. To spite them, they stood and then hugged and kissed. It was for the cause and turned lush and erotic. He felt her heart pumping with his and her lovely breasts on his chest and his manhood rose. He wondered if he was cheating on Stormy but forgot the question as her tongue slipped into his mouth. They felt invisible in their own private world.

The whole cafeteria got quiet, then low whispers, "Would you look at that?" A huge black football player jumped up with a glowering expression, but Harley got him calmed down, saying,

"They're just friends. They want to provoke everyone about racism."

For fun, some days she dressed in a white pantsuit while Devyn wore black jeans and a black T-shirt, and they walked around campus together. An urban black fox walking arm in arm with a blue-eyed blonde cowboy.

People stared.

They often hugged and kissed to shock them. She joked, "My roomie and I think you'd make a great Oriole cookie."

Made his imagination run wild.

Stormy was right to be afraid of him going off to college, but the only money he spent was to call her for three minutes, once a week. She didn't say much because her mother monitored her phone calls. He did all the talking. Something was wrong.

Had to drop a class. He didn't need to study in high school but at CSU, he spent hours outlining textbooks and typing notes. The other students drank beer, played Frisbee, and screwed their brains out. His social life was eating with Harley and Bianca in the dorm cafeteria. She was cool and didn't expect him to take her out since she knew he didn't have any money. Like him, she had grown up poor. "We'll have fun just hanging out and talking and…," she winked.

Devyn was falling for her and knew she wanted him to. It was the way she caught her breath and smiled when she saw him. It was how they walked arm in arm to class. They looked into each other's eyes as they talked about national issues and occasionally kissed each other's noses or cheeks.

On October 15, the Moratorium to End the War in Vietnam held a massive demonstration across the whole nation against United States involvement. Everyone but a few rednecks wore black armbands. Professors said if students wanted to protest, they wouldn't hold it against their grades. A lot of students stopped going to classes. At the rallies, he and Bianca sang protest songs and listened to speeches. A student told him that he shouldn't be there because he wore cowboy boots. Devyn said, "Hey, just 'cause I grew up on a farm doesn't make me pro-war."

Abbie Hoffman came to speak. He ranted against the Vietnam War and the establishment, calling it corrupt. "They're all pigs! We should burn the government down!"

A coed asked him what women could do to support men who resisted the draft.

He said, "Say yes to men who say no."

Guys scanned the room for that type of girl.

A big man with short-cropped hair stood up. "You're anti-American. We should support the troops."

He got booed by the crowd.

"Probably a returned Vietnam vet," Dev told Bianca.

Some guys burned their draft cards. He wouldn't get his for a couple of more weeks or he might have gotten caught up in the enthusiasm and burned it. He wandered arm in arm with Bianca back to the dorms, trying to sort it out. It was all confusing.

He and Bianca talked about Senator Edward Kennedy who had called for combat troops to be withdrawn from Vietnam by October next year and for all U.S. forces to be withdrawn by the end of 1972. President Nixon ignored the thousands who marched. Peace activists congregated outside U.S. embassies across Europe. Protests shut down governments. It was a world movement. "We're going to end the Vietnam War!"

Bianca wished this kind of energy was also going into ending racism and Devyn agreed. When they held hands in the cafeteria he got cold stares from whites and she got the angry ones from blacks. "Just ignore them," Bianca said. "We're confronting institutionalized racism with direct action."

Devyn thought it was the greatest thing he had ever done. He told Bianca, "Martin Luther King Junior said, 'Injustice anywhere is a threat to justice everywhere.'"

Stormy called for the first time, saying, "Mom ran off the road and we landed upside down in the river. I had to go to the hospital because I hurt my neck and back."

His heart jumped with anxiety. He had thought things were over between them but was suddenly back in love with her. "Are you alright now?"

"I'm still sore, but I'll be okay."

"Dang, I wish I could see you."

"Can you come over? I miss you."

Devyn was quiet for a moment. "I wish I could. I don't want to be here." He told her about the other students, their money, their coolness, and how he didn't fit in. "I don't have a car and I couldn't afford the gas even if I did."

She was silent, then said, "I lost your necklace in the accident. I'm sorry."

He had given her a little diamond necklace before he left. "Well, it only matters that you're safe."

"I have to hang up. Call when you can."

"I love you."

She didn't say it back. He was more than confused. He truly enjoyed Bianca and had believed it was over with Stormy, but now this. She wanted him to come see her, then she didn't say I love you. Women were baffling.

The next time he walked Bianca to class, she said, "I like you, Devyn. Why don't you give up that young country girl and fall in love with me?"

He said, "She just called. She was in a car accident but she's okay."

"Have you had sex with her?"

"Yeah, but it wasn't just sex, we made love." He caught her deep brown eyes.

Bianca said, "We'd make love." There was something in her eyes. "You've been gone long enough, she's probably with somebody else by now."

Slowing the pace, he couldn't answer for a minute, wondering about Stormy and the returned missionary. "I don't think so. We were both virgins."

Bianca grabbed the crook of his arm and giggled. "Aren't you curious what it'd be like with me?" She took a quick breath and caught his blue eyes. "This is the era of free love, no obligation."

His brain spun. A part of him still loved Stormy, yet he was completely attracted to Bianca. "If we did, I know I'd fall in love with you."

"Are you scared to fall in love with me because I'm black?"

"No way. Your skin is beautiful. I keep staring with wonder when we're holding hands. It's a still life of the end of racism."

"So why not come to my dorm room some evening?"

He took short breaths. "I…I…promised her. I…I've got to keep my word."

"You're silly but honorable. Maybe that's why I like you so much." She patted his butt as he stepped off the curb.

Devyn stumbled and fell on his face.

She picked him up by an arm. "I can think of better places for you to fall."

"I'm late to class." He took off running.

That evening she said, "Our relationship would be a political statement if we genuinely loved each other."

"Bianca, I'm all mixed up. I promised Stormy to be faithful. I love her and I like you more than a lot. I don't know how to handle this."

Her eyebrows wrinkled with anxiety. "To tell you the truth, my father would freak out if he knew I was seeing a white guy."

His mouth fell open. "I've been worrying because my family wouldn't accept you."

She shrugged. "We've committed to confront racism. Our children would be a beautiful blend of both of us."

He laughed.

"What's so funny?" Her tone was sharp.

"I just got an image of our baby's skin split down the middle, half white and half black." He saw her serious expression. "I'm sorry. I'm just afraid to love you."

She said, "Be brave. We are intellectually and physically matched. Your girl at home has problems and her mother hates you. It's simple."

He looked at her with fear and longing. To marry her was a life-long commitment to fighting for the cause. They would be constantly confronted with racism. He didn't know if he had the courage.

Harley invited him to a party with a live band. A couple of big guys came up to him, saying it was blacks only. Harley told them to back off because Devyn was his friend and then went dancing. Bianca waved at him to come in. They had a beer keg and the cover was five dollars. He had five on him but didn't want to spend it since it had to last him at least a week. He looked in and realized he'd be the only white guy hanging out with a bunch of muscular black athletes.

Jamir, the guy who wanted to date Bianca, glared at him for showing up. Devyn knew he wanted Bianca and would love having an excuse to pound a white boy.

He felt like an idiot walking home. "I'm a poor, stupid farm boy with a history of racism. I'm a total fake and have no business hanging out with Bianca."

Harley was concerned when he came back to the dorm room. "You don't want to party with blacks?"

"No man, I didn't have the money to get in."

He didn't believe Devyn was that broke. "Bianca was hurt. Now she thinks you're prejudiced."

"I only had a dollar on me." He saw the cynicism in Harley's eyes. "Honestly, I got scared when I realized I'd be the only white guy and Jamir gave me the look. I'm sorry, I really am. Guess I'm just a big chicken."

Harley shook his head, started to say something, then looked away.

Devyn longed for a simpler time back home with Stormy when his heart wasn't split in two. He needed to cut one of them off.

Bianca ignored him after that. He tried to sit next to her in the lunchroom and she barred him. She said loudly, "I don't sit next to cowardly bigots."

His jaw dropped as other students looked up.

Jamir took his place next to Bianca.

Dev dumped his tray in the trash and went to his dorm room. Harley stopped talking to him. He had never felt so alone. He was just too poor – too poor to party.

After receiving his draft card, Devyn caught a ride home with another student from Cedaredge. Surprising his parents, he said, "I'm quitting college. I don't fit in there. I'll get a job at the sugar beet plant."

The old Marine said, "You can't stay here without a job. Once a man is eighteen, he's on his own. You've got three weeks then you'll have to pay for rent and food."

His dad worked at Holly Sugar and could get him on. To get a job at the sugar beet plant, you put on a hard hat, boots, and gloves, and rode the rail. In the center of the three-story building between floors was a landing with handrails overlooking the staircases. They ran three shifts so Devyn was there at the beginning of every shift, seven days a week. Foremen pulled a man off the rail to work in his area. They asked his name and when he said Devyn McDowell, they'd take someone else. He realized Dad put the word out not to hire him. WTF? He thought Dad wanted him to fight in Vietnam. He got discouraged. It was the only job in Delta County this time of year. He didn't have the money to go to Mesa College in Grand Junction.

Stormy told him to go back to CSU so he wouldn't get drafted. She had no idea the risk with Bianca there. They snuck around to be together because he wasn't baptized and her mom kept introducing her to returned missionaries. This becoming an adult business wasn't turning out to be much fun.

In San Francisco on November 15, 1969, one hundred fifty thousand people marched, and in Washington DC more than two hundred and fifty thousand demonstrated in a symbolic 'March Against Death.' They marched at CSU and Devyn wished he was there to participate with Bianca, but he was trying to get a job in Delta so he could keep his girlfriend away from the returned missionaries.

Dad told him he owed $120 in rent and board if he wasn't back in college before Thanksgiving. Giving up, he left Stormy alone with her wacky mother and the returned missionaries. It was obvious she had been going out with one or another. As a consolation, his folks bought him a beat-up 1960 Chevy for $150.00.

On the way back to CSU he had a long talk with himself. He was going to break up with Stormy so he could see Bianca with a clear conscience. He imagined making love with her and it gave him courage.

Dev told Harley he went home to find a job because he needed money.

Harley said, "Dude, if I had known you were so broke and scared, I'd have paid for you to get into the party and hung out with you all night to help you get over your foolish racism. We thought you didn't want to hang out with blacks." Harley had made the football team so he was doing better.

Face hot, Devyn dropped his head. "No man, I think of you as my best friend here at CSU and I like Bianca a lot. She's smart and fun to be with and I'm almost in love with her. I'm just too poor to party."

"You're too late. Bianca is dating, Jamir, our fullback."

52. Busted To Buck Private

Anti-war protestors harassed me again inside the San Francisco terminal but I pushed through them, detached and neutral. Nothing mattered; my life was beyond reach, worthless even to myself. At this point, I was going about sabotaging my life. I was returning to Vietnam because my girlfriend insisted. Dove said we'd get married when I got back home, but I didn't trust her. She had Dear Johned me when I was in Vietnam. I had re-upped for another ten month tour, simply to get home for thirty days to talk to her, trying to win her back.

I kept thinking of Cây Lan, the beautiful young Vietnamese girl I was married to by an old Asian man under the ancient banyan fig tree covered in orchids. I was married! We had fallen in love during my choppers daily stops between missions to trade with the villagers. I had applied to marry her after Dove sent me the Dear John letter. But because of me, the Viet Cong had infiltrated the village. When command learned they were in the village, the Army blew the village and sacred tree to bits. I didn't know if she had survived. I wondered if somehow, someway, I could find her and we'd officially marry. I made my mind up to find her.

It was a gloomy day as the fog hung on. I got to OAT at 11:30 in the morning. If the line moved quickly, I may be able to check in by the noon deadline.

Like everything in the Army, it took forever to get to the desk. I couldn't cut. There were other guys in the same boat. I badly needed to take a leak but didn't dare step out of line. What was the worst that can happen? They would send me to Vietnam. They're desperate for helicopter door gunners.

Men moved forward with an indifferent shuffle. I felt condemned to participate in this macabre cluster bang. I finally made it to the desk and handed in my leave papers.

The sergeant exploded, "Soldier, you were to be here at 12:00 noon sharp. It's 12:30 now. You get 30 days; you don't get 31! Your orders don't say show up sometime during the day." Shoving the documents back into my face, the jerk pointed at the time on the form. "See – it says 12:00, not 12:30. You are AWOL!"

"My plane was delayed in Denver. We sat on the tarmac for two and a half hours until they got it repaired."

"There's no excuse!" His face was gleeful with power. "You should have flown here last night if there was a potential problem. You should have planned ahead!" He scanned my records. "I see you were late once before – you're AWOL for the second time!"

The men behind me watched my red-faced embarrassment.

"Where's your hat? Twice AWOL and no hat! I'm gonna bust you back to a buck private, and you're gonna take a pay cut. We can't have this in the Army!"

Men standing in line murmured with distress.

I looked the jerk in the eye. "I'm only thirty minutes late." I turned my palms up, asking for mercy with a soft voice, "You ever been to Vietnam?"

The asshole's face revealed he had not. Catching himself, he yelled, "You're begging for a fine, aren't you Buck Private Jaeger? Okay, smart-ass, you got it. One month's pay!" He stamped my paperwork in several places and aggressively shoved them in my face.

Shocked, it took all I had to keep from pulling the dickface across the desk and pissing into his thin-lipped mouth. I said softly, "Whatever. It don't matter no how. I've been sitting on an airplane and standing in this line for hours. I need to take a leak."

The jerk said to the guy behind me, "Next."

I found a restroom. *AWOL?* I was seething. Busted to a buck private, a pay cut, plus a month's pay for being half an hour late? *I gotta get out of here, this is too much.*

I became strangely sure of myself. The Army preached, "Make sound and timely decisions. You need discipline when it's hard – when you're cold, scared, lonely, hungry, and tired." A soldier went off to fight the spread of communism in a faraway land to protect everything sacred – family, country, my girl, and especially my deepest values about life. But this war was unjust. America had lost its moral compass. The values that once guided every step I made, every decision in my life, lay shattered on the ground.

On my return home, everything had changed...gone...my girlfriend was off with another man. While I risked my life, the coyote entered the hen house and took the prize. She was gone. Off in some distorted religious belief about self-sacrifice.

The Vietnamese government was corrupt; my war buddies were dead or badly wounded, and my identity as a courageous man of principle was destroyed. And nobody cared or understood. I corrected myself, well, maybe Devyn does.

The Jody who stayed home got sympathy, and you got shafted. Which battle was more important – to get rid of communism or to get rid of Jody? Was Jodi the guy who took your girl or was he bigger and much broader? The government lied and corrupted its own values, claiming to be the highest in the world, yet it was committing genocide in Vietnam. Maybe Jodi was the loss of an ethical basis in American society. Who can you trust? Not your girl, not her family, not your community who ignored what was happening in Vietnam, and certainly not your government that preached a good line but walked another.

My will to fight left. Puff! It was gone.

There was nothing left, nothing worth giving my life for. There was no Cây Lan. Dove was a religious slut who couldn't tell the truth from a lie. Wasted lives and billions of dollars down the drain in a war with little to do with the security of American citizens. It was sure a money maker for the defense industry. I went to Vietnam with false beliefs and idealistic values that had no substance. The truth was, people are predators and I was a pawn.

I had civilian clothes in my duffle bag. They'll keep me AWOL for thirty days before labeling me a deserter. My papers already say I'm AWOL and I'm busted back to buck private. I may as well take a month to think about my choices.

Devyn would say, "Let fate be the guide." It was a mystical approach; if the plane had landed in Grand Junction when he tried to enlist, Dev would be in boot camp, training for Vietnam, instead, he was headed to college.

Stepping into a toilet stall, I changed clothes and packed my Army uniform away. Something told me, "If you don't go back, you'll never get your purple hearts and the bronze star." I laughed, saying out loud as if I was talking to Rayferd, "I'd throw them in the trash along with my uniform."

I walked out of a bad movie and headed from the huge terminal to step outside into freedom. No one stopped me; no one so much as looked at me. Lots of guys were returning home, their commitments completed. I had one hundred dollars left. Devyn was right; I should have kept the money.

There was a lone sunbeam poking through the grey overcast San Francisco sky. I caught a bus for San Jose to talk to Bruce, Big Owl's brother.

The bus was crowded. Seeing a man with short-cropped hair who looked like a veteran, I sat down next to him.

Opening the official U.S. Army sealed envelope from my company clerk, I remarked, "I was a half hour late."

The tired veteran glanced at me. There was no fear on his face. He was merely resigned and numb. "Yeah, me too, but it don't matter no how."

For a long moment, I listened to the wind of my soul, and then unfolded the letter.

It was official Army orders permitting me to marry Cây Lan.

53. Fleeing The Army

Big Owl's brother, Bruce, looked nervously suspicious when he saw me at the door. "What're you doing here? Aren't you supposed to be in Vietnam?"

I explained I was back on leave but went AWOL after this sergeant busted my rank and pay for being a half hour late. I planned to report back in 29 days. "I just need some time to get my head together."

"They'll be looking for you. Did you use this address when you enlisted?"

"No, I gave my parent's address in Cedaredge." I was exhausted, scared, and nervous. Nightmares of killing people in Vietnam and of Dove's cold eyes when I had told her I didn't want to go back haunted me.

Bruce let me spend the night in his little camp trailer parked out back, making it clear it was one night only. It was tough because that's where we stayed when Dove came out before I left for Vietnam. We had formally announced their engagement, and she had pulled off my condom, declaring she wanted to carry my baby. I didn't sleep. I felt impotent. How could I wrest something good from this nightmare?

Sheer fright in the darkness. The continuous wop-wop-wop of chopper blades. The ominous sound of a rocket-propelled grenade, a boom as a ship got downed by enemy fire. My chopper took rounds through the floor, igniting a box of smoke grenades used for marking LZs. In seconds, bodies were reduced to bloody pulps and twisted into lifeless forms. I woke up screaming.

After giving me breakfast, Bruce said, "Don't go anywhere near your parents in Cedaredge because that's what most guys do. They'll pick you up and throw you in the stockade, then send you to Leavenworth." Leavenworth, Kansas, was a fabled military prison with rumors of torture.

I touched base with my older brother, a driver for a general at the Presidio in San Francisco. Maybe he'd help. I walked in and saw him playing Ping-Pong since he had nothing to do.

"What the hell are you doing here?" Mark looked scared. "You're AWOL, aren't you? You can't be here; you'll get me in big trouble. Get out of here. I don't want to see you again!"

I took off within minutes. Standing at the bus station, I thought, *I'm screwed. Where can I go?*

I took a bus to Phoenix where a gunner in Vietnam called home. He had discharged about the time I got the Dear John letter from Dove and said to look him up sometime.

Dave welcomed me but freaked since I was AWOL. "Shit man, if they catch you, they'll throw you in the stockade. You better turn yourself in before thirty days are up."

I stayed two nights. Despite Dave's strong encouragement, I wasn't prepared to return to Vietnam. I just couldn't do it. I couldn't kill anymore. I hadn't wanted to kill before I went there and it scared the living piss out of me that I started enjoying mowing people down, regardless if they were Viet Cong or old farmers in their fields. I had laughed manically and yelled, "Take that, you pigs!"

The Army had taught me to look at my position from the enemy's perspective. *Where am I vulnerable? Where will they get me?* Indecision was a decision. The army had legal authority but had lost its moral authority. And without moral authority, I could no longer consent to follow their orders. I decided to desert.

Devyn lived in a dorm in Fort Collins so there wouldn't be any place to sleep. I remembered a high school friend had moved to Wichita, Kansas. *They won't look for me there.* Barely had the money for the long bus ride, but I was in luck. Ryan got me on at the mom-and-pop store where he checked groceries. Ryan drummed in a local band and had lots of cute chicks hanging around. Marijuana helped ease anxiety about being AWOL but I was constantly on edge, thinking the FBI was after me.

I asked for the night stocking shift so I could work when the store was closed. I seldom went outside during daylight hours and I let my hair and beard grow. I started wearing store glasses or shades, hoping the FBI wouldn't recognize me.

For fun, I joined Ryan's band, playing the harmonica. Girls threw themselves at us and we were living the life of sex, drugs, and rock and roll. If I wasn't worried about being tried for desertion, this was living the life.

An older blonde gal working at the store was Mormon. She asked if I'd like to learn about the church. Some dreams die hard. I took the missionary lessons and got baptized, imagining there was still a chance with Dove. The Mormon gal started banging me, thinking I would marry her in their temple. I pretended she was Dove although she was a bit homely.

Anti-war protests were going on all over the country so I didn't tell anyone I was in the Army or I'd get spat on because of that darned song, *The Universal Soldier,* blaming servicemen instead of politicians. It was all messed up.

On November 12, 1969, journalist Seymour Hersh revealed the charges against First Lieutenant. William L. Calley at My Lai. I had seen many similar atrocities. The story brought back all the guilt and horror, affirming I wasn't going back. And it planted a seed: If Seymour Hersh could break a story like that, maybe I could also. If I was an investigative journalist who uncovered government corruption, it might make up for some of what I did in Vietnam. How could I get into college to study journalism? The colleges wouldn't admit me due to my deserter status, or if I was accepted, the FBI might locate me. I had to hide out – nothing else I could do.

I wrote Devyn, "I deserted. Come out and join our band. Bring your guitar. Lots of young cute girls hanging around. It'll be a blast."

Devyn wasn't surprised that I went AWOL since the U.S. was pulling out of Vietnam. Holly Sugar had laid him off so he went back to CSU and learned the dorms were closed until two days before classes started.

With nowhere to stay, he made the eight-hour drive to see me in his beat-up 1960 Chevy with two dented fenders and nearly bald tires. He hoped it wouldn't snow. Dev thought he might as well go out there and play in Ryan's band. Maybe he'd drop out of college and at the last minute, join the Navy. He didn't want to claim he was homosexual, escape to Canada, or go on the run. The old man would disown him after he kicked his ass. And worse, Grandpa might think he was a chicken-shit. His family didn't have political connections to get him into the National Guard like George W. Bush and other rich kids. If he went on a Mormon mission, it was good for a two-year Type D deferment, but he doubted it would win over Stormy's mother since she thought he was a manipulator and lied about being converted. Two years was a long time and Stormy would meet another returned missionary.

The Peace Corps was also two years, but if the war wasn't over by 1972, he was still toasted because it didn't look like Nixon's 'Peace with Honor' was going anywhere. They had spent months negotiating the shape of the table and where participants would sit. The only way you got a Conscientious Objector (CO) deferment was to prove your grandfather was a Quaker or Mennonite. The Mormons and Presbyterians were warmongers like all the other churches. Devyn told himself that his relationship with Stormy was on a moratorium. Things would work out. Or was he tricking himself and it was over forever? His heart burned like eating too many of Mom's hot enchiladas. Made him want to throw up and you know how it feels to puke hot peppers.

We agreed that life sucked the big one.

We lived in half of an old house with peeling paint in the bad part of Wichita. Devyn slept on a spring-sprung, lumpy couch from the Great Depression. Ryan and I worked at the mom-and-pop store and Devyn had nothing to do. He listened to Neil Young's song over and over, "Know when you see him nothing can free him. Step aside, open wide. It's the loner."

I was banging the blonde from the store who had talked me into getting baptized Mormon. "I pretend she's Dove. I'm wondering if since I got baptized in her church, she might take me back."

Devyn shook his head. "Only if you go on a Mormon mission for two years. Shit man, she couldn't wait a few months when you went to Vietnam, and she's still hooked up with Gabe for the Falcon money. She's a gold-digger. She'll dump him if somebody with more money comes along because Gabe is odd."

"Nobody has more money around Delta than the Falcons so I still have a chance."

Devyn said, "My ass!"

We drank cheap wine and smoked pot. The joints had stems and now and then, a seed blew up in your face. Devyn pretended to smoke because marijuana made him paranoid. He thought people could read his mind and imagined the police were knocking on the door and arresting everyone. He had too much time alone with us working at the store. Our band didn't have any gigs so he had hauled his guitar and amp out here for nothing. He tried writing songs for Stormy but nothing came, so he let it sit in its case.

We went to some weird party where everyone was stoned out of their gourds. Me and Ryan had fun, but Devyn sat on the couch, thinking about Stormy. Some guy told him to move so he stood up. The guy and his girl started doing it right there in front of everyone. Devyn couldn't keep from staring.

I didn't watch. It was just sex and it made me nauseous because I started thinking about my Mormon girl and how I used to make love with Dove. With her was sweet and sensual and full of love and romance and dreams of loving each other for all time and eternity, but with this plain girl, it was just mutual masturbation – empty

Dev was freaking about the couple fucking right there in front of everyone and all the drugs and smoke. He talked me into leaving the party.

My Mormon girl's old boyfriend showed up at the house right after we got home. He was in a greasy green army jacket and looked rough with wild brown hair standing up in all directions. He confronted me about doing his girl.

I said, "How was I to know she was your girl? You weren't around."

The guy said, "We were supposed to get married in the Temple and she dumped me after I got back from my mission. That's why I ended up in the mental hospital." He looked crazy and had prescription drugs in his pocket. He offered us some. He also had a gallon of cheap wine.

Ryan showed up and said, "Heck, let's party." He grabbed the cheap wine and poured everyone glasses of the vinegar-tasting stuff.

Devyn asked Wild Dude, "You were on a mission? Where? What was it like?"

The guy told a scattered story of being sent to California where he was on a walking mission, one without a car, and he never converted anybody. "It's hard man. You have these missionary lessons you're supposed to memorize and cite word for word. A lot of people slam the door in your face. You're supposed to study the scriptures and pray all the time. My missionary partner ratted me out for masturbating and I got into trouble with the church authorities."

"So you were engaged and planned to marry in the temple when you got back home?" I asked.

"Yep, she promised. I bought her a big diamond ring and everything."

"So how'd you end up in a mental hospital?"

"She broke it off with me. Said I was different, and she didn't know me now. I gotta admit I went a little crazy when she rejected me. You can't blame me because I went on a mission at her insistence. Heck if I believed their nonsense theory about become a god. I threw a bunch of shit around and threatened to kill her and myself with a kitchen knife. She got called the police."

Devyn asked, "How long were you in the hospital?"

"Three months." He grinned. "I just escaped two days ago. I went to the store where she works and that's when I learned about you." He stared at me.

It was nearly three in the morning and Ryan said he was going to bed.

The returned missionary said, "Hey, it's okay you banged my girl, but I need a place to crash tonight. Just tonight – I'll find another place tomorrow."

He had wild eyes. We weren't sure if he was psycho or if it was the prescription drugs and wine.

Ryan said okay.

Devyn didn't want to stay out in the living room with the strange guy so he crashed in the little bedroom off the kitchen with me. In the middle of the night, Dev woke up, hearing noises in the kitchen. He went out to see the escapee going through utensil drawers,

"What you doing, man?" The guy didn't have on a shirt and that wild look was in his eyes.

"Looking for a good knife." He pulled out a foot-long roast knife. "Think this would feel good going into your friend's body?"

"Man, you better put that away and go crash on the couch before you end up in prison."

His hands shook like he might use it on Devyn.

"Don't do it, man. You'll regret it to the day you die."

Mental dude slid it back into the drawer.

Devyn woke me. I had slept through the commotion since I had lost hearing in one ear from the artillery near my barracks.

Whispering, Devyn told me what was going down in the kitchen. We moved a chest of drawers to block the door and piled everything we had to give it bulk. It wasn't long before the mental escapee tried to push it open. We waited and he kept trying.

Devyn stood and yelled through the door, "Dude, you better be gone in the morning or we're calling the police, and they'll put you back in the ward." The noise stopped.

In the morning he was gone.

Devyn figured he'd better go back to college.

Like him, I decided Wichita was too weird after the Mormon girl I was banging broke it off and went back to the mental dude. She said, "I have to help him, he's madly in love with me."

Mad all right, I thought. I had this idea that since I was baptized Mormon, Dove might take me back. I wondered about playing on her sympathies like the crazy guy had talked his girl into coming back to him. Maybe I could claim what they called battle fatigue or shell shock. I had it. There were days I'd be working at the store and all of a sudden, I was killing someone with my machine gun or Cây Lan's face floated in front and I'd reach for her. People looked at me strangely. I worried that the FBI would track me down in Wichita.

I headed to Glade Park above Grand Junction where Tom Knutson immediately put me to work. He had a contract building fallout shelters for the Federal Government. They wanted to know what shelters could be built using primitive tools in rough, snowy conditions. The Feds were prepping for a nuclear war with The Soviet Union.

Hunting for downed timber in four feet of snow way out in the woods may sound like a lot of fun, but in truth, it was a far cry from playing in the snow. Once you found a log, a guy had to snag one end with a cable choker and then drag the winch hook to it from the bulldozer. Once you had it, the operator yells and you quickly got out of the way. I clumsily worked through wind-blown snow as cold sweat turned into icicles, hanging off my eyebrows. Underneath the snow, a log bumped into another, and what I thought was solid ground, rolled. I went over backward and was dragged along in a churning, tumbling mess.

The other guys asked, "Wasn't Rowdy standing there a minute ago? Where the hell did he disappear?"

On January 14, Biafra capitulated, ending the Nigerian Civil War. Everyone hoped Alayna was safe. She'd be done with her commitment in a year, but they sent her home early. It was too dangerous.

At every chance, I tried to talk to Dove but during and after having sex, she was distant. I couldn't figure it out. I told her about combat and my nightmares without going into the gory details, but she didn't seem to listen or care. I didn't get it. How could that crazy Wichita guy get his girl back after threatening to kill her and himself? I was a complete gentleman to Dove and very respectful, soft, and sweet.

It made no sense.

Like my life.

54. The Stockade

The ghosts of the dead came in the night seeking revenge. Responding to pressure from Dove and my father, in late March of 1970, I took a bus out to California with my younger brother. Toby had a high draft number and didn't have to worry about Vietnam. He had dropped out of high school to smoke dope and listen to music. We stayed with a sister in Calistoga, then looked up our brother Mark – a driver for a general at the Presidio. We walked onto the base and found him playing pool. He was shocked to see us. "You'll get me in big trouble!"

I said, "I'm turning myself in. Thought maybe you could help."

Mark got permission from a sergeant major to drive me to Fort Ord in Monterey.

On April 28, I turned myself in. Maybe if I did the time, Dove would love me once more. I was twenty years old. The sign above the stockade read: "Obedience to the Law is Freedom."

They locked me in a five-foot-wide by five-foot-high, eight-foot-long solitary cell. They took my shoelaces and belt so I couldn't hang himself. A bare bulb was on the ceiling and a small food tray opened in the door. I was to kneel by that door every hour on the hour, sixteen hours a day for fourteen days and recite my name, rank, and serial number.

Inside there was a stainless steel toilet and boards chained to the wall. I could put the boards down for seven hours each night. One wool army blanket and no pillow. Breakfast was a bowl of cornflakes without milk, a glass of water, and four pieces of bread, no butter. Lunch and dinner was a bowl of salty stewed tomatoes, one glass of water, and four pieces of white bread, no butter. After fourteen days, a guard took me to the showers. After

I cleaned up, I received a set of prison clothes but no underwear or socks. I got a pillow, a small pencil without an eraser, and a little notepad – back to solitary.

I wrote in the notebook:

Cây Lan, my jungle orchid, floats like a ghost before my eyes – a face I cannot escape. A face of youth and beauty. Patriotism, let's do our duty. We must defend the land, the home, and the family. Simple values. How proud were your family and especially your girlfriend who had promised to screw your brains out once you're in uniform.

You heard the rotor blade, chopping and vibrating; you heard the M60 machine gun and smell the gunpowder, feeling the heat from the barrel. Then you saw the stampede and blood-spurting bodies as they run from you. It's a shooting gallery like God makes rain and thunder. I am that god. The sky falls on their heads. I'm the one that makes it fall. Pull the trigger and you feel the gun come to life. It rains death at your command. What power! What terror and horror! What joy! You kill the pigs and the water buffalo the same as you kill Vietnamese peasants. It feels like an orgasm when it is over. You're drugged by the spell of power, of death over life, and drugged by the touch and throb of an exploding rod of steel – a phallus that gave escape through the rush of getting your rocks off. How can we keep killing these people to teach them that killing other people is wrong?

Darkness will not drive out darkness. Only love can drive out hate.

I will never kill again.

55. My Court Martial

The Fort Ord prisoners protested a whitewash tour by congressmen looking into mistreatment complaints. In anticipation, the prison commander changed all of our records. On the day of the investigating team's arrival, the prisoners were told to fall out at parade rest.

Several prisoners left for the latrine and the idea spread. About 80 men held a sit-in near the officer's quarters to bring attention to their grievances. The captain called individual names to return to formation. Most did because the refusal of a direct order put you back into solitary.

Fort Ord is five miles northeast of Monterey near the San Andres Fault line and several small earthquakes occurred. The deserters believed the quakes meant the peace movement was sweeping across the nation and they'd be freed. It was like the Lakota Sioux's Ghost Dance.

It accomplished nothing.

After 28 days, I was moved to a barracks with other deserters. I participated on May 16 when GIs organized Armed Farces Day. When the brass got word another demonstration would be staged for the visiting congressmen, they trenched a deep ditch along Route 1 and rolled out miles of concertina wire in case marchers charged the base. Outside of Fort Ord's gates, three to four thousand people and over a hundred GIs protested. MPs were called out for riot control.

A few days later, I was among three hundred prisoners singing amen and clapping hands. It didn't achieve anything but it felt good. Military discipline was unraveling and sabotage grew in every branch. On May 26, 1970, as the USS Anderson prepared to steam from San Diego to Vietnam, someone dropped nuts, bolts, and chains down the main gear shaft. A major breakdown resulted in thousands of dollars worth of damage and a delay of several weeks.

On June 8, I was automatically court-martialed and found guilty of desertion without facing my accusers. Under the military criminal code, the penalty for desertion during a declared war was death. In an undeclared war, the maximum punishment was five years in prison, but the Army wanted door gunners back in their combat units.

Determined to never kill again, I was one of 65,643 deserters. I felt a profound sense of betrayal by the government and feared they'd send me back to Vietnam. A knot tormented my stomach that I'd soon be back fighting the Vietnamese in the immoral war.

Contraband literature recommended deserters claim conscientious objector status. Each time we were told to do something for the army, we should say, "I freely choose not to bear arms or to serve, either as a combatant or noncombatant, a policy which I consider immoral barbaric, and reckless. I will answer no call to arms. I no longer consider myself under the authority of the US Army, and I pray for the strength and grace to hold to my beliefs."

Article 18 of the Universal Declaration of Human Rights said, "Everyone has the right to freedom of thought, conscience, and religion; this right includes freedom to change his religion or belief, and freedom, either alone or in community with others and in public or private to manifest his religion or belief in teaching, practice, worship, and observance."

The United States never signed it.

I read that Just War Theory was created to reconcile violent warfare with Christian compassion to justify the crusades as a holy war against the Muslims. It worked. Good Christian men could kill without feeling guilty.

The Department of Defense defined conscientious objection as a firm, fixed, and sincere objection to participation in war in any form because of religious training and/or belief. It must be an objection to all wars rather than a specific war. The only men granted the CO exemption at this time were Quakers,

Jehovah's Witnesses, and Mennonites. All the other religions supported Just War Theory.

On July 7, I applied to be released from military obligation as a conscientious objector. Immediately, I was called into an office. "Sir, Private Jaeger reporting, sir."

The commanding officer said, "Sit down, private."

I sat on a fold-up metal chair placed in the center of the commanding officer's office.

"Sargent Major Hamilton says you're a real live one. Says you got a line of bullshit."

"Pardon me, Sir?"

"Wait a minute." He went to the door. "Come in gentlemen. This is one you'll want to hear." The company XO and other men from HQ staff filed in. They faced me. The atmosphere was tense. Commander big butt picked up a manila folder from the desk. "You want out of the Army because you're a conscientious objector."

"Yes, Sir."

He turned to the other officers. "This boy claims to have suddenly become a conscientious objector." Glaring at me, he said, "I see you volunteered to be in the Army and also volunteered to be a door gunner on a helicopter. Is that right?'

"Yes Sir."

"You went out on over 100 missions with only a wound to your right calf. Is that correct?"

"Correction sir, three shrapnel wounds to my right calf, another injury from an ammo can when the helicopter crashed, and that doesn't count several head concussions."

"There was a recommendation for a bronze star for bravery after a mission where you had provided the intel and set up the Viet Cong. Our forces killed over three hundred of the gooks that day. Is that correct?"

"The number is inflated, but yes Sir, the commander said he'd put me in for a Bronze Star."

"But you didn't get the medal or any of the purple hearts, did you?

"No, Sir."

"You're pissed about that, aren't you?"

"No, Sir."

"You participated in many village raids where VC hid, didn't you?"

"Yes, Sir, we attacked friendly villages, Sir." I fought to keep calm, but sweat was running from my cheeks and forehead.

"You're pissed that you fired on a friendly village. Did it occur to you that the Vietcong infiltrated that village because your group landed there for lunch?"

"Not until later."

"It's true that your chopper and about five others landed at the village many days for several weeks. You got friendly with one of the girls and wanted to marry her, didn't you soldier?"

"Yes, Sir." My gut spasmed with guilt.

"So if anyone is to blame for the village getting shot up because the Vietcong moved in, it was you. Am I right, soldier?"

"Sir, I did not choose to land at that village." I felt springs of sweat running down my sides.

"Come on door gunner. You were the one that got chummy with the peasant girl – isn't that true?"

"Yes, Sir."

"Now you're pissed at the army and want to get out as a conscientious objector since you set up that village."

Guilt made me angry. "Yes Sir, I set them up. It's my fault the Vietcong came in there." I looked at the floor. "Just kill me. I don't care." I meant it. I'd rather die than live with this knowledge that it was my fault.

The XO stepped up. "Enough, Soldier. Answer yes or no, nothing else."

The others in the room occasionally threw in a yes or no question.

I could not explain, could not describe my nausea and utter horror at having set up Cây Lan's village. I couldn't say that I lay in a desperate fever with guilt, had nightmares, and I had fought to keep from turning a gun on myself.

"Isn't it true that you had a bout of illness after your last shrapnel wound and they found nothing physically wrong with you?"

"Sir, I was told that I had an infection in my leg."

"It was in your head. You're a goddamned mental case."

My throat went dry and I had trouble speaking. The small office heated up with each verbal assault. I sat erect and still as they shouted. Suddenly, it got quiet. My ringing ears felt hot from their insults, and my uniform was soaked with sweat.

The CO began softly, "You were so fed up with the war that you," he shouted, "Extended for six more months, knowing that meant thirteen months in a war zone, didn't you?"

"Yes, Sir, it was the only way to get out of there."

The XO stepped in front of me. His 6'3" frame of raw meat and hard muscle bulged as he pointed a at my face. "Answer yes or no, Soldier, nothing more, or I'll have your ass on a rack before you know what happened!"

I felt his rage bouncing off my body, but said nothing.

The commander continued, "We've researched you and know everything about you. We know where your brothers and sisters are, where your barber dad works, and what your mom does at 10 AM every morning." He turned it over to a subordinate officer who described where my siblings lived, their jobs, the cars they drove – everything. The officer described how my father was in the resistance against the Nazis, then he faced me. "He didn't lack courage, did he?"

"No, Sir."

The officer told about Big Owl being laid up at the Denver VA hospital. "He's no chicken. He did his duty and nearly lost an arm and a foot. He said to tell you to get your ass back to 'Nam and kick butt on the gooks who mined the road where his truck got blown up near DaNang. "That's right Soldier, your buddy, Alvin, is recovering in the Fitzsimmons hospital while you're lying here in the stockade out of harm's way. Why'd you turn into a chicken?"

"I did not turn into a chicken, sir. The war is wrong. We are like the Nazis–"

The XO stomped on my right foot.

Pain shot through my arch.

"I told you, Yes or No. That's all!"

I fought tears, gritting my teeth. It felt like the middle of my foot was broken. I thought, *How ironic it would be if I couldn't walk because the officer stomped it and they couldn't ship me back to Vietnam.* Helped a bit with the pain.

The commander said, "Your fiancé Dove knows you're here. She's sad you're afraid to go back and fight the communist aggressors who are killing Christians." He spat on the floor. "You claim you're a conscientious objector but you don't believe in God, damn-it! You expect us to believe this crap?" He put his mouth to my ear, "NOW YOU TELL ME WHY YOU CAN'T FIGHT - YOU COWARD? WHAT DO YOU BELIEVE IN?"

My aching foot said not to answer, but the CO repeated it in my left ear, screaming at the top of his lungs, "I'll bet you want to go live with your buddy, Devyn, who's marching around his university chanting, "Hell no, we won't go!" He backed away and looked at me expectantly.

I glanced up at the XO and back to the CO who motioned the XO away. He nodded for me to speak.

Slowly and sincerely, I said, "I believe in the right of all living things to live. It is the law of nature. A flower cannot grow if the bud is clipped and neither can an apple tree bear fruit if its limbs are hacked off. If the seeds are to survive it must first blossom for the fruit to ripen. If humankind is to survive, his seed must also be allowed to mature. To destroy his own is cannibalism and if he eats the young, he too will be eaten by someone stronger."

Their faces looked confused. The commander said, "Do you expect us to believe that horse shit!? Can you tell me one good reason why you should be so damned privileged?"

No one stomped on my other foot so I went on, "That is exactly what you're doing to me, to the other guys who've been to 'Nam and saw the gore, the innocent people dying. What the US is doing is morally and ethically wrong. That is why the Vietnamese turned against us. You can't win the hearts and minds of a people with body counts. The US is committing genocide."

The XO took a step at me. "We're trying to stop the god-damned communists. Don't you understand that? The communists in North Vietnam want a piece of your ass for dinner and your balls for desert. How are you gonna make an apple pie without any balls if you let the commie in the kitchen?"

I risked my left arch but said, "All human life is sacred and I will no longer be a party to killing innocent people."

The only substitute for wisdom is fast reflexes. The XO stomped, but this time, I was quick, moving so fast that the XO slammed his boot down hard and missed. He winced and reached for me with gorilla arms.

The commander said through gritted teeth, "That's enough! Get this butthead out of here before I bust his legs!"

Knowing my application for CO status was denied, I stood and proudly limped out.

56. Frightened Free

On August 12, the men staged a demonstration at the Fort Ord Stockade. It began when MPs arrested two prisoners because one didn't have a hat and the other didn't have his shirt tucked in.

We heard about the jailing of three black WACs and it pissed the men off. The women were arrested because they associated with militant black GIs on base.

The news of the injustice spread. Fifty GIs gathered near the gates of the SPD complex to let the MPS know they didn't like the harassment of our brothers and sisters.

The MPs radioed for support and large numbers of CID personnel and military brass converged.

The men responded with a volley of rocks. The crowd of GIs grew larger. They trashed the mess hall and smashed all the windows, then broke down doors and entered three buildings. They overturned tables and threw chairs out windows. Someone set fire to the mess hall.

Fire trucks arrived and turned hoses on us while allowing the buildings to burn to the ground. It was as effective as tossing ice cubes into a roaring fireplace.

I couldn't participate in the demonstrations because they took us deserters out to clean trash on the bombing range. The sergeant ordered us to pick up every little shard of metal. We were upset about being taken away from the demonstrations. Some guys refused to get off the buses. There were close to a thousand prisoners and the buses held 60 or 70 guys.

A sergeant announced, "So you wanna be wise guys, listen to this. If you don't work, you won't get any food or water. If you want to sit on these hot buses all day and not eat and dehydrate yourselves, go right ahead. Anybody that gets off in the next 15 minutes and works gets all the water he wants and he'll have a fine lunch."

A few guys trickled out but it didn't take long for the rest of us because the buses got hotter and hotter sitting in the sun.

I started picking up trash and soon, everyone climbed off. The prisoners were pissed. Someone started a fire and quickly, a brush fire roared up several draws.

They called out all the fire trucks. To punish us, they took us back to the base and put everyone on cleanup duty although it was getting dark. Like the other deserters, I was regarded as a suspicious malcontent, a leftist, and a deviant.

They assigned me to dust, mop, and scrub headquarters. First chance, I started opening drawers hoping to find my file, and low and behold, there it was. I skimmed the records. My orders were to ship out in a little over a week to Vietnam. *Holy shit... I've got to escape from here.*

While people protested outside the fence, on September 3, a few days later, they put the prisoners into a formation of 40 men deep and 20 wide. At roll call, I was called up front with a bunch of other deserters who were on the bombing range when it suddenly shot up in flames. Two MPs took me under guard saying they were my escorts until I got on the plane.

To process out, you went through a bunch of different lines to clear your files and take them with you to Vietnam. There were long lines since they were getting rid of all those who rioted or refused to work. The MPs escorted me to supply. It was a long wait. They got bored and hot, so the two men rotated who watched me. One went to the can and then the other went.

I got through supply and medical, next was finance for my pay. It was very hot and the lines didn't move at all.

One of the MPs spotted a donut shop across the street. He told his partner, "Look, man, I'm gonna get a coffee and a donut, then you take a break and we'll trade off."

The line still didn't move and we saw the other MP sitting in the shade, relaxing in a chair, reading the paper, and eating his donut *real* slow. Now and then, he'd look over to see that we hadn't moved.

The MP with me got angrier by the minute because the first MP didn't come back. He said, "Look, I can see you from there. I'm going to go over and make him come back. You don't go anywhere. You stay right here in line like a good soldier to get your pay and you won't have any trouble."

"Yes sir, I'm not going anywhere – I want my pay." Right after the MP left, the line started moving faster and faster and I got $285.00 in brand new bills. I looked around and both MPs were contently siting in the shade reading the newspaper and drinking iced tea. They weren't paying a bit of attention to me.

I walked out.

I went to my barracks. Packing my duffle bag, it struck me – *this is my only chance – I could put on civilian clothes and escape.*

At that moment, my sergeant walked in, "What are you doing Jaeger? Where are your buddies?" Referring to the two MPs.

"They're supposed to be watching me. I'm not supposed to be watching them. I don't know where they are."

Sarge nearly gave an order but stopped. "You never saw me today, did you?"

"No, sir, there was no one in the barracks when I packed my gear."

"You're about to make a tough decision. Good luck with whatever you're up to." He walked out without looking back.

I stripped down, put on several pairs of underwear and T-shirts, then two shirts and extra socks in my pockets. I found a narrow box about the size of a small briefcase and put in my letters. Sticking the box under one arm, I walked to the main gate. Those guards didn't say anything because there was too much chaos. They weren't interested in some guy in civies who didn't carry much.

I couldn't go to Vietnam again. I walked out from Fort Ord without looking back. The fog slowly rolled in with spells of onshore winds. I went to the bus station but Army MPs were patrolling.

I figured it was safest to head to the beach. There was a sandy cliff I slid down and I walked toward what I hoped was Monterey. The sun moved down the horizon.

The sand was easier to walk on where water packed it tight. All that I knew as true, right, and correct had been turned upside down in Vietnam. The only way to get out of this war psychologically intact was to refuse to go back. I mourned, not in self-pity, but because I had lost a reason to live. Dove would never be mine but this was better than going back to kill Vietnamese peasants. The army had legal authority but had lost moral authority, and without it, I could no longer follow their orders. Paradoxically, the only way to be brave was to walk away from the war and tell people what was going on over there.

I walked along the ocean to Lover's Point and then on to the Point Pinos Lighthouse at Pacific Grove. I was stunned by the power of the thirteen-year high tides as waves crashed high and sprayed all around me. It was hypnotic. I wavered and nearly jumped off the rocks into the raging water.

The surfers ran what they called, "The Boneyard," in this area. Just past Ulu, at the very top of the point, the Boneyard had a gnarly-looking reef within a bowl of rocks, rocks, and more rocks. Not the friendliest surf spot on the California coast, the Boneyard was where the winter swell hit the point directly on the nose. The waves were big and the takeoff area was small. It was known as "The Red Triangle" thanks to the shark attacks on surfers, swimmers, and divers.

Someone said to avoid beaches with large seal populations as they were 500-pound TV dinners for great whites. I'd be a skinny meal for a shark, but I nearly waded in where a pack of fat seal slept.

My guilt was two-fold. It was the pain of having possibly killed Cây Lan and her people, and it was also the pain of disappointing and embarrassing my family and myself by deserting because it made me not only a criminal to the government but in the eyes of many, I was a yellow chicken shit.

Dancing around the dark waves coming in higher with the rising tide, the aspiring hero in me died.

I was frightened but free.

57. Rendering

It was CSU or Vietnam. Devyn had chickened out of going on the Mormon mission because Stormy again started dating a returned missionary who had been accepted on a full ride to BYU. Dev hadn't applied for financial aid and his parents were paying on farm debts. Dad said, "I could declare bankruptcy and get out of it, but I'm the one who borrowed the money so I should pay it back."

To go back to college, Devyn borrowed five hundred dollars from his grandmother at five percent interest. She made him sign a loan agreement. "You need to pay me back as soon as you graduate."

Renting the cheapest room available in Fort Collins, he bought a fifty-pound bag of oatmeal, butter, and brown sugar for food. He took a job driving a truck for Longmont Rendering because it paid the best. Heart in a freezer, he didn't write Stormy.

The Women's Strike for Equality took place on August 26. It celebrated the 50th anniversary of the Nineteen Amendment which gave women the right to vote. Congress debated the Equal Rights Amendment that would make it against the law to pay women less than men for the same work. Eventually it would be up to the States to pass it, but the conservatives didn't like the idea of equality and it never passed.

Devyn drove a route picking up grease from fast food places, bones and blood from butcher shops, and help out in other areas as needed. When he stopped at a store to get a drink, he stunk so badly that the clerk backed up as far as possible.

A sudden snowstorm hit the front range and thousands of sheep died in muddy corrals. Devyn helped drag the carcasses out of the slime and threw them on a truck. The sheep's skins peeled off and he pulled the meat and bones things off the field – some with their guts hanging out and twisted. Smelled worse than it looked. He only threw up once.

Make that twice.

No, honestly, it was three times.

The boss sent him home looking green and very weak.

I had asked Devyn's parents for the address and that afternoon, I showed up at his place on Remington Street. "Can I stay with you for a while?"

He cautioned, "Only if you get a job. I'm eating oatmeal three times a day. I'm so hungry my stomach thinks my throat's been cut. I sold my car to pay for tuition and books. I'm riding an old 350 Honda motorcycle way down to Longmont for my job picking up barrels of grease and bloody bones from butcher shops. I'm barely scraping by."

We negotiated with the landlord a slightly higher rate for an extra bed. I got a job in the auto shop at the local K-Mart. I had bought a 1956 Ford pickup truck that needed engine work, shocks, and brakes. It had chrome exhaust stacks and chrome on the engine. I sold all the chrome parts for money to repair it.

About that time, Jimi Hendrix died of a barbiturate overdose in London. I told Devyn about the dude in San Francisco who had lost his leg from barbs. We agreed we'd only drink and smoke cigarettes, no drugs.

Having a friend around took the edge off the pain of losing Dove. We got into deep discussions about love, free will, and the power of the State. I lived with self-punishment and doubt. "What was I supposed to do? I couldn't go back and kill more women and children. Now I'm on the run. The Feds might pick me up anytime and toss me in prison." My brain was addled. "Does might equal right? Must we obey higher authority or get punished? Try to strangle a man and he'll fight back fiercely but choke him slowly and he doesn't realize he's suffocating. War is death and chaos bobbing up and down that makes you numb and brain dead until you're finally home, then you realize everything you were doing and believed in was wrong."

I walked around in a daze, feeling bitter and confused. We were too young to vote but I had been killing people in Vietnam. "Vets can't vote the bastards out of office that sent us there."

Devyn said, "You made a good moral choice. Why beat up yourself for that? To me, you're a hero. You made the best choice and were powerless to change the orders you were given."

"I choose out of the situation. I had nothing but bad choices." At the moment, I just wanted to feel safe and die quietly like an insect on some car's windshield.

"You were a pawn in a worldwide political game that has nothing to do with you. War is a racket that makes big corporations big money." He went on, "You're feeling guilty because you volunteered so you're punishing yourself. But hell man, you were in love. If Stormy wanted me to join the Army and I didn't have the chance to explore what it meant before I went in, I'd a done the same thing. The only reason I didn't go on a Mormon Mission is I had the chance to dig into the religion enough to realize it is total BS."

I lite a cigarette. "Now you're paying the price for having done the research. Maybe if you hadn't, you'd be down there in Guatemala, converting people hoping Stormy was waiting for you."

"Yeah, but there's no guarantee she would stay true just like Dove abandoned ship when you were in Vietnam. Or like that crazy dude in Wichita on a mission. And the Mormon religion is a crock. No way I could convert people to something I don't believe."

I said, "Who's to say a woman won't leave after you are married? Times can get tough."

"Maybe it's good they dumped us. We love them and fantasize about being married to them, having a family and all that, but it'd be worse if they didn't have the strength to weather the problems we're sure to face."

He offered me a Camel Filter and I took it. Devyn said, "For sure, Dove didn't have the strength or courage to wait. It's better you found out now instead of after you had four kids, then she left you."

One night I yelled, "Incoming!"

"What?" Devyn raised up from sleeping.

I thought someone had woken me by the toe. I was back at Dong Tam. "I felt this tug on my right toe and a voice said, 'incoming,' which means the VC are walking in mortars. I yelled and everyone scrambled to the bunker. We waited and no mortars came in. Everyone was upset about getting woken up and we went back to the bunkhouse. As soon as my head hit the pillow again, mortars began walking in so we headed back down to the bunker. Sure as hell, they hit our barracks and blew it to smithereens. We would have all been fried meat if I didn't have that dream."

"Must have been intuition. You were supposed to live," Devyn said, "You must have some purpose. Rowdy, you've got to come to terms with your ghosts."

"I don't know why I'm alive." I swallowed hard. "We go through life thinking we're making free choices. But culture is so embedded in our consciousness we don't know we have alternatives."

Devyn said, "In a sense, we're always innocent. We make the best choice we see at the moment."

"Few of us have the awareness that Jesus did before he was crucified. Did Adam have awareness? Did he understand the consequences of being exiled from God's presence, from the garden? If he had spent a week out in the desert before he ate the apple, would he have resisted Eve's request?"

"The Garden of Eden is a metaphor about our innocence. You are actually a hero. Over there, you learned it was wrong to kill innocent people. It took balls to desert." He took a deep breath. "I admire you."

"Thanks, but I feel like I lost my soul over there."

"You didn't lose your soul – you lost your naivety. You lost faith that our government tells the truth and does the right thing."

I said, "If you think about it, Jesus was foolish. He should have taken off right after the Sanhedrin trial. Maybe he would have lived a long life."

Devyn laughed. "There's a theory he did. Some claim he lived in southern India into his late eighties as a great guru."

I shook my head. "A guy never knows what is true does he?" I started to tell him about Cây Lan but couldn't. I choked up and couldn't. It was like my guts were tied up and knotted like those dead sheep Devyn had picked up for the rendering company.

58. Turkey

Like Jimi Hendrix, Janis Joplin whacked herself with drugs and went to hippy heaven. In the middle of October, Nixon announced the U.S. was pulling 40,000 more troops from Vietnam before Christmas. I was happy I wasn't over there. I felt better about the decision to desert because all the helicopter door gunners remained in 'Nam.

On his birthday, Devyn called Stormy. For once, instead of hanging up, her mother said, "You made your choice when you didn't go on the mission. I'm not letting you hurt her again. She is dating a returned missionary and they are a good fit. She will be married in the temple after she graduates from high school. You are evil to the bone. Don't call and don't write – I destroy everything you send Stormy."

He felt like a total turkey. Better than being a dork but the consequences were the same. Devyn couldn't bring himself to talk to the college girls because he didn't want to get his heart broken again.

At the end of October, Halloween parties fired up all over campus. We went to one at the Theta Chi house across from the university on Laurel. I picked up this cute redhead dressed like a carrot. Her firm boobs were all but hanging out of her tight orange top. Bringing her back to the little room, we had great fun.

It drove Devyn crazy as he tried to sleep. The girl sighed and giggled. Reminded him of Stormy. He missed her more than ever, fantasizing they were married and living together right here in this little room on Remington Street. He imagined them having a baby because he was taking Human Growth and Development. Comforting, but a fantasy. Devyn cried himself to sleep thinking of their lost love while I got taken care of.

On November 4, The United States turned control of air bases in the Mekong Delta over to South Vietnam while pulling out more U.S. personnel. "I knew that was going to happen," I said, "I'd still be over there firing my machine gun to protect the helicopter."

Devyn rode his 350 Honda motorcycle to class. Out of nowhere, the car in front slammed on its brakes. The choice was tail-ending it or dumping his bike. He squeezed hard on the right front brake. The front tire locked down and he did a complete flip over the handlebars, hitting his head on the pavement and sliding on his back feet first. *This is it, this is it!* He came to a stop under the car's rear bumper. He pushed himself from under the car and jumped up.

The truck driver behind him came to a stop with its front end over his motorcycle, blocking traffic.

Waving thanks to the driver, Devyn tipped up the bike. The handlebars were twisted in a knot, but with a surge of adrenaline, he pushed it to the curb.

A passing student asked if he was okay. "Yeah, shook up, but I'm in one piece." The back of his black jacket was ripped to ribbons, his helmet was cracked, and his bad knee hurt like a.... His right wrist was dislocated. Taking a deep breath, he pulled on it until it popped back in. *Dang that hurts!* He thought, *I gotta buy a car before the snow.*

I told Dev, "It's fate man. You're alive for a reason." We laughed.

A couple weeks later, he introduced me to sandy-haired Sue, a cute blonde-haired Mormon girl. We started seeing each other.

Devyn called her Susie Q after the song by Credence Clearwater. "So you seeing Susie Q again tonight?"

"Reckon so, she's a horny one."

It was close to Thanksgiving when the guys at the Theta Chi house offered their basement for half the cost of the room on

Remington. We hung old sheets on the ceiling and walls to keep dust off their beds. The old forced air gas furnace was loud when it kicked on. It didn't bother me since I had lost hearing in one ear from the artillery near my barracks in Vietnam.

Devyn rolled a barrel of bones, blood, and fat off a butcher house dock. Slick with frost, it slipped and the barrel edge landed on his left foot, breaking several toes as blood and fat spilled all over his shirt and pants. He managed to make it through the day but quit that night, telling the boss, "I can't handle this job anymore. I'm tired of stinking, my wrist hurts, and now my toes are broken."

A week later, I took him to get his last check from Longmont Rendering. The boss said we could have one of the half alive turkeys they picked up from a farm. "We keep them if it looks like they might make it."

They were roosting in a shed. I got a tire iron and smacked one on the side of its head. It smelled like the rendering company so we tossed it in the back of my pickup truck.

Fitz was from Nebraska and constantly talked about hunting geese, ducks, and turkeys. He loved Wild Turkey whiskey. We got to drinking beer that night and decided it'd be funny to put the rendering company turkey on his bed. We propped its little gobbler head up on Fitz's pillow and laid it out on the bed all cute and smelling nasty. Getting toasted, we forgot about it and went to bed.

Late at night, Fritz came home. We heard him stomping around above our heads, yelling at the top of his lungs, "Who put this fucking turkey on my bed? It stinks!" Doors slammed as Fitz threw it outside.

The next day, we thought about plucking and roasting it for a Thanksgiving dinner but nobody wanted to fish it from the trash barrel because of its wonderful bouquet – puke. I was hungry for meat. "If you get me Fitz's Wild Turkey whiskey, I'll dress and pluck it."

Devyn snuck into Fitz's room and snagged the bottle. "Let's chug it and I'll help you."

We drank the whole fifth and staggered by the time we had it gutted and plucked. The next morning we cooked it for hours. The American Indians seized a replica of the Mayflower that Thanksgiving, but heck, our turkey was the best dinner everyone had in a long time.

"I can't believe you put that god-awful stinking turkey on my bed," Fitz said, "I nearly lay down on it because I didn't turn on the light." He forgave us for drinking his Wild Turkey whiskey. "I don't blame you. That thing smelled like puck and shit."

Devyn got a job in the psychology department filing papers and helping the professors tabulate research results at half his Longmont Rendering pay. At least he didn't stink after work and his toes and wrist healed. He saved enough to buy a car after he sold the motorcycle. It was a yellow Pontiac Lemans with a black vinyl top and an automatic. Black leather seats and an eight-track player but the thing was gutless. "Someday, I'm *not* going to be poor. Maybe then a girl will be loyal to me."

Although he never heard anything back, Devyn sent letters and songs to Stormy. Her mom tossed everything but maybe she'd miss one. He hoped her returned missionary wasn't like the ones he met at the Mormon youth conference one summer. All of them were only interested in getting laid.

He bought a poster with a butterfly leaving someone's hand. It said, "If you love something, let it go. If it returns, it is yours, if it doesn't – it never was."

We stared at it every night before we went to sleep, trying to understand how love works. It was as pointless as going on a Mormon mission or to Vietnam for a woman. But the Thanksgiving turkey was good.

59. Psych Survey

On January 2, 1971, they banned cigarette advertising on TV but everybody kept smoking like there were health benefits. I liked my job at Kmart enough to stay in Fort Collins. I bought a 35mm camera on a blue light special and took a photography class at Front Range Community College since they let anyone in without checking records.

Winter semester, Devyn took social psychology. The major assignment was a field research paper. We thought it'd be fun to interview girls in the dorms about their sex lives.

I broke it off with sandy-haired Sue. "She reminds me too much of Dove. She wants to get married in the temple but she's nowhere near as beautiful." Maybe we'd meet a nice girl, at least one better than Big Kate, this waitress I picked up late one night in a college bar.

She was pretty if you were drunk. We called her Big Kate for her double Ds. If a guy was stoned, she looked like Gracie Slick of the Jefferson Airplane. She'd pop over after her shift as a waitress in the bar after two in the morning and do me.

Devyn listened to us grunting and groaning and tried to imagine he was up on Grand Mesa at the Milk Creek beaver dams hanging around with Stormy and catching little brook trout. He kept wondering if their love meant anything to her. *Why am I so self-deceptive? Stormy might have hooked up with a returned missionary while I was in Guatemala and I would have been destroyed.* It was better this way. At least he wasn't selling Mormonism in a foreign country while she married a returned missionary in the temple

I had enough of Big Kate. I told her to quit bothering me so she went over to Devyn and gave him head. He nearly said stop but damn, it felt good, and he pretended she was Stormy. He wouldn't let her crawl on to satisfy herself. "No Kate, I'm a married man." He lied for self-preservation. Better than lying to convert someone to Mormonism.

Big Kate went through most of the other guys in the house, and one by one, the guys told her to stop coming to them room. She circled back to me. By that time, I was horny. When I got tired of her again, she'd slip over to Devyn.

After a month or two, the guys held a meeting. One night, we *all* stayed up late and told Big Kate to stop coming over.

At first, she didn't believe us, but when she realized we were all serious, she ran out of the house yelling, "I don't understand why you guys don't want me!"

Guess she didn't think that we all knew all of us were sampling her big boobs and big fat…

Devyn and I came up with a list of twelve questions to understand what college girls thought about sex. We piloted it at Ingersoll Hall. Some of the girls slammed the door in our faces when we said we were doing a survey of sexual behavior for a psychology class. Several were nice and took the survey seriously. Sexual attitudes were all over the map. Some thought it fine to have a quickie, others said it was immoral unless you married. Devyn got an "A" on his paper.

His first.

Dev's writing was improving but at midterms, the professor in his creative writing class pulled him into his office. Pulp crime writer, James Crumley, lit a cigarette and blew smoke in Devyn's face. He said, "I don't know how to tell you this but if I'd known how bad a writer you are, I wouldn't have let you in the class."

Felt like the professor had stuck a sharp pencil in his gut. "What do you mean? There's no hope for me to be a writer? I'm a junior and I thought this was a sophomore-level class."

"It is and you're not good enough to be in it."

Bubbles floated in his eyes. Devyn said, "What can I do? It's too late to drop the class. If you had told me earlier, it wouldn't be a problem." The sucker hadn't bothered to read their stories until now.

After some back and forth, they worked out a deal – Devyn would take a C and not come back to class.

Crumley said, "If I don't have to read your crap, it's worth it to pass you." He unnecessarily added, "You're so bad you couldn't even learn formula writing."

Devyn was devastated and quit trying to write fiction for years.

In the process of researching sexual attitudes, I met Paige. She took the survey seriously and answered honestly. She said if you cared deeply for the other person and were honorable; it was okay to have sex outside of marriage. She was a cute teen from New York State with a tight body that made me consider lifting weights. But mostly, she had a sense of humor and genuinely liked me. We saw each other regularly.

Devyn found himself without a buddy to have philosophical conversations with. Made him miss Stormy even more. Some nights he'd pretend to call her and imagine what she might say. When the fantasy stopped, he was lonelier than a prairie dog in a foxhole. He sent Stormy a song he wrote for her. "I love you in the winter when leaves begin to fall." She never wrote back. Probably engaged to her missionary.

Near the end of January, a hundred soldiers testified about Vietnam War crimes. The Winter Soldier Investigation gave me daymares. I'd hear a truck backfire and hit the ground. But reading the articles convinced me that if I became an investigative journalist, he could make a difference. I started a journal about my Vietnam experience.

I was always with Paige.

Devyn remembered Susie Q. A Business Finance major, she couldn't hold deep conversations but was open-minded. She agreed the Mormon religion was pretty much BS, although she still wanted to get married in the temple. She grew up in Grand Junction so they had rural Colorado thinking in common.

One Saturday after she spent the night, she wanted to take a bath together. He said, "Why not?" There were two bathrooms in the Theta House so he told all the guys the one with the tub would be occupied that afternoon. Neither had taken a shower or bath with someone of the opposite sex. It was an interesting experience, to say the least.

All the guys were jealous. "How'd you talk her into it?"

"She's the one who suggested it." Wasn't long after that Sue got serious but Devyn told her the truth. "I'm married to Stormy in my heart. I don't think I'm capable of loving anyone else. My heart is too broken and my truster is dysfunctional."

She wanted to heal him, but Devyn said, "I like you, you're charming and will make some man a good wife. I'm sorry, but I love Stormy. I think about her day and night. It's not fair to you. We shouldn't see each other anymore."

She took it like a man. For several weeks she stuffed her feelings, then came over to our place and blew up. "You're such an ass, you led me on, and you used me. You never loved me. I hate you, and you should be condemned to hell."

Didn't make either of them feel any better even if there was some truth in it.

One day Albert walked into the house holding three baggies of marijuana in his fist, "There are lids all over the lawn." He looked like Al Hirt and strangely enough, played the first trumpet in the CSU band. He was from New York City and planned to be a music teacher.

We were watching a *Star Trek rerun.* "What are you talking about?"

He dangled baggies in front of us. "I swear there are full lids all over the lawn, come see."

We ran outside and sure enough, all bagged up, fat one-ounce lids of marijuana were scattered around the front lawn, right there on Laurel Street across from the dorms where the police cruised on the hour.

Devyn yelled, "Far out!" One of the guys in the house had a dog called Garth, and it tossed the lids of marijuana around the lawn like they were Frisbees. Afraid the fuzz might see it and bust us, we gathered over a pound's worth and took it into the house. We divided the weed among the guys.

Smoked like good Mexican stuff. We found a short carpet roll and poked a hole in one end for the joint. A guy huffed and huffed until the tube filled up with marijuana smoke, then the man at the other end uncovered it and THC smoke blasted into your lungs. You'd stagger around higher than a kite.

We called it Big Kate.

They were building a restaurant on the lot next door. A couple of days later, we saw some long-haired hippy frantically digging in the dirt that the contractors had piled up from excavating the foundation. I said, "He probably buried his pot in the dirt and Garth found it." We called him pot hound after that. Great dog and excited to jump for Frisbees. Had a nose for weed.

Some girls rented the house next door and pot hound made friends. The cutest one, Jackie, went for Harold, the strangest long-haired dope head in the house. He slurred words and stayed stoned day and night. Maybe marijuana was the answer.

One of the guys was a nerd with wild hair that stuck out all over. Randy wanted to get into CSU's Vet MED program, but he seldom studied. One night we were playing Risk at the girl's house and Randy said, "Oh heck, I have an organic chem midterm tomorrow." He disappeared for twenty minutes and came back to the game.

I asked, "I thought you had a big chemistry test tomorrow."

"Yeah, I flipped through the chapters. That's enough."

"You're kidding me."

"Nope, when I take a test, I mentally look up the right page and find the answer."

Randy was shy and never dated, yet he ended up with Mary Ann, who planned to be an English teacher.

Like usual, Devyn didn't have a girlfriend because he was still in love with the Mormon female who dumped him for a returned missionary. In the meantime, I was falling in love with Paige. "She's a good woman and a great lover."

A couple of weeks later, me and Devyn got the munchies after smoking weed. We took my pickup to the 7-11. Stoned, it took a long time to decide what to get. We kept picking up snacks, staring at 'em, and putting them back – up and down every friggin' lane until the clerk came over and helped us find something. Guess he was used to this. On the way home, we got to talking and I missed the turn in to the house. I drove around the block. Devyn said, "Pay attention this time." We talked and missed the house again.

I said, "Let's concentrate. You tell me when to turn into the driveway." It happened four or five times before we finally caught the turn. We were living in a Cheech and Chong show.

Every time something came on the news about Vietnam, I had nightmares. Par for the course, I woke up screaming and cursing.

Devyn sat beside me as I told him about killing villagers and people working in the rice paddies. He said, "Rowdy, there is something else that happened over there. I can sense it. Tell me about it."

I shook my head. "No. It's stuck down in my craw. I don't know if I can ever talk about it."

The U.S. table tennis team visited the People's Republic of China. They called it "Ping Pong Diplomacy." Nixon went to Russia and everybody thought the Vietnam War might end.

Paige had to drop out of CSU because she ran out of money. She asked if I'd move to New York with her. I told Devyn, "We might get married. I'm going." During Spring Break, we drove east together.

After the burning of Old Main last spring, the big war protests died out at CSU but students were still upset about the Vietnam War. On March 10, the 26th Amendment was passed to lower the voting age from 21 to 18. Ironically, I was already twenty-one.

The same month, Calley got a life sentence for his role in the killings at My Lai.

In April, the Vietnam Veterans Against the War staged a series of protests, and other demonstrators engaged in mass civil disobedience with 12,000 people arrested. Vets flung medals on the steps of the Capitol, threw medals over the White House fence, and marched to the Pentagon and Congressional hearings. Servicemen roamed congressional office buildings to make their case. The former Pentagon aide, Daniel Ellsberg, leaked the Pentagon Papers to the New York Times. On April 24, two hundred thousand marched again in San Francisco.

Devyn wrote that the fraternity guys checked out The Library, a topless bar in Greeley that just opened. Devyn couldn't believe he was having a beer with cute topless college girls serving. No touching allowed. Made him feel crazy. Stupid to look and not touch – better not to look at all. He'd rather dream about Stormy and make himself nuts wishing he could hold her. Damn, no matter what he did, he ended up thinking about her. It was like somebody had drilled a hole in his heart and kept scraping it with a piece of salted celery.

I understood because oftentimes, I still ached for Dove.

60. Portraits

Paige was from New York and planned to attend the university at Syracuse. I took a job at a giant steel mill and we lived together. The factory covered several square miles and had more employees than many towns had people. A lot of the workers were WWII vets, tough-as-nails union men, and the brotherhood. They were as strong-willed mentally as they were muscled. You peddled them no bullshit, and you got none in return. After work, the men drank beer, told stories, and laughed at the local pub.

No one got a raise at the factory unless he moved up the ladder by taking a more difficult job in the plant. Job openings were posted weekly on a bulletin board in the cafeteria and had a rating number next to them corresponding to the level of difficulty and pay scale. I found one nobody wanted. The job had been open for years and was never filled successfully. It paid twenty-five cents more per hour than I made. They tried me and soon, I figured out the machinery and got the raise. Heck, after working in the Glade Park sawmill, this was a piece of cake.

I took night classes at the local college in photography and journalism. As a result, I became very artistic with black-and-white photography, learning how to capture emotions on film. I studied journalism at night and picked up an enlarger to develop photographs.

Paige posed for me around Syracuse. Together, we found ways to turn common, ordinary structures and buildings into political statements; she was the subject but the object was to end the Vietnam War. Some of my photos were picked up by the local newspaper and a couple of them went out on the AP.

Paige knew my story – the whole thing from Dove to Cây Lan, and her heart broke for me. She loved me back to normal but she would not marry me with the desertion hanging over my head.

At one point, we had a pregnancy scare and she said, "I will never ask you to go back to the Army. I'm proud of your courage and the honor you've shown by deserting that immoral war, but how can we get married and start a family with it hanging over our heads?"

"I understand what you're saying. It would be the pits if they picked me up and you were expecting."

Tears of frustration and sadness ran down her face. "The problem is, we don't know how long it might take to get out of prison or the Army. They may send you back to Vietnam because the US is still ferrying the South Vietnamese in our helicopters – you could get killed."

"They might send me to Leavenworth this time because I've deserted twice."

"How long could they lock you up?"

"Five years, more or less." We talked about moving to Canada, only four hours from Syracuse. But that was a permanent decision. I would never be able to come back to the U.S. and I would never see my family or friends again.

It weighed Paige down; I saw the changes in her face from the photographs I developed in my darkroom. She became thin and drawn. It was the weight of me, of my legal problems with the Army.

"Listen, Paige, I'm setting you free from me, from my problem with the US government. I love you, I enjoy you and I want to have children and make a family with you. God knows you'll be a wonderful mother but this is draining the life from you." I showed her the difference in the photographs of her from the time we met until now.

She agreed.

No woman deserved to have my crime hanging over her head. I got in my old pickup and drove three long hard days to Glade Park, where I asked Tom Knutson to put me back to work.

A safe harbor, I could work there until the Vietnam War ended.

61. The Sawmill

There was still snow in the mountains when I arrived back to Western Colorado in mid-April after leaving Paige in New York. The sawmill had sat idle over the winter months. Tom Knutson hired me to get the mill ready which he hoped to start up around the first of May. I was hurt from losing Paige. It was lonely since I mostly worked alone. The other crew members began arriving near the end of the month.

In May, I had a crew of thirteen men. Mr. Knutson wanted me as his foreman because of my military background. "I know you won't be afraid to tell the men what to do." He knew I had deserted and understood the consequences because he had served in the Korean War. Tom thought I was brazen to desert, and anyone with balls like that could probably handle just about anything.

I learned to operate bulldozers, tracks, big tire loaders, and diesel trucks. I sharpened chainsaws and took them apart for repairs.

Tom taught me how to fall big, straight pine trees, and how to calculate the number of board feet before it was touched by a blade in the mill. Tom was seldom around since he did the business and marketing of the lumber products in town. So it was up to me to keep things in order and running smoothly. It meant keeping a crew of young, uneducated rednecks and hippies focused on the job instead of killing each other during downtime.

The *New York Times* published the first installment of the Pentagon Papers on June 13, 1971, and Americans learned the true nature of the Vietnam War. It contained stories of drug trafficking, political assassinations, and indiscriminate bombings. The government officials thought foreign communists were fomenting the anti-war movement. At nights, I was killing from my door gunner position and often woke up screaming. The good thing was my men knew I had killed during the war and that made them wary to cross me.

I also cooked lunch and dinner. It was easy to please these meat-and-potatoes guys. All I needed was fire and a big cast-iron skillet. We ate illegally harvested deer. My little brother, Toby, worked in the mill for three months, but he hated being told what to do by me so I nearly fired him for being lazy.

Some of the workers wanted to smoke pot during work hours but I put a stop to it to keep them from chopping off a body part. Still there were broken bones and mangled fingers. We found the remains of a finger still stuck inside a work glove a few days after an accident. It belonged to the green-chain operator, Taylor, who was recovering in the hospital. But his pinky had taken up residence at the mill. When placed on the window sill of the cookhouse, it quickly mummified and turned brown.

A fun trick good for a knee-slapping laugh was to plant the dried fingertip between slices of a bologna sandwich during lunch and offer it to an unsuspecting new employee or hide it in a steaming bowl of hearty bean soup. It became a popular initiation rite that everyone looked forward to whenever a fresh hired hand showed up.

A friend of Tom's son came to work at the end of May and he brought along his wife, Bertha. They had a baby girl. Bertha took over the cooking duties. She constantly bitched about having to live and cook at the mill with a bunch of foul-mouthed men who had the table manners of starving dogs.

I got together with Dove and again tried to explain the horrible carnage and my reasons for not going back.

Her fiery blue eyes became remarkably cold. An indefinable, faint expression on her lips turned into a mocking uneasiness.

I felt her energy shrink, leaving only darkness as if I had walked into a freezer warehouse. Anything to dry her tears:

"Dove, if you could only understand – the creep was reading me the riot act, gonna bust me to a buck private, and he had no idea of what it's like to be in combat. I know this is hard on you and it's hard on me too. I'm so sorry, but I can't go back. This war strategy of killing anything that moves is absolutely wrong. People are dying who shouldn't be. It is an immoral war."

She walked away.

As I stared at her tight ass, I thought, *I should have had sex with her before I brought that up.*

I wrote Devyn, "Hey if you need a summer job, I can get you on at the sawmill. Free room and board and a dollar and a quarter an hour."

In June, Devyn arrived. Soon, he wasn't happy to have committed to work far up in the mountains since he couldn't swing by the Dairy King to see Stormy. Even if she wouldn't look at him, he could watch at her serving people at the Dairy King. He didn't appreciate it when we stuck the mummified finger in his scrambled eggs. "This is gross. Why the fuck did you do that to me?"

"It was just a joke, man. Don't get so upset," I said.

I used a big claw loader to pick up a log and took it to the four-foot diameter circular saw. The sawyer sliced the bark off, using a hook mechanism to turn the log on each side. Once it was square, he sliced off boards. When he got to the core, the sawyer cut a fat railroad tie. The next man pulled the boards off the rollers and ran them through the edger saw that came out on rollers. The ender used a radial arm saw to cut the end of each piece and shoved the trimmed boards down rollers to stackers that placed them in different-sized piles. It took two men to pick up and stack the heavy railroad ties.

Devyn was a stacker at the very end of the "green chain" and got covered with wet sap as he sweated under the tin roof.

"Take a shower over there." I pointed.

The water was cold and the food was always beans and macaroni or some variation with a bit of hamburger. Devyn started calling the cook, Bitchy Bertha. He said, "I need to see some normal people. Anyone besides these smelly hairy legs."

The next weekend, I took him down the mountain. The dirt logging camp road has a long series of switchbacks and was narrow. You might meet someone coming the other way. "You're going too fast, slow down," Devyn cautioned.

As we made another turn on a switchback all of a sudden, my hands slipped off the wheel. We went straight off the road.

Devyn screamed, "We're going to crash!" The front end flew up from the ground as our heads hit the headliner. He yelled, "Hang on!" Grabbing the roof handle.

Wham! The back of the car hit the dirt and the front came down hard and rocked up as the car fishtailed.

"Ha, ha, ha." I laughed hysterically.

His face was white, Devyn panted. We were on the cutoff. I steered the car back onto the main logging road, still laughing so hard that tears ran down my cheeks. I stopped the car to catch my breath.

"You jerk! You knew about that cutoff."

"I couldn't resist. Tom did that to me the first time I came up here. It's the sawmill initiation."

"You got me good!"

Seeing the dark place on his jeans, I laughed again. "You peed your pants!"

He looked down. "Dang, this is embarrassing!"

We grabbed snacks at the Glade Park store and Devyn changed into a swimsuit. I took him over to the Pot Holes, a swimming hole. Girls!

Devyn was excited. High school girls from Grand Junction hung out in bikinis on the slick rocks overlooking the falls. He tried to talk to them but they weren't interested. We realized their boyfriends had jumped into the pool below and were climbing back up.

The work was hard and Devyn couldn't sleep because half the guys in the bunkhouse snored, others farted and most didn't bother with the cold shower so they stunk. He pushed me to go to Delta so he could get a glimpse of Stormy.

I said, "Why are you trying? Her dad says she's dating some guy who's back from BYU for the summer. He's a returned missionary, probably the same one she dumped you for."

Devyn didn't care. He hoped if she saw him, it might give her a heart pang, and she'd stop and think. After getting a soda at the Dairy King and not seeing her, we went to the drive-in movie to see *Little Big Man* with Dustin Hoffman. We had tried to see it two years ago and I started having bad flashbacks so we had to get out of there. I said, "Let's try it. Maybe I'm better. I heard it's a great movie."

We pulled onto the hump to get a speaker and I said, "Dev, you've got to let Stormy go. She's gone."

"Have you let Dove go? I mean completely? You still fuck her once in a while."

"In my dreams. Since I deserted the second time and told her that I couldn't go back, she won't look at me. It's over."

"Yeah, but you still love her, don't you?"

I couldn't answer because I wasn't sure. Probably, maybe, yes, and no.

We enjoyed the beginning of *Little Big Man*, but when the fighting between the Calvary and Indians started, the sound of gunfire got to me and I was back in Vietnam. "Sorry, man, you gotta get me out of here."

"It's still bad, huh?"

"Yep." I was nearly hyperventilating.

On the way back to the sawmill, the radio played, "Everybody's talking at me. I don't hear a word they're saying – only the echoes of my mind."

At the end of June 30, The United States Supreme Court upheld the right of the New York Times and the Washington Post to publish classified Pentagon papers about the Vietnam War. It inspired me. I sent letters to the editor and short articles to newspapers regarding political issues hoping to gain name recognition. Nothing progressive got published in conservative Western Colorado.

Tom Knutson had a couple of dirt bikes that he let us take riding after work. It was a blast and we rode hard, shaking out our muscles from the stress of lifting tons of wood each day. It was great until Devyn wrecked when he popped up over a rise and met a log that had fallen overnight. Didn't hurt him, but it tore up the bike. We weren't allowed to ride the dirt bikes after that.

Bitchy Bertha kept serving only beans and hamburger, macaroni and beans, or hamburger and beans, meal after meal. The guys complained and Devyn was pissed when he figured out that Tom was taking a quarter per hour out for food. "This sucks. He should be serving us ham, steak, and chicken at that rate. I thought it was free room and board."

I shrugged, saying I'd talk to Tom about the meals next time he was around.

One weekend, we went to the Escalante Potholes and stopped at Captain Smith's stone cabin. Seems the man was a Civil War vet. After it ended, he came out here and became a hermit. "That's where I'll end up in about a year," I said.

"You don't mind being way out in the mountains with no women, other than bitchy Bertha around?"

"I do, but what choice do I have? I'd love to be in college majoring in journalism, but I'm sure the FBI would nab me. They'd send me back to Vietnam as a door gunner since Nixon's Peace with Honor isn't going anywhere."

We liked going to Tom's Tavern, a bar on Delta's main street, to play pool. This tall muscular fellow, Jack, worked at the mill. He claimed he was a black belt. It wasn't my job to find out.

One weekend, some dude got mad when Jack beat him at pool, and he swung his stick at him. Within seconds, Jack had him on the floor with the pool stick pinned to his throat.

The bartender yelled for all the pool players to get out. After a bit of an argument, it was clear Jack hadn't started it. He booted the fellow and let us stay.

Devyn heard about a prank someone at college had played in a bar, and he talked us into trying it. We went to Tom's Tavern the next weekend. The bar served food and people brought their kids in. We ordered a pitcher and held a chugging contest.

Out of nowhere, Devyn acted like he puked, using a hot water bottle with warm chicken soup under his shirt, and he blew it all over the table.

Everybody jumped back.

A girl screamed, "Oh God!"

Jack and me had big spoons and said, "Don't worry, we'll clean it up." We took spoons of the soup that looked like puke and put it to our mouths. I got it up to my nose and it smelled like vomit. I nearly threw up for real.

Everyone in the bar stared in shock. Women screamed and our waitress gagged and threw up.

Using a spoon, Devyn acted like it was delicious as he stuffed his mouth with chicken soup.

The bartender yelled, "Hey, you can't do that in my bar!"

Devyn jumped up from the table as we followed close behind. He called out, "Sorry 'bout that, I didn't mean to puke."

Folks were horrified.

Outside the bar, our sides split with laughter. I said, "I didn't think you'd do it."

"You challenged me to. Where's my twenty bucks?" Devyn said.

I handed him a twenty and we laughed our tails off.

The bartender came out. "You guys don't come back in here, you hear?"

I said, "Hey man, you can't ban a fellow for puking. He didn't mean to."

"Heck, you guys, I've got to clean that up nasty stuff." The bartender stomped his foot and pointed. "Don't come back." He slammed the door on his departure.

Devyn did a Clint Eastwood pose. "That was groovy man."

Everyone laughed.

Nixon announced that the United States would no longer convert dollars to gold at a fixed value, ending the Bretton Woods system. He also imposed a 90-day freeze on wages, prices, and rents because inflation spiraled out of control. Australia and New Zealand withdrew all their troops from Vietnam.

I liked being up in the mountains where the Vietnam War was a distant memory. I avoided the news and didn't have nightmares except when the wind pounded through the pine trees. In the back of my mind, I wrote an investigative piece akin to the Pentagon Papers story. Something that would put Johnson in jail for getting us into the Vietnam War.

Devyn left his 450 Honda motorcycle at a shop in Delta. The agreement was he'd pay the mechanic every week. After he made a payment, we saw *The Summer of '42*, a movie about a kid seduced by an older woman. Devyn said, "This is the Bummer of '72. No Stormy, and no other options while eating beans, hamburger, and macaroni and stinking of pine sap while listening to hairy legs snore and fart in the bunkhouse." He complained so loudly about the food that Tom Knutson permitted us to poach a deer.

Devyn and I snuck up to a pond that deer frequented and lay down in some tall grass. Suddenly, there was thumping and a whole herd of does and fawns ran to the pond. They began drinking while I sat there without taking a shot. If Devyn had the gun, he would have immediately popped one.

I lay there watching. A deer nearly stepped on us and Devyn said, "Dang it, shoot, knock one down, Rowdy. They're about to trample us."

I plugged one in the neck and she fell. We stood up. The other deer didn't see us as if we were invisible. Some still drank at the pond although one of them was laying at its edge, bleeding out.

Devyn yelled, "Get outa here, shoo! Run you crazy deer."

They scattered in all directions.

I stood staring. I was back in Vietnam and these deer were villagers. I just killed a woman.

Devyn jerked my arm. "Look there's a fawn that won't leave. You must have hit its mother."

I shook my head, trying to come back to this place. "Oh shit. Damn it. That's why I was taking so long. I didn't want to kill one with a baby."

"Dang it, now you need to kill the fawn. Look at the tits on the deer, it has a full udder. You got to shoot the fawn too."

The fawn frantically ran around its mother, panicked, it bleated.

"Shoot it, dang it." Dev reached for the gun. "If you don't shoot it, I will. Put it out of its misery."

I let him take the rifle because I was about to throw-up.

We gutted both carcasses and carried them back to the camp. Mr. Knutson was nervous about getting busted for poaching and said we needed to hang them in one of the fall-out shelters.

Devyn skinned them out while I paced around outside the shelter. I was back in Vietnam.

We left the meat hanging. Tom said it needed to cure for a while before eating it.

Weeks went by and every night, the men asked Bitchy Bertha why she didn't cook the venison since they knew it hung in a fallout shelter. She shrugged. "I haven't been given permission."

Sick of beans and hamburger, we went to the shelter. Maggots crawled through both carcasses. I was especially sickened. I told Devyn what had run through my mind after I shot the doe and the other deer ran around like frightened villagers. "Man, you have no idea what it was like in Vietnam."

He looked at me without really understanding.

The last weekend Devyn worked before going back to college, I stopped on the way to town at Cold Shivers Point. We walked out to the edge where I pointed out the logging truck lying on its side at the bottom of the canyon. "The driver lost his brakes and couldn't make the turn down the Monument. He managed to jump out, but they still haven't been able to get the truck."

I yelled into the canyon. "Fuck the war! War…war…war echoed. I screamed, "I'm not going back." Back…back…back.

Before we left, Devyn yelled, "I love Stormy…"

It echoed, Stormy…Stormy…Stormy.

I understood.

62. Cedarberry

The next June nine months later, Devyn graduated with a bachelors and he hit the road to see his love. Stormy had moved into her own apartment just south of Eckert. A white car sat outside. He knocked and stood back politely. It was a clear day with blue skies and just the right temperature. The apple trees had green leaves and were just starting to bud.

Her emerald eyes opened wide as she stood at the door, blinking. "Well, this is a surprise."

"Can I come in or do you have company?"

"No, it's just me. Yes, you can come in."

It had one-bedroom, was neatly arranged and sparkling clean. They talked casually for several minutes; Devyn couldn't hold back the question eating him. "So are you seeing someone?"

A shy smile. "I'm engaged."

His heart dropped down through his gut and hit the floor where it wallowed. He almost said 'Shit!' out loud. When he caught his breath, he asked, "Is he a returned missionary?"

Shaking her head, she smiled. "No."

A touch of relief. "So what is he? Where did you meet him?"

"I met him at the Dairy King in Delta. He's Catholic."

"Catholic?" He said aloud. "You're shitting me."

A slight chuckle. "No, for real, he is Catholic like the rest of his family, and they are wonderful, loving, and warm."

"Your mom didn't have a fit?"

"Oh, she did, but I'm eighteen and on my own, and she can't do anything about it."

He damned near dropped to his knees to beg but looked her straight in the eyes. "I thought you'd wait for me. I've graduated and it looks like they might stop drafting guys for

Vietnam so I can decide what to do with my life. I might go to graduate school or the Peace Corps or maybe work construction, but I wanted to see if you were available and if so, we could decide together."

She held up her left hand, showing a cheap diamond engagement ring. "I'm sorry, it's too late."

Devyn took a deep breath and exhaled. Fighting tears, he turned for the door and then stopped to look at her. "I'll love you my whole life." He ran from the house, started his car, and took off, wondering what the hell he was going to do. He could still get drafted so maybe he'd go to graduate school.

He stopped by his grandmother's trailer, thinking to have her read his palm and maybe spend the night. She said, "Since you graduated from college you can start paying back the money I loaned you."

Dev had hoped she might make it a graduate gift. He sat for several minutes, then asked, "How much do you want for the monthly payment?"

"Twenty-five dollars and I'll start charging you five percent interest since you're out of college."

"Okay, Grandma. As soon as I get a job, I'll start paying you." At least she didn't charge him for rent and food like his dad when he stayed the night. Going to graduate school might be a plan.

He went up to my house since we were his second family. I was there. I had an ice business with a string of machines and vending locations.

To Dev's delight and surprise, my sister, Hetty, trailed a four-year-old and was divorced. They had liked each other through junior high and high school, but he had fallen in love with Stormy while she had run off with her now ex-husband. They hadn't talked since graduation.

She gave him a big hug and kiss. It felt like old times. They used to joke that she and Devyn would get married, and I would marry her best friend.

I said, "I knew Stormy was dating some Catholic. Her whole family is upset. She's probably doing it to rebel against her mother. I doubt she'll marry him."

"She acted very confident when I talked to her a half hour ago. Said she loves his family."

He and Hetty had a lot to talk about. He stayed with his grandma for a few days, then drove up to Hayden to see his parents and tell them about Stormy.

His mom was sympathetic, but his dad hit the nail on the head. "You're lucky she's engaged. We always thought she'd have troubles since her mom is so up and down, and Devyn, she's biologically a Falcon. You know how he is, and she probably inherited his cunning. She took you for a ride." He took a puff on his cigarette. "Jesus, you was gonna go on a mission for her, and she still dumped you."

"Mind if I spend one night without paying?"

Mom insisted.

It was good to feel welcomed by his mother, but since he was over eighteen, he had to leave in the morning or the old man would charge him rent and food.

Devyn needed to find a job.

He asked all around but the energy crisis was worse. There were long lines at gas stations. Nobody was hiring long-haired hippies fresh out of college, figuring he was a draft evader. The country was in a recession. He camped at night using the floor mats for cover because it was cold and he didn't have a tent or sleeping bag.

Devyn didn't feel sorry for himself because the draft might expire. He felt free and full of hope, if sad, about Stormy. He kept thinking about Hetty and decided to go back to

Cedaredge. He got hired to drive a route for Delta Coca-Cola and rented a dumpy trailer in Eckert.

Hetty thought he was handsome in the Coke uniform, and they started seeing each other. They already knew everything about each other and agreed on everything from politics to the best brand of cigarettes. They were both hurting. It was a rebound, but each needed someone.

On June 30, 1973, the government ended the draft. Devyn said, "I did it! I avoided Vietnam and I'm free." He started seeing Hetty seriously.

Dev and I rode motorcycles all around and one night coasted off the Grand Mesa with our girls. It was a full moon so we shut down the engines and lights. We listened to the chains clicking and the tires humming in the moonlight. It was magical.

In midsummer, Devyn drove to Grand Junction and took the operator's union apprenticeship test since the Cola job didn't pay well. Wasn't long before they left a message he was called out. He was to report to a controversial site way up in the mountains near Reudi Reservoir outside of Basalt not far from Aspen. They were tunneling to divert water to the front range. He had just enough money to rent a room and buy groceries, and then he reported to work as a brakeman.

The next week, Devyn called Hetty.

She left the kid with her parents and came to visit. He and Hetty were in love or maybe it was lust, but it didn't matter, it felt good and they'd known each other for a long time. He was a part of our family so it made sense.

There were calls for Nixon's impeachment after he ordered Attorney General Elliot Richardson to dismiss Watergate Special Prosecutor Archibald Cox. Cox was investigating the Watergate issue. Things were going crazy at the top. It inspired me. I became more determined to get a degree in journalism so I could write some incredible investigative piece that made a real difference. "The problem is my military record. I don't think a college will admit me and there's always a risk of the FBI picking me up." I passed the GED and bought a bunch of college textbooks to educate myself.

Devyn stayed in a tiny room at an old mining hotel and avoided the drinking men below in the bar. He wrote a poem for Hetty, "Dancing to the Essence of Love," sending it to her.

She wrote back, saying, "Come see me. I got a job in Montrose."

I was confident since I had a business and money. I had pretty much stopped worrying about the FBI picking me up and especially being shipped back to Vietnam as a door gunner since the US had pulled out. I dated different girls, got laid, and felt that maybe I had a decent life ahead of me.

Stormy married the Catholic guy and went off to live happily ever after. I cut their photograph from the local paper and gave it to Devyn.

"Geez, thanks for nothing." He threw it in the trash.

Dove still wasn't married but flaunted money from the Falcons. I felt nothing but despise for her. I wouldn't have minded having sex with her again because she was so darned beautiful, but the last time had been flat without feeling. I told Devyn, "It's just sex. I felt like I was doing it with a hooker." I thought a moment. "No, the girl in Vietnam was better. Heck, she's not even a good prostitute."

I had finally stopped loving her.

In mid-October, it dumped two feet of snow and Devyn got laid off. With no hesitation, he headed for Hetty and moved in with her. One of our older brothers got him on at Montrose Distributing, and then after a couple of months, he took a job at Russel Stover's new candy factory.

Dev and Hetty had fun playing house but struggled with her boy, Mick, since he was a handful. They had constant arguments about how to handle him. Devyn thought he was right because he had taken a course in child development, while Hetty knew she was right since she was his mother. They had some hellish fights but always made up. It was a cycle of intense love-making spliced with yelling but they genuinely liked each other and could talk about anything.

The apartment walls were so thin you could hear the neighbors pee and flush the toilet. The couple in the next apartment banged their bed on the wall and hollered during sex every night. Devyn knocked on their door, asking if they could move their bed to the other wall.

The guy said, "Hell, we can hear you too, move yours."

He and Hetty moved their bed to the other wall to get some sleep.

In November of 1973, Nixon said, "I am not a crook," confirming he was. By the end of the month, it was revealed there was an eighteen-and-a-half-minute gap in a White House tape recording. They had the smoking gun and were after Nixon's ass.

I cheered them on. "They'll get that asshole. He's keeping our Army helicopters in Vietnam. I just wish they'd go after Johnson, he's the one that got us into the war." I was incredibly happy I deserted.

At Christmas, everyone went to my family's house to celebrate. We played chess and cards, laughed, told stories, and joked. It was warm and everyone loved each other. Dev couldn't believe we treated him like one of the kids.

Both Devyn's and my Dad had been abusive so he and Hetty knew exactly what buttons to push. His psych professor said couples get married to do therapy on each other and were like a grain crucible, grinding wheat into flour. God, did he and Hetty grind.

He asked her to marry him.

She said, "I'm not ready." A month went by and she asked him.

He said, "We've got a lot to work out."

His dad said he should marry her because it wasn't good for the child with them living in sin.

Mick caused a heap of trouble at the daycare center. They were about to kick him out so Devyn spent hours there watching and thinking of suggestions. Nothing worked. He finally started paddling the boy as his father did to him, but instead of just wacking him, he had a long talk with Mick, explaining why he was paddling him and it helped. Social Services called. The caseworker implied Devyn was abusive. He was twenty-two and he'd be tried as an adult. The bed-banging sex fiends next door had just moved out. Dev figured the neighbor turned him into social services after he complained to the manager about their noise.

He talked the bank into financing a trailer house. He knew he'd better get away from the child before he got arrested for disciplining him.

63. Montrose

On August 8th, Richard Nixon resigned and Gerald Ford became the President. In September, Ford pardoned Nixon and the resulting outcry pushed him to proclaim conditional amnesty for Vietnam War deserters and draft evaders. I told my family, "I'll believe it when I get an official letter."

One weekend, Devyn and Hetty were at our parents' house. A couple of weeks back Devyn said something about me always bumming smokes. I walked up and shoved a carton of cigarettes in his face. "Here, god-damn it. This for all the cigarettes I've bummed off you."

Dev stood up. "Hell, I didn't mean anything. I was being an ass. I don't want your cigarettes." He pushed them back.

I shoved the carton into his chest again. "Take them."

"Seems like you want to kick my ass. Hell, I'm game."

We went outside and beat the shit out of each other. I thought I could take him in a heartbeat but Devyn was strong and quick. We pounded each other, back and forth, bloodying each other's faces and hands.

Hetty dragged a water hose over and sprayed them with cold water, "Yelling, Stop it, you two. I love you both."

We quit punching and stared at each other for a couple of seconds, then walked away. Guess it was one of those best friends guy things. Who knows?

It was over a month before we spoke again. Dev and Hetty were dancing in a bar in Montrose and I walked in.

Dev nodded, and I nodded back.

Hetty waved me over so I sat down with them.

Dev bought me a beer.

"Thanks."

Things were good again.

Hetty was upset that Devyn didn't ask her to move into his newly bought trailer with him, but he was scared of social services. He didn't want to treat the child like he had been and for sure, he didn't want to end up in jail. But he loved her, me, and everyone in our family as we did him. They kept dating and spending the night once in a while, going back and forth about getting married.

Although he had moved to the trailer without Hetty and the boy, they often went to one of my brothers to play pinochle and no one said anything. It was strange because every time Dev asked her to marry him, she said, "Not yet."

She started dating other guys and on occasion, he'd see her out dancing with one. It broke his heart. We hung around and neither of us brought up the matter. A weeks went by and Devyn called her. They got together since she wasn't seeing anyone. A month went by and Hetty stopped taking his calls. He gave up and tried to find another girl, but a month later, she called him. They were experts at grinding each other into flour.

I finally received the amnesty letter from President Ford in November. Five years of paranoia, being on the run, and losing girlfriends when I told them the truth. I was tired of being afraid to sign my real name to newspaper articles, of thinking the FBI tailed me, and of moving without a forwarding address because the stockade hung over me like a ten-mile high thunder cloud.

Devyn said. "Good for you, you're a free man now. You can be yourself again. Like I said, you're a hero in my eyes."

"I'm no hero. I should have never enlisted. Got a lot of guilt over what I did in Vietnam."

"No need to punish yourself the rest of your life. Move on, be a free eighteen-year-old again. You've been frozen."

I drove to Denver to sign the papers. The drive over the passes was spectacular with snow on the mountains. The rules required two years of community service. The agent handed me a list of approved agencies where I could complete the two-year obligation. "Hey, these are all in Denver. Isn't there anything in Western Colorado where I live?"

Nope, everything was in Denver.

I was pissed – the government had no right to tell me where to live. On December 20, 1974, I was discharged with *other than* honorable conditions, but I did *not* feel free. Guilt and carnage haunted me.

I blew off the community service. "What are they going to do? Send me to Vietnam as a door gunner?"

Devyn said, "You never know. The U.S. Army is still over there ferrying South Vietnamese troops around,."

"They'll have to find me."

The year struggled by and Devyn was lonely anytime he didn't see Hetty. His ninth-grade basketball team did poorly during the season but took the league tournament to everyone's surprise. It saved his job because he had been put on probation for yelling at his students like his dad had yelled at him.

At one point, he was called into the office about his car being seen at DeJulios' bar.

"They have a restaurant and I often eat there."

"This is a very religious community and people are saying things."

Devyn started parking way down the block. Montrose was too small of a town.

My 162nd Airborne Helicopter unit finally pulled out of Vietnam. The Khmer Rouge was taking over Cambodia and the U.S. bombed the hell out of them and Laos. The last American combat troops were out of the country, but there were still U.S. military advisors and those guarding the U.S. Embassy in Saigon. South Vietnam was losing the war to the communists. The U.S. initiated the evacuation of American civilians and at-risk Vietnamese from Saigon on April 29, 1975. Within two days more than 7,000 people were evacuated by helicopter. I watched the images on TV with my family and friends in Cedaredge.

Devyn said, "We should be glad neither of us are there. If you had enlisted for another three years on top of your initial enlistment of three years you might still be."

"No, I would have been done in January of this year."

Devyn shrugged. "The point is, I'm happy you deserted, and I'm glad I didn't enlist. It's been a waste of billions of dollars and millions of lives. The Vietnam War is finally over for the U.S.."

We high-fived.

I said hopefully, "Someday I'm going to write a piece that makes maybe prevents a war like Vietnam." I was surprised that my buddy didn't smirk. Someone believed in me.

That summer Devyn rode his motorcycle to Mesa College in Grand Junction to earn credits so he could move up on the school district salary schedule.

I had also enrolled in college. I worked as a motel night clerk and lived in a basement apartment. Dev started staying with me ever so often. The landlady yelled at him for being there, threatening to kick me out. One night after a horrible nightmare about killing Vietnamese, I jumped up and started tearing the place apart.

Dev joined and we nearly destroyed it.

In the morning we realized what we had done. I said, "We'd better get out of here."

We packed up. I found a shitty room in a two-story house on Pitkin avenue. The room had a frig, hotplate, and an outside door.

I started banging this girl named Marta I picked up at a bar. She was plain as the fields of Kansas, nearly featureless with a flat nose and no eyebrows. And she wasn't smart. Turned out she was raised in a Mormon sect. We briefly talked about getting married in the temple.

Devyn asked, "You sure? She's kind of odd."

I shrugged. "At least she's a blond. She's better than nothing – she drinks like a fish and is great in bed."

I majored in journalism and was on the road to becoming an investigative journalist. Since I had self-taught for several years, I was way ahead of the other students. The college newspaper hired me as a reporter.

Since he and Hetty were on another break, Devyn hooked up with this recent Cedaredge High School grad, Cindy, another Mormon. She was wild in the sack. One weekend I brought Marta and we camped out on Grand Mesa in the same tent. Everyone got sloshed. We watched each other do it. Pretty awesome.

Before she left for CU in Boulder, Cindy promised she'd be true to him. "Someday we'll get married in the temple." She often called and wrote, saying she loved him.

Since things were off with Hetty, he started thinking, *Well maybe…*

The next school year, Devyn transferred to Olathe because the school district was moving ninth grade to the junior highs.

His old coach from Cedaredge High, Alex, was now the assistant principal at the small junior-senior high school. They traded off driving to work. Alex advised him about class management and how to motivate students without being too stern. "You don't need to yell. In fact, its better to lower your voice and talk seriously to get the kid's attention."

Devyn traded his GTO in on a brand-new 260Z to be like Coach Alex. My family accused him of thinking he was too good for us since he wasn't seeing my sister and also had bought a trailer house and a new car.

"No way!" To make up for it, he called Hetty. They started seeing each other again, but like usual, they fought, made up, didn't see each other, and then got back together. Every time they broke up, he thought about Stormy.

He heard she was in Grand Junction and tracked her down. She opened the trailer house door, looking surprised. She was six or seven months pregnant.

"Well, what are you doing here?"

He couldn't hide his shock. It took a minute to say, "Heard you were in town and wanted to make sure you're doing okay."

She pointed at her womb. "I'm expecting." Two toddlers waddled over and hung on her legs.

"I can see that. Guess you're happy."

"I'm alright."

There was anxiety in her eyes and a slight tremble on her lips. It was clear things weren't going well.

She didn't invite him in, and he wouldn't have gone anyway. It was over.

He called Hetty when he got back to Montrose. "What ya up to?"

During a separation from Hetty, Cindy came home during Thanksgiving break and spent the night, then she went back to CU. Devyn kept itching down there. He realized Cindy had given him the crabs. He quit taking her phone calls.

She showed up again during winter break in December, claiming she had been loyal. She asked why he quit talking to her.

"Cindy if you're going to sleep around, you should check yourself once in a while. You gave me the crabs the last time you were here. I had to boil the sheets and use Blue Ointment. It was disgusting."

I told him about Cindy trying to do me up on Grand Mesa while he and Marta were asleep.

"Geez, man, wish you'd told me back then so I would have known she was a slut. I wouldn't have had all those dreams about marrying her in the Temple."

I was probably the only guy who understood. I still periodically had vivid dreams of marrying Dove in a Mormon Temple.

64. Gunnison

Before heading to Western State for his master's in counseling, Devyn came to Grand Junction to hang out because suddenly, Marta had ghosted me. I was dumbfounded since she was so plain she was all but ugly. I couldn't imagine she had found another guy.

We went out drinking and dancing, and since Hetty was seeing a new guy, we picked up a couple of girls. I picked up this looker, and Devyn got stuck with the big one.

The girls said, "Let's go skinny dipping. Our apartment complex has a pool."

It was late at night and no one was around. The foxy lady stripped and we both drooled.

The big one took off her clothes and jumped into the pool, causing a huge wave.

Me and my new flame sensually swam around together while Devyn did laps. The big gal was on her back and her huge honkers stuck out of the water. Squirting water from her mouth, she said, "Look, at me, I'm a whale."

Everyone laughed so she kept doing it, over and over. "I'm a whale, I'm a whale."

We got out of the pool and the fox took me to her bedroom while the big gal expected Devyn to follow her. He couldn't do it. He kept thinking of Hetty and Stormy, both who were petite and skinny. He said, "I'm sorry, I'm engaged and I can't."

"It's because I'm big and fat isn't it? You're making an excuse."

"No, truthfully, I've been seeing someone for the last three years. I'm sorry I didn't tell you ahead of time, but I'd like to be with your friend."

She was upset, yet accepted it and let Devyn sleep on the couch.

The next day as we headed out for breakfast, Devyn asked, "So was she good? You going to keep seeing her?"

I shook my head. "No, she was on the rag."

"What? She went swimming, and I didn't see a string hanging out."

"I know – fooled me good."

"I didn't know a woman could go swimming while on her period."

"Guess some kind of special tampon."

"So why did she take you to bed?"

"Her friend asked her to. She wanted to make sure you would do her, so she took me to her room." He grinned. "So how was the whale?"

Devyn laughed. "I told her I'm engaged to get out of it."

It was a good joke on us.

He bought his grandmother's old camper trailer and her even older 1952 Chevy pickup to pull it with. The darned thing barely dragged it up Cimarron Pass. It struggled to keep it from running away on the way down with smoking brakes. Blue Mesa pass was worse. People flipped him off as he chugged up the pass at eight miles an hour. It was a relief to make it into Gunnison.

He found a trailer park and got it hooked to utilities, then had a phone installed, and first thing, he called Hetty, "I made it!"

She'd come up next weekend.

It was a relief when Hetty arrived. She said, "When you finish the program, maybe we can get married."

"Sounds good to me."

Jimmy Carter beat out Gerald Ford as the next President. On January 21, 1977, Carter granted a full presidential pardon to hundreds of thousands of men who had evaded the draft during the Vietnam War, including deserters. I was finally free! And I was writing articles for the Mesa College newspaper. Life was good.

Devyn and Hetty continued their on-and-off pattern, and he finished the master's degree in record time. He went to summer school to have fifteen more credits on the salary schedule. Hetty and I met him in Lake City on the 4th of July.

It was an old-time celebration with a cattle drive down the main street. Cowboys shot blanks and roped each other. We sucked down a beer in one bar and some dude rode his horse in.

The bartender pulled out a shotgun, hollering, "Get that fucking horse out of my bar."

The cowboy saluted, "Just having some fun." He rode back out.

It was exciting.

We got too drunk. Devyn suggested riding back to the Gunnison with this guy he knew, and we'd get our cars in the morning when we were sober. Hetty sat on his lap because the car was full. She had on tiny white shorts. Devyn couldn't resist. God, she was sexy. They made out and rubbed all over each other, nearly making love.

From the back seat, a girl said, "No wonder she drove up here to see you."

Watching Dev and Hetty, the driver nearly ran off the road.

I was in the back seat between two coeds and tried my best, but they fought my hands off to my utter disappointment.

When the three of us got out, the diver said to Devyn, incredulity in his voice, "You're going to be a high school counselor? If you keep acting like you did today, you won't last long."

After graduation, Devyn drove all over the State looking for a job as a school counselor. Despite the low pay, he accepted one at a Catholic High School in Colorado Springs.

Hetty was upset. "I might as well start dating again."

"It's the only offer I have," he shrugged, "Maybe in a couple of years and some experience, I can get something closer to Montrose."

I worked up to being the Chief Editor at the Mesa College newspaper and received positive feedback for every editorial I wrote, preparing to become an investigative reporter. Someday, I'd find corruption and take the crooks down.

Hetty started dating around. Nothing serious since she still thought things might work out with Dev. They had been through this so many times; she figured that at some point, he'd get a job within driving distance.

To everyone's surprise, at the end of the school year, Devyn married a divorced Mormon girl and they moved to Grand Junction because he was offered a job in a high school. I dropped by his rental house in Grand Junction. Didn't stay long. As we walked outside, I said, "Man, you don't have anything in common. Why did you marry to her?"

"She's pregnant."

My head dropped. "Oh, that's tough. You'll end up with child support." We looked up at the Grand Mesa. There was a patch of snow people called The Bear on the Mountain. Next to it is another big snow patch called The Swan on the Mountain looking as if it was about to get eaten by the bear. As predictable as could be, you could plant your vegetable garden right after the Swan on the Mountain's neck broke. Nothing got frosted if you waited. If you weren't patient, your garden froze every time.

"What are you thinking of doing?"

"See what happens when the baby is born. I think she quit taking the pill."

"When did she stop taking them?"

"Don't know, she doesn't tell me much. I'm not sure when the baby is due."

"Well, man, you'll figure it out. I learned Marta was pregnant when she left me. She's never asked for child support because she didn't want me around because I'm a sinner."

"You're lucky."

"Well, good luck. You deserve it after what you went through with Stormy."

"Same to you. You went through hell with Dove and are still paying the piper." He kinda of chuckled. "She's probably the most expensive piece of tail you ever got." He grinned. "You ever put a pencil to it?"

Fuck me, I hadn't thought about it that way. Probably a couple hundred thousand not counting the fear, revulsion, and stress.

The college president wanted to turn Mesa College into a university although it would cost the taxpayers a large fortune. He was never in his office since he was over in Denver playing politics, button-holing congressmen, and talking to people with decisional power. This was my chance to establish a reputation for taking down corruption in the government. I wrote a scathing editorial, criticizing the college president, implying backroom deals and corruption.

It blew up.

Everyone in Grand Junction talked about it. The Daily Sentential printed a story about his editorial on the front page. I was elated and called Devyn. "Did you see the Daily Sentential? I made the front page!"

Devyn said, "I don't know, Rowdy. My parents know President Kiefer. He's a good man and is very popular. He teaches classes at a big church that they go to."

The day the president got back from Denver, I was called into his office, read the riot act, and fired from the paper.

In a fit of temper, I quit the journalism program with only one quarter to go. It was a hard lesson that the power of the pen is nothing if you piss off a powerful politician.

65. Oklahoma

With nothing to do, I thought of Martin Montoya, my buddy through boot camp and advanced infantry training. He should be back in Aztec, New Mexico since his service obligation as a draftee was only two years.

After quitting Mesa College, I loaded my old Ford Bronco to the brim and took off at four in the morning.

Marty was surprised to see me to say the least. He was smoking a cigarette and drinking a beer while sitting on that old stump his grandpa had marked with nails of family birthdates. "Well, look what the cat drug in and the dog won't eat." He said. He was half-stoned since he didn't have any handyman work for the day. Marty looked like he had been in a fight and had gotten flattened.

I grinned from ear to ear. "Hells bells, long time no see." We hugged each other and looked into each other's bloodshot eyes.

Marty asked, "Want a beer?"

"Not at ten in the morning but coffee would be great."

We went into the house to catch up. Marty had married a Vietnamese girl. He showed me her picture. She was cute, but not pretty like my Cay Lan. "She was sweet and innocent until I brought her over here. She got Americanized within a year and there are guys with a lot more money than me. She left before we had kids so I guess that's a plus."

I told him about Dove and Paige.

Marty said, "You're still trying to be the hero, aren't you?"

I took it like a man, which means you eat shit and say thank you. "I need to learn to say no to women. I try to prove I love 'em, then get dumped."

Marty said, "Yeah, we're still into the knighthood code of chivalry and service to the ladies."

He told me about this older gal he had met when playing pool who was constantly hitting on him. One night, he took her out to his pickup to shut her up. They had sex in the parking lot. "I wasn't attracted to her, but she wouldn't let up, so I did her. You know what?"

"Tell me."

"She showed up at my place a day later and wanted to have a relationship. When I told her I wasn't interested, she got mad and said I had to get tested for STDs to prove I was clean. I said 'I'm clean. You're the first female I've been with since my wife left.'"

"So what happened?"

"She said if I didn't get a test and prove I didn't have any STDs, she'd report to the police that I had raped her.

I blew her off and the next thing you know, I was sitting in jail. I got a lawyer and had to go through a psychological evaluation, all kinds of stuff."

"Did you get off?" I grinned, "I mean off the court case?"

"Yeah, but only because there were lots of witnesses in the bar who knew she kept trying to get me to have sex with her. They dropped the charges, but it cost me a small fortune and frightened the piss out of me."

"And made you more scared of women, didn't it? That's where I'm at now. When are we going to learn to stop trying to please them?"

"Yeah, we're hen-pecked, pussy-whipped, scared, low class, good-for-nothing wimps."

The conversation shifted to the war. Marty confessed to having PTSD. "I wake up in the middle of the night screaming.

That's probably why the wife left. I still sleep with my .45 under my pillow. Can't get over it."

"The only hearts and minds we won in Vietnam were big American businessmen's," I said. "I was thinking, given that 10% of the population has sociopathic tendencies, they should draft only those guys since they can kill without empathy and have no remorse. It's us guys with a conscience who get PTSD because we were forced to do wrong things." I shared that over 63,000 Vietnam Vets had committed suicide. "I've thought about it."

"Me too, but I ain't gonna let them push me into it. Wouldn't prove anything."

We smoked weed and drank beer for three days. Marty blew off a couple of handyman jobs. He'd rather sit on that old stump on his grandfather's farm. One night, we went out for a beer and played pool. When we were leaving, some idiot pulled up right behind me and wouldn't move so I couldn't back out. I honked and waited. I flashed the brake lights. Nothing. The guy was by himself and sat there, blocking us on purpose.

I got out and went to the driver's side window.

The guy rolled it down.

I said, "Hey fellow, we're trying to back out and leave, would you mind pulling forward a little instead of parking right behind us?"

I went back to my truck but the man didn't move his car. I honked and flashed the lights. Nothing. This time I was pissed when the guy rolled his window down. "This is the second time I've asked you to move. Are you looking for a fight?"

The guy grinned and stepped out of the car.

I hit him with a twisting punch square in the mouth.

He dropped onto the asphalt.

"I can kick the tar out of you or you can move your car. Which do you want?"

The guy got to his knees. "I'll move."

"It would have been easier if you had moved the first time I asked."

I went to the emergency room because the guy's teeth tore a hunk of skin off my knuckles and the human bite is the worst of all animals. Had to get stitches. Reminded me of taking shrapnel.

Back at Marty's, we were shaken up. The fight brought back feelings from combat. We sat up all night talking. I said, "It was supposed to be a short war. We were supposed to come back heroes but all we got was rejection. Everyone blamed us peons." I told him about the time my helicopter had given Marty's platoon a lift.

"I'll be darned. Why didn't you say something?"

"It was noisy as hell and I hated having to drop you off in the swamps, figured you might get mad at me since I had a nice dry bed at night."

"I wouldn't have gotten mad. I'da been happy you were still alive." A wry grin. "We got pulled out and ended up in Hawaii while you door gunners had to keep ferrying the South Vietnamese around. So I was the lucky one."

I didn't tell Marty that I went AWOL and then deserted.

We talked on and on. Drinking beer and shots of whiskey, and smoking weed and cigarettes added clarity to the discussion.

The next day after sobering up, I headed on to Oklahoma. My goal to see my son, but I stopped in Durant since I heard Big Owl was living there.

"Well, I'll be…" Big Owl said, slurring his words. "Never thought I'd see you again. Come on in."

It was the filthiest place I had ever seen. Beer cans, dirty plates of food, piles of cigarette butts, and clothes were scattered everywhere.

"Want a beer?" Owl asked as he opened a fresh one.

"No, I'm driving. Headed outside of Antlers to see my son."

"You got a kid?"

"That's what the mother says. She wrote my mom and said I can visit."

"I'll be damned. Who was it?"

"Some woman I met in Grand Junction. I thought we might work something out, but all of a sudden, she disappeared. Guess she's in this sect of Mormons and didn't want me around."

"You always were a bad influence." He finished his beer and opened another one.

"What about you?" I asked.

"Oh, hell, I got married, and she ran off with some guy. Said I drank too much and my nightmares scared her."

"I know that one."

We smoked cigarettes. Owl popped open another beer. I asked, "So what are you doing for work?"

Owl shrugged. "Nothing right now. Lost my license and can't drive. I need to take a bunch of alcohol classes and pay some big fines to get it back."

We talked a few minutes but I didn't stay long. The trailer smelled of man sweat, beer, and cigarettes. The toilet was crusted and smelled like an old outhouse. No way I wanted to spend the night there. I drove until I couldn't see, then slept in my pickup, looking forward to seeing my son, assuming I had one.

When I saw Martha again, I realized that she had the perfect face for radio. My two-year-old boy was called Paul.

They greeted me with reserved hospitality. It was a farming community on the plains of Oklahoma without electricity or power motors. They did everything by hand. They weren't Amish, but like the other women, Martha wore a brown dress with a white bonnet like in colonial times.

She said, "I could not raise a child in that party environment at Mesa College, therefore, I returned to my childhood faith community and made them my family. My son should know his father, but if you do not choose to live with us and practice our religion, you will not have any contact except on his request when he is of age."

I was shocked. Marta had been a drinking, drugging sexpot with me and had barely mentioned she was in a sect of the Mormons. If brains were dynamite she couldn't have blown her nose, and here she was telling me about religion. The only way to win an argument with her was to keep my mouth shut.

Everyone was courteous but when I declined the leader's invitation to learn about their faith, everyone, including Marta and the kid, politely turned their backs. They would not speak directly to me.

Shunning was a strange experience. Marta said to my child. "Your father is leaving."

I got the message.

All the way back to Grand Junction, I tried to understand it. We had partied with the best. Suddenly she had disappeared.

A guy never knows what a girl's going to do, does he?

66. Melanie

I sold advertising placements for several months to get by and then got on as a copyeditor for the Delta County Independent. The publisher and chief editor were impressed with my hard work and writing talent, so they gave me an assignment to write a feature article. My photos were remarkable. One article about an old rancher was sensitive, showing the struggles and courage of the fellow's life in Western Colorado. People called the paper saying how much they enjoyed it.

The publisher assigned me as a feature writer along with copyediting. "Take all the photographs you want, they are sensitive and descriptive."

Having landed on my feet, I wanted to find a woman worth marrying. A friend introduced me to Chrystal. Her husband had died of a stroke at the ripe old age of 36. She was 26 and had a three-year-old boy that was funny and bright. We went to lunch and Chrystal talked about how wonderful her deceased husband was, what a great father he had been, and how the little boy looked like his dad.

During the next months, I did everything I could to get Chrystal to fall in love with me. I was gentle and kind. I played with the little boy and bought him little toys and ice cream. I took them out for dinner and to a park where I pushed the child on the swings. I took them to movies. But nothing made Chrystal come out of her grief. She couldn't bring herself to kiss me. "I feel like he's watching me from above. I feel like I'd be cheating on him."

She was beautiful, kind, and smart. Didn't hurt that she had a paid-off house and a small fortune from the life insurance. I kept trying and trying, but she'd pull back when I leaned to kiss her. I realized I could never compete with a ghost who was the most perfect husband and father that ever existed in the history of mankind.

After several feature articles that the community liked, the publisher permanently moved me from copyeditor to photographer and reporter. I started looking for good stories.

I met a strawberry blonde woman who worked for an attorney. Melanie was smart and cute. I was spellbound by her intellect and energy. We had deep conversations about religion and politics. We agreed the individual should be sovereign and everyone should be free and equal. We ranted about racial injustice and the way big corporations ran the world, causing wars on poor people. Her economic and political philosophy was formed by John Locke and Milton Friedman – the free market should distribute resources based on the individual's contributions.

Our discussions left us stimulated. We made passionate love that put our souls on the ceiling. To me, this was the real thing, pure love.

Melanie was me-deep in conversation, but I didn't notice because she was bright and fun. She had grown up in the Reorganized Mormon Church but didn't attend anymore.

I moved in with her and admired the photos of her on the walls. Each one included her or her family. We agreed to split the costs so it was a good deal for both of us.

Melanie was a radical feminist, believing patriarchal power was the cause of the world's problems. She constantly ran down the male-dominated system and advocated the abolition of marriage because it suppresses women. She also believed in free love – everyone should have the right to have sex with anyone they want.

I was mesmerized by her flexibility in the bedroom. She could do things I didn't know were possible, especially when she was in her favorite position – on top in reverse cowboy.

When Devyn saw us together, he figured we'd be getting married and soon pop out a baby.

For the first time in my life, I was doing a job I loved with a woman who loved me. I agreed with Melanie the government should be eliminated – people needed autonomy to do what they wanted. There shouldn't be laws against victimless crimes like prostitution, gambling, and drugs. She was a free thinker, supporting homosexual and women's rights – everyone should be equal.

We often had other couples over for dinner. To my surprise, she prepared everything and wouldn't let me help, even with the dishes. I got to thinking that despite her avowed feminism, maybe deep in her heart; she was a traditional woman like Mother. The one time I met her family, that's the way her mom acted – helping everyone and being supportive of her husband.

I thought about marriage but didn't bring it up because Melanie would say I was trying to dominate her and marriage was an oppressive institution.

People came up to us at the store, saying, "You look like a happy couple." Everyone thought we were married because we fit. Young couples invited us over for cards, drinks, and dinner.

We especially liked this real estate agent and his wife. Donna was a looker like Dove with shining blonde hair and blue eyes. She and I subtly flirted when we were pinochle partners. In retaliation, Melanie flirted with Clint and made jokes about trading partners like in the movie, *Bob, Ted, Carol, and Alice,* but no one took it seriously.

Money flows uphill to power; in this case, it was power generation. Right after moving in with Melanie, I began a complex investigative piece regarding Colorado-Ute, a coal-fired power generation company. I received a tip that the company was cooking data to convince the Colorado Utilities Commission to approve the construction of additional coal-fired power plants. It was unclear why. One bit of information led to another. I took a trip to Denver to analyze the Utility Commission filings.

Melanie was fine with me being gone, saying she needed to work.

I went from Denver to the Hayden Colorado Ute plant to talk to the plant management. I stayed with Devyn's parents and interviewed Mr. McDowell who was a shift supervisor at the Hayden power plant. I poked around at the Craig, Colorado Ute plant before going back to Delta.

Melanie was fascinated with the information I collected. She helped me go through the confusing mass I had assembled and showed me how to organize and compile data in a legal case. Intrigued, we worked together, mapping out an investigation plan.

During the next months, I interviewed workers and managers in power generation and the electrical grid throughout Western Colorado. Many of the Colorado Ute employees were under tremendous pressure and were unhappy with the company. They gave me documents to support their misgivings. I was often on the road but on return, Melanie was welcoming like a full moon that drowned out the nearest stars.

I felt secure and happy for the first time in my life. Growing up with nine brothers and sisters, we had suffered from constant poverty with never enough to eat. Life was good. I sang to Melanie, "Loving you is easy 'cause you're beautiful."

Each time I went on the road, tracking down some lead for my potential Pulitzer-winning story, I said to Melanie, "Remember, we are under the same moon and I am with you."

Melanie responded, "My love for you isn't perfect, but it is constant."

We agreed we had no right to control each other. She demanded a high level of privacy, which was fine with me. I had things I didn't want to talk about, especially that I deserted. Remembering Paige, I was afraid of where it might lead.

When I was in town we often went out. "Dance with me, I want to be your partner."

I was surprised one day when Melanie's father showed up at the newspaper office. He wanted to go for a walk. Not a big man, but very intense with piercing gray eyes, her father gave me a rehearsed speech, "You're living with my daughter. She's a good young lady, she's smart, and she will someday be a lawyer. I understand you have a child, is that right?"

"Yes."

"What went wrong? Why aren't you with the mother of your child?"

"I don't know. She left suddenly. I didn't know she was pregnant until several months ago when she wrote my mother saying I could visit the boy. She lives in a religious commune down in Oklahoma."

"That doesn't make sense. You must have some weakness, some incapacity to be a father. You don't have a relationship with your child, do you?"

"I only met him once."

"My point exactly. You aren't responsible. I can't let you marry Melanie, you understand. She's my little girl, and I must protect her from men like you who don't have good careers and who won't be around to help raise any children."

I was nearly speechless but caught my breath. "I'm not sure she ever wants to marry, but if she did, I'd do my best to be a good husband to her." We looped around the block.

"Your best could never be good enough – you don't have a career that will ever amount to anything."

We were back at the newspaper office.

Melanie's father offered his hand.

I declined.

"I'm glad you understand." Turning, her father walked away.

I was more befuddled than upset. I talked to Melanie about it.

"Oh, Daddy is like that, – he's very protective."

That was it; she wouldn't talk about her father. But it was clear they had a special relationship because Daddy often stopped when he was in the area on a business trip. Melanie immediately left with him like they were on a date. Me not included.

One night because it was gorgeous out, we drove to Switzer Lake. We stepped out of the car to breathe the fresh air. The moon flooded the hills and fields with fresh beams that made everything appear ghostly. Holding each other, we slowly swayed back and forth until we were dancing. I twirled her and we two-stepped around the parking lot. Soon we were swing dancing under the moonlight as a song played through the radio, "It's a supernatural delight. Everybody's dancing' in the moonlight."

A pack of coyotes howled nearby, making the frogs go silent, but the moon held the space without judging or attacking. A solitary dark cloud extended its finger across the moon's face. We shivered with the mystery of romance.

67. Damned Depressed

Devyn held his wife's hand as much as possible but had to take breaks. He felt bad because they had been through a natural childbirth class and he was supposed to be there to catch the baby. It was a difficult twenty-three-hour labor. "Can't you do something? She's exhausted, please?"

They gave her a spinal. She still struggled. The doctor finally did an episiotomy so the baby could come out. It was a star gazer, turned upside down. It was a beautiful baby boy with blue eyes.

When she came home, Dodie was extremely tired and depressed. He tried to kiss her, talk with her, and hold her, but she scrunched away. He had to go to work.

One evening while she was asleep, he lay on the couch holding the baby to his chest. They had the same blue eyes, blond hair, and the same crooked smile. He knew it was his. They bonded.

Three days passed. He came home to her lying on the couch. "Are you okay?"

"Who's going to take care of the baby?"

"Huh? You and me, who else?"

He called her OBGYN. She had postpartum depression, according to the doctor. "She should come out of it in a couple of weeks." He talked his mother into coming to help but she could only stay a week. For some reason, her mother wouldn't come.

The next week, they were in bed and she said, "I want a divorce."

"What? That's ridiculous. We just had a baby."

"I don't love you, you don't love me, and I want a divorce."

"No way. Let's give this a chance. I'll fight for our marriage."

"You'd fight for anything. You coach football. You're violent!" She jumped up and ran for the door. Getting it part-way open, she ran into it with her shoulder. "Ouch!" She yelled.

He went to her. "Are you okay, did you hurt yourself?" He tried to put his arm around her.

"Stay away from me!"

The next day, a deputy showed up at his school. "Are you Devyn McDowell?"

"Yes."

"I suppose you knew this was coming."

"What was coming?" It was Monday, May 13th.

"I'm sorry." The process server handed over the documents.

His hands shook. Nothing says I love you like divorce papers and a restraining order. "What does this restraining order mean?"

"You can go to the house and get some essential things during the next twenty-four hours but once you leave, you can't go back. You have until two o'clock tomorrow afternoon to get what you need. However, you're not allowed to take anything that could be defined as a marital asset."

"What's a marital asset?"

"Anything you jointly bought or own like furniture, bedding, and stuff like that. Don't take anything that is hers."

Devyn was in shock. Hadn't seen it coming. It was like someone clocked him in the back of the head with a two-by-four board. He went to his Principal, "I have a family emergency. I need to go home."

Hyperventilating on the way to the house, he was surprised no one was there. He walked through and everything looked the same. *Was this some mean joke?* He packed a suitcase and grabbed his toothbrush, guitar, and some essential tools. He didn't have any money so he went to the credit union. Dodie had drained their accounts. He had $15.00 on him. He drove around town, trying to figure out what to do.

Using a pay phone, he called me.

"Man, I'm sorry, but I'm not surprised. You two weren't at all compatible." I listened to what had happened and said, "Sorry, I'm living with Melanie, and I know you couldn't commute from Delta."

He went to the high school and talked to one of the coaches. Chuck said, "Why don't you stay on the couch in the coaches' office for a few days until you find a place? At least you can take a shower."

He was upset; he had shared all the subdivision plans with Dodie, how they would split the lots off and build four-plex units. He calculated that if everything went right, they'd make over a hundred grand after the dust settled. But with this divorce, it couldn't happen; they'd be lucky to break even if he sold the house. The papers said she was taking possession of the property because it was in the best interests of the child to stay in the marital home. He was on the street. The temporary orders said he had to give her 80% of his paycheck each month in child support and maintenance. That meant he had to survive on $200 a month. Couldn't be done unless he worked two jobs. He was up a creek.

Nervous wrecks don't sleep at night, especially on the coach's couch in the locker room. In the morning, he took a shower and went to work as usual. He had a suitcase of clothes on the front seat of his 240Z, his guitar and music books, and an electric typewriter. His tools and a box of memories sat in the back. That was it. He was starting over. *Don't lose your job, Devyn. Don't lose your job. Stay focused at work.*

He canceled all the credit cards so she couldn't run up more bills, then drove past the house. He saw her parents loading everything into a big U-Haul truck.

He talked to several attorneys. They all wanted retainer fees. Predators. They said even if the house was empty, he couldn't stay there. "You'd have to get written permission from her since she has possession."

The restraining orders said he was abusive.

One divorce lawyer said, "That's a common allegation." He read on. "It says you bruised her shoulder."

"She got mad at me, jumped up in the middle of the night, and hit the door with her shoulder."

"Huh," he shrugged. "You'll need to pay a thousand dollars up front if you want to retain me."

Leaving, Devyn felt like a piece of shit.

Her parents took her and their baby to Colorado Springs. The house sat empty.

He went back to the house. They had stripped it bare, leaving only the wires to his stereo. She even took his Atari game and tools. All the furniture had been his. She hadn't contributed anything to the household, but they took every single thing, including his tent and sleeping bag. He found half of a stale package of macaroni in the trash. He was so hungry; he wanted to eat it but had nothing to cook it in. Ignoring the attorneys, he moved back in and slept on the floor without a blanket or pillow.

Devyn started reading, *The Greatest Salesman on Earth*. It said, "The blood of defeat does not course through my veins." His old man had taught him to be courageous when being abused physically and mentally so he clenches his jaw and made a list of what he should do. Shutoff notices for the phone and utilities came in the mail. She had quit paying her share two months before she left, apparently planning to leave. He called the companies and begged for time. "I get paid at the end of the month. I'll pay you, please leave them on."

He never had a good basketball shot but was great at rebounding – that's where all his points came from. He went outside that night. Rising over the Grand Mesa was a thin sliver of the moon. He needed to rebound again. Within a week, he got a half-time job at the City Market freezer warehouse working from 4:30 PM to 1 AM with no breaks. He got a few hours of sleep and then back to school at eight in the morning, determined to survive.

Figuring he might have to live in his car, he traded the 240Z for a pickup with a camper shell. At least he could stretch out and be dry if she got the house. His first purchase when he got paid from the freezer warehouse job was a sleeping bag and pillow.

Three different lawyers asked him the same thing, "Is she alcoholic?"

"No."

"Is she a drug addict?"

"Not that I know of."

"Is she mentally insane or incompetent?"

"No, not legally, but I think she's depressed"

"Is she a known child abuser?"

"No."

"You have no legal standing to get custody of the child."

One explained the Tender Years Doctrine which presumes a child should be with its mother and the baby should be in the marital home. "You're lucky she left. Since you're living there, possession is ninety percent of the law."

"You poor sucker," one lawyer said.

He worked at the freezer warehouse for over three months and was exhausted. One night he collapsed on the freezer floor. His bad knee from high school football had given out. "Come back tomorrow," the shaggy-bearded freezer boss said.

"I've got to quit. My knee is gone and I'm toasted."

He hobbled into a doctor's office and a week later, had surgery. The surgeon said old scar tissue had torn loose and locked up his knee. He went back to school on crutches. Kids gave him a bad time, "Hey Mr. McDowell, you stick your foot where it doesn't belong?"

He thought, *How did you know?*

Sunday afternoon, Dev talked to the Mormon bishop who was an insurance agent with six kids. Ray was shorter than Devyn and weighed three hundred pounds. He waved at a chair. "Have a seat. What do you want to talk about?"

He had been in several times, trying to figure out how to earn back full membership and also have Dodie's temple marriage annulled. "Can you call Dodie and talk some sense into her? Isn't marriage sacred?"

"As I've told you before, she was sealed in the temple to her first husband. Your civil marriage doesn't count and isn't sacred."

"It was sacred to me."

Bishop Harding shrugged. He said seriously, "Since his mother is sealed to a good Mormon, the baby is his son in the eyes of the Church and God."

"What?" Devyn's mouth fell open. "How can that be? He's my biological child."

Ray shook his head as if Devyn was feeble-minded. "They were sealed for time and all eternity and she will be with him in the Celestial Glory, so your son belongs to the man. He's *not* your child."

Devyn nearly jumped from his chair and said, "That's nuts!"

The Bishop leaned back in his big black office chair. "Devyn, do you know why I'm a Mormon?"

"No." He expected some lecture about the angel Moroni and the golden tablets and that it was the true church the only true church and the only way to get into the Celestial Glory was to do everything they said.

"The Mormon religion, the Mormon church, and its teachings, work for me. I'm comfortable with it. It may not be the right church for you. If it isn't, you need to find a church that works for you."

"Well so far, it certainly hasn't worked for me. This idea that my son belongs to another man is absurd."

The bishop turned up a palm. "You probably need to find another church. One that works for you."

He limped out of the office on crutches, feeling shocked, angry, and confused. He got to thinking. The bishop hadn't said Mormonism was true, he simply said it worked for him and Devyn should find a church that worked for him. The only reason he had joined the Mormons was to marry Stormy in the temple for all eternity and she ran off with a Catholic. He realized that being married for time and all eternity was a myth like Santa Claus, the Easter Bunny, and Democracy. For the last decade, he had tried to believe their bullshit, but there was no way he'd ever accept that *his* biological child belonged to another man. It dawned on him; *I'm free from the Mormon Church! I should find one that works for me.*

He found Dodie's first husband's phone number and called him out in Salt Lake City. He told what had happened.

The esteemed elder said, "She often gave me the cold treatment too. And she kept getting depressed. She's lay on the couch and wouldn't talk. She accused me of being abusive when we divorced. I was hoping she'd get over it with a new man."

Devyn said, "I kept trying to get her to have the temple marriage with you annulled but she wouldn't, so I guess she's still married to you."

The priesthood holder chuckled. "Sure, she'll be one of my wives in the Celestial Glory."

Dev went back to the bishop. "The Mormon Church isn't right for me. Pull my records and take my name off the church rolls."

Ray was a good man and got it taken care of. Devyn was free to believe what he understood was the truth which was the Presbyterian thinking that everyone has the right to worship according to the dictates of his conscience.

Dev stood in the checkout line at the grocery store. He glanced down at a little girl with blonde hair, thinking about his child. The child tugged on her mother's sleeve, "Mommy that man with a beard is staring at me."

The mother pulled her close and glared at Devyn.

He looked around, expecting to see some older man behind him. No one was there. It hit him, *I'm a man. I'm grown up, and I need to start acting like it.*

The temporary orders hearing rolled around and he was finally out of school. He couldn't pay an attorney and argued for himself, "Your honor, I don't make that much money. I can't afford the mortgage, utilities, buy food or pay for gas."

The judge looked at his paycheck stub. Devyn showed proof of her paychecks, saying, "She was a checker at City Market." The judge ordered him to pay a third of his salary to Dodie.

He took a job driving a gravel truck while working at a radio station on the evening shift. Drought-stricken trees held onto scattered raindrops as the big truck pummeled the ground with its tires. People pulled out in front of him and he yelled, "I'm in a big truck, I can't stop on a dime." Didn't help. Sullen people leaf work, the swish of traffic. He read marital law books for the five minutes it took to get loaded. He bought a two-wheel trailer and rebuilt it and then sold it for a small profit. Found another one and did the same thing. He needed money. No time for anything but work. Dodie's lawyer demanded half of everything, including the projected profits from the subdivision and from the sale of the four-plexes that would never be built. His dream of being self-sufficient disappeared in a puff of smoke.

He drove to Eckert to see Grandma. She read his palm. "I saw it in your palm, Dodie was just using you to have a baby. It's such a shame."

"This is the worst time of my life. I don't know if I'm going to survive."

"I've had several times I thought I wouldn't survive." She told him about her mother dying and their father leaving afterward. She and her oldest sister were only sixteen and eighteen. They had to take care of the younger ten children by quitting school and getting jobs. "But we got them all raised."

"Wow, I didn't realize you were so tough."

"The roughest period was when your grandfather got burned in the gas station because a fellow threw a cigarette into a gasoline pan. Your mother was playing there and Will grabbed the pan and ran it outside, the flames flying all around him. He caught on fire and rolled in the sand."

"Is that how he got those scars all over his body?"

"Yes. They took him to a hospital down in Las Cruces. A doctor told me he might not live. I stayed in a tiny room for months with your mother, just getting by. There I was with a five-year-old and no job." Tears came into her eyes. "We went to see him every day. Somehow he lived, but the doctors said he'd never walk again because he had been burned so badly. You can't imagine how terrible it was. Back then there were no government benefits and no insurance. A church gave us food and paid the room rent. As I recall, it was $3.00 a week." She looked up at the ceiling as she wiped away tears. "The most wonderful day of my life was when we went to the hospital and there your grandfather was, hobbling down the hall on crutches. He said, 'I'm gonna walk, Skinny.' He called me Skinny although I'm fat. You can't believe the relief I felt."

Devyn said, "I guess getting divorced isn't the worst thing that could happen."

The courthouse stood out from other buildings like a middle finger. In July of 1974, Devyn attended the final divorce hearing. Not that he wanted drama, but it was anticlimactic like his wedding to Dodie had been. There was a crotchety old judge, a court recorder, Dodie's lawyer, and him in the judge's grey office with a picture of Colorado Governor John D. Vanderhoof on the wall, framed by Colorado and U.S. flags. Her lawyer presented the signed documents and the judge scanned them. He asked a couple of questions of her lawyer and one of Devyn because the child support was at the minimum.

"I don't make much money."

He asked her lawyer if the marriage was irretrievably broken and he said yes. He asked Devyn the same thing.

"I don't believe in divorce. Marriage is a sacred promise for better or worse and no marriage is irretrievable."

The judge asked, "Then why did you sign this divorce decree?"

"Thought I had to."

"Do you agree the marriage is irretrievably broken?"

Her lawyer explained that if Devyn didn't say those exact words, they'd have to renegotiate everything and he'd push Dodie to take the property back.

"Okay, I agree the marriage is irretrievably broken."

The old judge stamped the document. "You are hereby divorced."

Devyn was surprised. It was as empty as their wedding had been, like sex with a hooker, not that he knew what it was like. Walking down the courtroom steps into the hot sun of the Valley of the Ute Curse, he told me later that he felt like he had committed a crime and was found guilty. "It was group sex. Dodie screwed me in front of the judge, her lawyer, and the court recorder."

The next weekend, he drove six hours to see his baby son.

She wouldn't let him. "You're supposed to notify me in writing. Talk to the judge."

Life was tough enough without getting kicked in the heart. Devyn went back to his hotel room with feelings so mixed you couldn't call it a scramble. It was more like eggs on the wall, cheese scattered everywhere, bits of meat and veggies on the floor with spinach sticking to the ceiling. How could he work so hard for so long with only a gas receipt?

He drove all the way home and got drunk. The radio played, "How can you mend a broken heart?"

I was in Delta living with a woman. Hetty was married just like Stormy so he was all alone in the world.

He enclosed the two porches to convert the house into a duplex and took in a housemate to make ends meet.

When he started school again in August, the principal said, "I need you for meetings after school." He was taken out of coaching. The only real joy of working in the schools disappeared. He went back to being an evening shift radio disc jockey. He got home at one in the morning and back to work in the schools at seven. Sure better than the freezer warehouse.

After Thanksgiving, the principal called him into his office. "You need to pull yourself together. You're just wandering the halls and teachers say you're spacy. People think you're doing drugs. If you don't get your act together, I'll recommend you aren't rehired next year."

I stopped by for a visit. "You don't look so good. You're pale and you're a skeleton. Have you seen a doctor? Maybe you have cancer."

Devyn shook his head, "No time and no money, I'm working eighteen-hour days. The tires on my truck are so worn you can see the air in them like when I was in college. My motorcycle seized a piston over the winter. Plus, I need to work on this house before I can sell it." He was damned depressed.

The radio said it would be cold tonight and the communists might take over the world.

68. Myeong

Somehow, Devyn made it through the school year with light snow, occasional rain, and episodic wind howling past the windows. In the spring he painted houses after school and on weekends. Life was slowly improving.

At a bar, he met a beautiful Korean girl who didn't speak much English.

She wasn't a typical bar girl. Myeong was only twenty-one and lovely. Her father had died. Korea had no opportunities for a single girl without a dowry. She now worked at a small factory assembling electronics.

He took her to Delta to meet me and Melanie.

It happened that Hetty was visiting with her two children in tow. Her son, Mick, ran to Devyn and hugged him.

Devyn patted him on the head. "How are you doing, sport?' He and Hetty hugged.

Myeong didn't understand much English but knew they were close.

Devyn felt the same old energy he always had for Hetty. She smiled warmly, trying to hide her attraction. He asked, "How's married life?"

There was yearning in her eyes as she met his. "Oh, it's going okay." She nodded at the tiny blond girl hanging on her leg. She pulled Dev off to the side. "You said you were getting married. A couple of months later, I figured that since I was pregnant, I might as well marry the father because I was finally ready. If you hadn't gotten married, maybe we would have."

"I wish I had known and I wouldn't have married Dodie."

They stared into each other's eyes until Myeong grabbed his arm.

Devyn gave Hetty a quick hug goodbye. She pulled him in. They kissed deeply and held each other's hands.

Myeong yelled, "Hey!"

He said they went to high school together and once had dated.

She didn't understand. When they got into his car I saw her yelling and then she slugged his shoulder. He suppressed a laugh and flipped me off.

On another weekend they met me and Melanie at the Delta park. We walked along the sparkling irrigation canal. I snapped impromptu shots of Melanie in patches of snow and caught her reflection in the slowly running water.

While the girls walked ahead, I asked Devyn if things were serious between him and Myeong. "She hardly speaks English and gets mad when I don't understand what she's trying to say, but the sex is fantastic."

"You planning to stay with her?"

"As long as possible. She seems like a good woman. Dobie never talked to me, so I'm used to being quiet." He shrugged. "I probably won't let her move in because things change once that happens." He asked, "How's it going with you two?"

"Great, couldn't be better. If she wasn't such an ardent feminist, I'd marry her in a heartbeat."

As we left, we wished each other good luck and happiness.

He and Myeong struggled to communicate. He couldn't learn Korean and she couldn't learn English, but their bodies communicated like angels.

However, one evening, she blew up because she was frustrated with his inability to understand her. She stomped out to her car and wouldn't take his calls after that.

Feeling like he must have pissed off God again, Devyn went to see his grandmother in Eckert. She read his palm and suggested another degree was in his future. It seemed like a good idea. He applied for doctoral psychology programs and law schools all around the country. To his dismay, the only one that accepted him was the University of Northern Colorado in Greeley – The University of No Credit.

Devyn sat outside his duplex watching the sun go down on a lonely evening the Friday after Memorial Day. He wished Hetty would call and say she was getting divorced. He'd marry her the moment she was free.

Not gonna happen.

69. Bury It

"Devyn, can I drive down to talk?"

"Sure, I've got a cold beer in the frig."

The day withdrew as I drove west in a trance. I shut my car off, slowly got out and sat down on the step next to my best friend.

"Want a beer?" He offered a Miller Genuine Draft.

"Sure."

My face was pale. "I was in Durango following a lead on the Colorado Ute story and returned to Delta about two in the afternoon because my contact got scared and didn't show." My fingers trembled as I lit a cigarette. "I stopped at the office and the publisher sat me down. He said my investigative piece was canceled due to businessmen saying they'd pull all their advertising if we ran the story. They wanted the construction jobs and the ongoing jobs when a new power plant was built outside of Delta." A puff and a swig of beer. "I quit on the spot and left for home. I had some flowers behind my back when I walked into the bedroom." I sucked on the cigarette. "Man, this is hard to talk about." I felt water in my eyes.

"Want a shot of Irish whiskey?"

"Sure, that might help." My hands shook.

Devyn brought a bottle out to the step and said, "Give me one of those smokes."

We did two shots.

After he lit up and took a deep drag, I spoke, "I opened the bedroom door and there she was, Melanie's naked back to me. She was rocking and squirming her hips on Clint."

"Who's Clint?"

"Fuck, I thought he was a friend. We played cards with him and his wife. Donna is gorgeous with a great body. She has blonde hair and blue eyes like Dove. Don't know why he'd want Melanie. We had joked about swapping but I never thought it was serious."

"Oh, man. I feel for you." He took a drink. "So did you kick his keister?"

"No. I was too shocked to say anything. It was minutes before she looked up and saw me because she was into it with this ass hole. She didn't jump off the creep. She said, 'What are you doing home so early? You weren't supposed to be back until after eight tonight." My eyes narrowed as I shook my head. "She just kept humping him."

"Another shot?" Devyn poured.

I knocked it down without moving, watching the scene over again. I shook my head and stared into the gathering darkness. "At least Clint tried to wiggle out from under her. His eyes were big. He must have thought I was going to shoot him. He knew I'm a Vietnam Vet and have a gun." I held out the shot glass.

Devyn poured more whiskey.

"Melanie had this look of entitlement. I dropped the flowers, turned around, and walked out. That's when I called you."

"She's a feminist isn't she?"

"Now I know why she didn't mind me going all over the State to research my Colorado Utilities story."

"You wanted an exclusive relationship and she had an open one. Cuts to the core."

I explained that I had spent several months investigating a proposed series of power plants by Colorado Utilities – a coal-fired electrical generation company that Devyn's dad worked for up in Hayden. "The company officials claim there is a power shortage in California. It's been running all existing plants at 180% of capacity to fake the need for more power. The PUC monitors how much above-capacity plants are running to determine whether to permit new plants. I discovered they're forging the data because they're nearly bankrupt. The only way they can stay solvent is to get cheap loans from the federal government they use to pay off existing debts, but the feds only loan on new construction. So they are forging data to show there is a need for new power plants."

"That's cynical. So what happened?"

"I had the data, the documentation – everything, including tape-recorded interviews of former employees. Colorado Utilities had proposed to build a plant in North Delta. If I published their scheme, it would end the whole thing and they'd be out of business."

"Isn't your job as a reporter to investigate and publish significant information that is the truth and impacts many citizens?" He offered another shot and I accepted, knocking it down.

"The Delta Chamber of Commerce got wind of my story and a dozen big advertisers went to the publisher, saying if we ran the story they'd pull all their advertising. They want the plant built because it would stimulate the Delta economy and bring in high-paying jobs. Anyway, my boss killed the story this afternoon, so I quit."

"All of this shit happened today?"

"Yes. My whole world just blew up. I feel like I'm back in Vietnam and I just got that letter from Dove."

"Geez. I feel for you, man." He looked sick.

I couldn't speak.

Devyn said, "So much for independent reporting."

"The reality is that all news stories are controlled by advertisers – that is why the news is only about crime, sports, or feel-good crap. They don't want anything published that might affect their sales."

"So our press isn't free, it's controlled, not by the government, but by businesses?"

"Hard truth isn't it? But that's the way it works." I was rattled, my dream of writing a Pulitzer Prize-winning Pentagon

Papers type of story was destroyed right as my relationship with Melanie had blown up.

"Didn't you say she had a strange relationship with her father?"

"It was odd, to say the least. I told you about him coming to the newspaper and walking me around the block."

"Yeah."

"He'd take her out to dinner anytime he was in town and they'd be gone for hours. It was like they were on a date."

"Sounds like something Cheri's dad might have done if he had a chance."

My eyes opened as I recognized the facts. My voice hardened, "I knew there was something weird about her dad. They acted like lovers instead of a father and daughter. He did everything he could to keep her from being close to me."

We did the man thing.

We went out to the Escalante Potholes and spent the night drinking, burning memories in a campfire and scattering tobacco to the four winds. The night was clear and warm with billions of stars glowing across the Milky Way. We built a sweat lodge with tarps to get the poison of infidelity out of our bodies, and then sat by the campfire, drinking beer and doing shots of Irish whiskey.

Devyn asked, "You ever see Dove around Delta?"

I gave a half chuckle. "Around all the military bases, they have shysters trying to sell you stuff. They'll talk you out of your paycheck. There was a little booth near the bus station outside of OAT. Have you seen those big white family bibles?"

Devyn nodded. "Yeah, my mother has one."

"They're big," I gestured with my hands, making a box, "I bought one for Dove. This was in 1969. They mailed it to her and she wrote to thank me while I was in Vietnam. I made sure it was a Mormon Bible." I lit another cigarette. "When I went to work for the paper, she kept trying to catch me. I was hardly ever there because I was in and out working on stories." I laughed and took a drink of beer. "I thought she must be trying to get back with me."

"Hadn't you moved in with Melanie by then?"

"Yep. Apparently, the only reason she kept trying to see me was to give back the white Bible. She finally just left it at the newspaper office." I puffed on the cigarette and blew a smoke ring into the warm night filled with brilliant stars. "By that time I was an atheist, and no way I wanted a Mormon Bible, but it would have been nice to have seen her."

Devyn threw another piece of cedar on the campfire. "You still have feelings for her?"

"I suppose. Do you ever get over your first love?" I poked at the fire. "How about you? Do you have feelings for Stormy?"

Devyn did a shot of whiskey, then cleared his throat. "I still love her. Don't know why. Hell, I might even think about going to the temple if she suddenly called and wanted to work it out, even though I think she has two kids now."

"Jesus man, I wouldn't go that far. You need to bury it and bury it deep."

"I know."

He helped me tear pages out of the big white Mormon Bible and we slowly watched them burn as we drank, farted, and cried silently.

In the morning, we skinny-dipped in the potholes and sat in the sun until badly sunburned. That afternoon, every part was bright pink.

"Ouch!" Devyn gritted his teeth as he pulled on his underwear.

"Reckon you won't be using that for a while." I chuckled but had the same problem.

"Same for you."

"Doesn't matter. I won't be getting any for a while."

A few days later, I went to Melanie's house to get my stuff.

She was unrepentant. "I assumed you were taking care of your needs when you were on the road. We never promised fidelity. Why are you so upset? I wasn't putting it in your face – you weren't supposed to be home until much later."

I just shook my head.

Devyn was impressed that I could put my emotions in a box and turn it off. I was upset but wasn't devastated like he was about getting divorced.

"In Vietnam, you learn to bury it underground like we did that contraband from the supply depot, or you'd go crazy."

"Hah. If I buried all my crazy mixed emotions about females, it would cause an earthquake and split me right down the middle and blast out like a volcano."

I stared at his blue eyes.

He was serious.

70. July 4th

I moved in with him and we painted houses together. One afternoon as he rolled yucky brown paint on the siding, Devyn said, "Christian forgiveness is a myth."

"Add that to liberty and justice for all," I said as I painted the trim a nice off-white color.

We played the Eagles on guitar and harmonica, "You can't hide your lying eyes."

I couldn't stand being home because we'd end up talking about love, women, and infidelity. He'd go out for long walks and I started hitting the San Antonio Rose, a country dance bar. I swing-danced with the girls until the management kicked everyone out at two in the morning, and then got back to painting houses the next day. Once my sunburn healed, I got laid every few nights by different girls.

Devyn couldn't deal with the thought of getting close to a female. Instead of hitting the bars, he went for long drives out into the desert where he looked at the stars.

"Just have sex and leave when you're done." I teased him, "You might as well be a monk."

Devyn shrugged, "Might not be a bad deal. At least you get enough to eat. They're always plump." Said he felt like a can of mashed buttholes.

"I'm not willing to be condemned to a life of horny loneliness like you." I convinced him to go to the San Antonio Rose. "Come on, don't keep copping out on me, I'll buy you a beer."

Devyn sat at the bar with men who drank and looked over their shoulders without smiles while I danced with hot girls swinging their hair like whips above the sanded dance floor.

Divorce sympathy was as scarce as deviled eggs at a church picnic. One of the fellows at the bar said, "It would be better if divorcing couples went out and had a duel, winner takes all."

Devyn retorted, "The woman would have a sharpshooting lawyer while the man stood alone with a pop gun." At least his sense of humor was still alive.

After a couple of shots of tequila, Devyn got the nerve to ask a chunky girl to dance. She looked him up and down. Seeing his worn-out expression and beat-up cowboy boots, she said, "Sorry, I'm not your type – I'm not inflatable."

Devyn smirked. "Thank you. Coming from you, I'll take that as a compliment." He went back to the bar with the other sad men. Most were divorced. To the crusty-looking man on the next stool, Dev said, "The more women I meet, the more I like my dog."

The fellow knocked back a whiskey sour. "I couldn't get laid in a women's prison with a fistful of pardons."

They laughed and had a shot together. "Here's to men who lose women." Sounded like a book title but men don't read or take advice so it wouldn't sell.

On the Fourth of July, we went up to Indian Point on Grand Mesa because I hated the fireworks. I got flashbacks if there was a loud noise that sounded like gunfire. That point was the same place the Ute Chief had spread tobacco to the four winds and left the curse, "Your children who are born here shall never leave."

We watched the fireworks going off in Delta and Montrose. Although I couldn't hear the explosions, it reminded me of a firefight where my helicopter had tripped an aerial booby trap, and we were knocked out of the sky into the defoliated swamp. I relived the Vietnam War over and over. I refused to talk about it to anybody but Devyn and had to be drunk to do so. The worst memory was about Cây Lan, my jungle orchid, but I couldn't talk about her – even with beer and whiskey heating my belly. I remarked, "Celebrating the Fourth of July is false patriotism because America has been at war for over 200 years. It's a symbol of U.S. imperialism and corporate colonialism." I wished that my combat memories could turn to ashes. My sorrow for volunteering drove me down into the depths of my soul.

"You ever hear what happened to Dove?"

I shook my head. "Yeah, she took off with this former Vietnam vet. I'm sure she fell in love with his uniform and medals. They got married and have a kid now."

"Wonder if he has PTSD?"

"Don't know, don't care."

"At least she got away from the Falcons."

I chuckled. "Heard her husband is an Evangelical Christian."

"So much for her temple marriage."

"Hey," I said, "I heard Alayna went to Oklahoma and hauled Big Owl out of that filthy trailer. She got him sober and converted him to Mormonism."

"Wow. That had to be a chore."

We toasted Big Owl.

"Is he going to marry her in the temple?" Devyn asked.

"Sure as shit," I said.

"We can't go."

"Yeah, I know. I'm an atheist these days."

"I had my membership withdrawn. I'm not a Mormon anymore."

"Good for you."

We did another toast. Staring at the campfire, Devyn said, "I was just sitting here thinking. Why couldn't you and I marry Dove and Stormy? Owl was the worst drunk of our group and there's a stump out there with a higher IQ."

"I know. We're both smart and good-looking. What is wrong with the universe?"

"If the Mormons are right and you can become a God. maybe our God is just another Big Owl."

I grinned. "Or maybe like Gabe – a God with Asperger's syndrome."

"Gotta be one or the other as crazy and unpredictable as life here on earth is."

I asked about this pretty former cheerleader that Dev had dated for a few months.

"She won't take my calls."

I took a drink. "You're better off." I sighed. "I hate to tell you but one night, I picked her up at the Rose. We did it in my car in the parking lot. I was kind of grossed out by her because she was loose as you know what. When we finished, she went back in to the dance hall, probably to pick up another guy. She's a wild one."

Devyn couldn't speak for several minutes, then he grinned. "She sure had a sweet ass and a tight pussy when I dated her." He took a shot of whiskey. "I've wanted to marry her until this moment." Another silly grin. "Thanks for telling me." He lit another cigarette. "Man, all I want is a woman to love me. Is that a crime?"

"Don't think so."

We were blood brothers for life. Cutting our palms with a pocket knife once again like we had done at Harts Basin before Owl and I enlisted, we clasped hands and forearms, proclaiming we'd find a woman who would be true and bear our children. We promised we'd ask the other man to check out our honey before getting involved the next time.

Devyn said, "I thought we did that with Dove and Stormy. What did we miss?"

"You tried to talk me out of joining the Army to be Dove's hero. I should have listened."

"You told me Stormy was too young, too much like her mom, and that she get away from home before she'd be ready for marriage."

We were in that state where a guy had drunk himself sober, an odd paradoxical place of headache clarity as we looked at the crescent moon high overhead.

I said, "We should start listening to each other."

Devyn got out his guitar and I played my harmonica.

"Just yesterday morning they let me know you were gone."

We talked about the women we had loved and then scattered tobacco to the four winds and promised again we would never commit suicide over a woman.

I said, "You just need to make sure you never get involved with another Mormon girl."

"Okay, and that includes any of the Mormon spin-offs."

"Sure."

We toasted and tossed down another shot of Irish whiskey.

The End

Please, out of the kindness of your heart, leave an honest review of this book on Amazon, Goodreads, or Barnes and Nobles. I would appreciate it very much,

Danyl A. Doyle, coauthor